# BLACK BAPTISTS
# AND AFRICAN MISSIONS

# BLACK BAPTISTS
# AND AFRICAN MISSIONS

The Origins of a Movement
1880–1915

SANDY D. MARTIN

MERCER

ISBN 0-86554-600-2                                    MUP/H173

Paperback reprint, 1998

The paper used in this publication meets the minimum requirements of American National Standard for Information Sciences—Permanence of Paper for Printed Library Materials, ANSI Z39.48-1984.

*Library of Congress Cataloging-in-Publication Data*

Martin, Sandy Dwayne.
    Black Baptists and African Missions: The Origins of a Movement,
    1880-1915 / Sandy D. Martin
        xvi + 242 pp.        6" x 9" (15 x 22 cm.)
    Includes bibiliographical references and  index.
    ISBN 0-86554-600-2 (alk. paper)
    1. African American Baptists—Missions—West Africa. 2. Missions—Africa,
West. 3. Africa, West—Church History.  I. Title.
BV2521.M37  1989                                    89-39041
266'.6166'08996073—dc20                                    CIP

# CONTENTS

# PREFACE

This study traces the origins and developments of black Baptist interest in the Southern states and their efforts to evangelize West Africa in particular. Some general historians in recent years have given much attention to the African mission movement among black Americans, especially during this period. Their studies illustrate how enslaved people, formerly enslaved people, and their children expended time, energy, and revenues from their meager resources to make contact—albeit a Christian missionary one—with their racial kin in Africa. The work of these historians has contributed to our understanding of the self-concept of black Americans, their commitment to shed the bondage of racial discrimination, and the emergence of pan-African thought.

I wish to make further contributions along these lines. Furthermore, and perhaps much more significantly, this volume has the advantage of placing the missionary movement squarely within one of its particular religious contexts, that of black Baptist thought and activity. Thus far, no recent, critical, in-depth, book-length study of black Baptist involvement in African or foreign missions has been published. Also, the reader will discover within these pages another example of the use of religious themes by black Americans in order to give their disadvantaged conditions meaning and to suggest avenues and principles by which they may be liberated from these situations.

Many colleagues, former professors, friends, and others have contributed much to the completion of this manuscript. Robert T. Handy and James M. Washington of Union Theological Seminary read earlier forms of this work and made vital suggestions. Of course, they both have been more than professors; they are also advisers and friends. I am truly indebted to Chairman George Howard and the professors and staff of the Department of Religion at the University of Georgia and the university in general for their gracious support and confidence in the significance of this project. This publication is made possible in part by a grant from the University of Georgia. Phillip McGuire and Earl Sheridan of the University of North Carolina at Wilmington, Norman Rates and Heyward Farrar of Spelman College, Lillian Ashcraft-Eason of Clark College, and John Diamond and the Interdenominational Theological Center community have graciously provided collegial encouragement and support. Gratitude and appreciation are also extended to Albert Raboteau and David Wills, codirectors of the Afro-American Religious History Institute sponsored by the National Endowment for the Humanities at Princeton University during the summer of 1986. Their valuable insights into the history of religion for Afro-Americans as well as those of the institute's guest lecturers (Charles Long, Randall Burkett, Will B. Gravely, James Washington, and Preston Williams) and the twenty-plus coparticipants added immensely to my own understanding of the discipline. I hope that some of that increased understanding is reflected in the following pages.

Staff persons at the libraries, archives, and collections of Union Theological Seminary and the Schomburg Center in New York City; the American Baptist Historical Society in Rochester, New York; the Moorland-Spingarn Collection in Washington, D.C.; and the Robert W. Woodruff Library of the Atlanta University Center all gave important and patient assistance. I am deeply grateful to June Reddington, who typed this manuscript despite her demanding duties in the Admissions Office of Spelman College. My wife Danita has been a bulwark of support and comfort during the time leading to the publication of this work. There are many, many other friends and colleagues too numerous to mention.

Finally, but certainly not least in significance, portions of this book have appeared in previously published and copyrighted works: a segment of chapter 1 appeared as "Black Baptists, Foreign Missions, and African Colonization, 1814-1882," in Sylvia M. Jacobs, ed., *Black Americans and the Missionary Movement in Africa,* Contributions in Afro-American and African Studies, Number 66 (Westport CT: Greenwood Press, 1982) 63-76, Copyright © 1982 by Sylvia M. Jacobs, ed. Used with permission. Selected portions of chapters 2 and 3 appeared as "The Baptist Foreign Mission Convention, 1880-1894," *Baptist History and Heritage* 16 (October 1981): 13-

25; chapter 4 includes a segment from "Black Baptist Women and African Mission Work, 1870-1925," *Sage: A Scholarly Journal on Black Women* 3 (Spring 1986): 16-19; and chapter 5 includes portions from "The Debate over Interracial Cooperation among Black Baptists in the African Missionary Movement, 1895-1905," *Journal of the Interdenominational Theological Center* 13 (Spring 1986): 291-303. I extend my thanks to the above publishers for their permission to reprint these materials.

Of course, all shortcomings are my own.

# PREFACE TO THE PAPERBACK EDITION

This paperback edition comes essentially unchanged from the study published several years ago. Hence, the object of the study remains the same: a historical investigation of the African American Baptist movement for African missions principally during the years 1880-1915. While there are discussions of missionaries and their experiences, the predominant goal is the historical examination of the development and growth of American black Baptist interest, organization, and pursuit of African missions. This study retains the same significance as it did back in 1989: it demonstrates the interplay between spiritual and temporal salvation or liberation in black religious thought; it provides historical insight into the most populous group of black religious people, the Baptists; it points to the similarities, differences, and interactions between African American and white Christians regarding overseas, particularly African, missions; it examines the self-concept of African American Christians and their sense of spiritual and temporal connection with their continental African siblings; and, more fundamentally but crucially significant and especially illuminating to many readers, this study documents, along with other works, that African Americans actually manifested a lively, ongoing, organizational African missions movement extending back at least to the early national period of American history.

In the first edition I commented on the paucity of academic studies on African American missions, especially in reference to Baptists. That absence of study, sadly, is still evident and thus points to the continuing relevance of this work. With the increasing popularity of Afrocentric thought in some circles, one would have imagined that black American missionary interest in Africa would have received greater scholarly investigation, particularly as it cast light on the African memory and character of blacks in the diaspora. Perhaps greater interest along these lines will surface in the years to come.

At any rate, I have been quite elated at the warm and enthusiastic reception of the previous volume. Every review that I can recall was overwhelmingly positive and even laudatory. A number of scholars and students of religion have mentioned this work as part of their face to face introductory meetings with me. Many professors have commented favorably about their use of the book in courses on missions and American and African American church or religious history and have expressed the earnest interest that it be reprinted. These positive responses to the book, testimonies to its scholarly contribution, have proven both delightful and humbling. I hope those who are already acquainted with the study will employ the paperback edition and others encountering it for the first time will find it equally useful in their scholarly and pedagogical enterprises.

The professional and personal acknowledgments listed in the previous edition are still pertinent for this one. There are a number of important additions. I am grateful to Mercer University Press for reprinting this study and extend special thanks to Dr. Andrew Manis, editor for Religion and Southern Studies and an insightful and dedicated scholar of American, Southern, and African American religious history. The renowned American church historian, Dr. Robert T. Handy, graciously consented to do write a foreword for this edition. It is an honor to count myself among his students and deeply gratifying that he would lend his valuable word of endorsement to this study. The East Friendship Baptist Church, skillfully and lovingly pastored by the Reverend James Kendrick, has provided a wonderful spiritual home for us during our stay in Athens, Georgia. Mrs. L. V. Rogers and Miss Adlena Martin and Miss Hattie Martin are precious aunts who bring much joy in my life. Finally, since the publication of the first edition, my wonderful wife Danita and I have had the joyful addition of two fine sons to our lives: Terrance Ladale Purnell and John Wesley Michael. Of course all shortcomings, limitations, and errors in this work are mine.

Sandy Dwayne Martin
The University of Georgia
Athens, Georgia
January 1998

# BRIEF CHRONOLOGY:

## Some Important Dates
## in the Development of African Missions
## among Black Baptists, 1814–1915

1814 *The General Missionary Convention of the Baptist Denomination in the United States for Foreign Missions (also known as the Triennial Convention) is founded.*

1815 *The Richmond African Baptist Missionary Society is established by deacon William Crane and ministers Lott Carey and Colin Teague.*

1816–1817 *The American Colonization Society (ACS) is organized.*

1820 *Lott Carey and Colin Teague journey to Liberia as missionary-emigrants.*

1845 *The Triennial Convention divides into two organizations, the American Baptist Missionary Union (North), or the ABMU, and the Southern Baptist Convention (South), or the SBC, due to issues arising directly from the slavery controversy.*

1846 *Two black missionaries, John Day and A. L. Jones, are appointed by the Southern Baptist Convention for service in Africa.*

1847 *Liberia, a former U.S. colony, is declared a republic.*

1849 *A white missionary, Thomas J. Bowen, ventures to Nigeria upon appointment by the SBC along with two blacks, Robert F. Hill and Harvey Goodale.*

1875 *W. J. David, a white Mississippian, and William W. Colley, a black Virginian, are sent to Nigeria by the SBC.*

1879 *William W. Colley returns to the U.S. and begins campaigning for the formation of a national, black foreign mission convention.*

1880 *The Baptist Foreign Mission Convention (BFMC) is established in Montgomery, Alabama.*

1883–1884 *The first BFMC missionaries are appointed.*

1887 *The BFMC commissions its second set of persons for service in Africa.*

1893 *The remaining BFMC missionaries in Africa return to the U.S.*

1895 *The National Baptist Convention (NBC) is established.*

1897 *The Lott Carey Baptist Foreign Mission Convention (LCC) is organized in Washington, D.C., because of differences with the NBC.*

1900 *The NBC sends John and Mamie Branton Tule to southern Africa; the LCC commissions Clinton C. and Eva Boone for service in central Africa.*

1905 *The LCC and the NBC establish a cooperative arrangement that lasts until the 1920s.*

1915 *John Chilembwe, an indigenous South African educated in the U.S. and supported by the NBC, dies in a rebellion against the South African government; controversy within the NBC regarding its publishing house leads to the NBC's dividing a year later into the National Baptist Convention, U.S.A., Inc., and the National Baptist Convention of America.*

# ABBREVIATIONS

| | |
|---|---|
| ABMU | American Baptist Missionary Union |
| ACS | American Colonization Society |
| BFMC | The Baptist Foreign Mission Convention |
| BGAWST | Baptist General Association of Western States and Territories |
| LCC | The Lott Carey Foreign Mission Convention, later Lott Carey Baptist Home and Foreign Mission Convention |
| NBC | National Baptist Convention |
| SBC | Southern Baptist Convention |
| VBSC | Virginia Baptist State Convention |

# FOREWORD

It is good news to know that Sandy Martin's *Black Baptists and African Missions* is now available in a paperback edition. Thoroughly researched and thoughtfully written, the study centers largely on the motivation of African American Baptists in the southern states and on the way they developed organizations to fulfill their chosen commitments to bring the Christian gospel to Africa, particularly to West Africa (notably Liberia), but also to regions in South and Central Africa. The missionary enthusiasm and action of black Baptists came during a harassingly difficult time (1880-1915) for African Americans. The choking coils of Jim Crow laws largely restricted their voting rights, especially in the South. This in turn opened the way for strict segregationist legislation, and bound many of them to bitter poverty. Nevertheless, the black Baptist missionary drive of those years succeeded in raising sufficient funds to support both African American and indigenous African missionaries as they labored abroad in Africa. Readers do get some sense of what was going on in the missionary fields with their difficulties and achievements, along with the primary focus on home base problems and attainments in shaping such organizations as the Lott Carey Baptist Home and Foreign Mission Convention and the National Baptist Convention Foreign Mission Board.

In this carefully documented case study of an important chapter of black Baptist history, Martin has contributed much in revealing detail to a previously neglected area. In so doing, he points to ways in which the religious lives and achievements of African Americans are important for fully understanding the broad fields of American religious, cultural, and ecumenical history. Those missionaries and their supporters drew much from prevailing similar movements among the white denominations of the period, such as the search for Christian civilization, but in distinctive ways that also, slowly at first, eventually affected those of the white majorities. In part this came from cautious cooperation with other religious bodies, including participation in the founding of the Baptist World Alliance (1905), and sending of twenty-five delegates to the famous Ecumenical Missionary Conference at Edinburgh (1910).

This convenient second printing of a pioneering study makes it readily available for college, seminary, and university courses—and also for church libraries and study groups. The book's selected bibliography and several indexes add to its usefulness. A graduate of Tougaloo College who has earned three advanced degrees from Columbia University and Union Theological Seminary, Martin is a prolific writer and speaker. He currently teaches in the Department of Religion of the University of Georgia.

Robert T. Handy
Henry Sloane Coffin Professor Emeritus of Church History
Union Theological Seminary
New York, NY

# INTRODUCTION

## LAYING THE FOUNDATIONS
## FOR A NOBLE ENTERPRISE,
## 1815–1879

This study traces one of the most fascinating aspects of modern religious history, the development of African missionary interest among black Christians between the years 1880 and 1915. We shall examine this development by a case study of black Baptists. The object is to investigate the origins and development of this movement among Afro-American Baptists in an effort to acquire a fuller understanding of the meaning that Christianity held for black Christians during this period. The principle objective, then, is not to chronicle the activities of individuals and groups on the mission fields, but to explicate a significant phenomenon of American religious history.

The central, controlling thesis of this endeavor is simple: that black Christians in general and black Baptists in particular actively engaged in an effort to evangelize Africa during the late nineteenth and early twentieth centuries; that they understood redemption or salvation of non-Christian Africans in material or temporal as well as spiritual terms; that this enterprise demonstrated their sense of racial identity with all peoples of African descent—a proto-pan-Africanism, if you will; and that this missionary quest on behalf of the ancestral homeland contributed to the development of and conflicts among black Baptist denominations.

Certainly one aspect of nineteenth-century evangelical, Protestant Christianity, of which black Baptists were participants, was the belief that the entire world should be converted to Christ, even though such attempts often entailed physical and mental suffering and even death on the part of some brave and committed individuals. Black Baptists embraced this tradition fervently. Even the bonds of slavery and subsequent lynching, Jim Crow laws, and other forms of overt racism would not deter them from carrying out the Great Commission—to go into all the world and proclaim God's salvation.

But something else was transpiring among Afro-American Christians. It was the realization that blacks the world over faced similar oppressions and threats and that their separate paths all led to one destiny. In their encounters with Europeans, they observed that all peoples of African descent were placed at the periphery of significance in social and religious intercourse and at the very bottom of the economic and political pyramid—defined by most Europeans as beasts of burden rather than as siblings in humanity. They were discovering an idea that Europeans already shared concerning themselves—a concept of race that transcended national, "tribal," and cultural boundaries. Thus what the reader will observe in the following pages is an enterprise that encompassed various facets: the spiritual and material, religion and race, Africa and America.

It is appropriate to examine black Baptists for at least two significant reasons. First, so little scholarly work has been devoted to this community of black Americans. James M. Washington's recent *Frustrated Fellowship*, Mechal Sobel's *Trabelin' On*, and Leroy Fitt's *A History of Black Baptists* are notable exceptions.[1] Second, this neglect of black Baptists by both general and religious historians is even more surprising in light of the fact that the number of Baptists has always been at least equal to the much-heralded Methodists; indeed, since the Civil War, Baptists have constituted the clear plurality among Afro-American Christians. This populous, diverse, and geographically distributed group thus provides an important insight into the ideas, goals, and strivings of the total black community.

In addition to the above points, a case study of the African mission movement as a black Baptist phenomenon of American religious history is a valuable contribution to our understanding of the development and institutionalization of religion among Afro-Americans. Of course, it should

---

[1]For recent studies of Afro-American Baptist history, see James Melvin Washington, *Frustrated Fellowship: The Black Baptist Quest for Social Power* (Macon GA: Mercer University Press, 1986); Mechal Sobel, *Trabelin' On: The Slave Journey to an Afro-Baptist Faith* (Westport CT: Greenwood Press, 1979); and Leroy Fitts, *Lott Carey: First Black Missionary to Africa* (Valley Forge PA: Judson Press, 1978).

be remembered that non-Baptist black Christians were also involved in this
enterprise before, during, and after the 1880–1915 period, as recent works
by Walter Williams and Sylvia M. Jacobs reveal.[2]

It can be argued that practically all chronological demarcations are
rather artificial. Nevertheless, the period between 1880 and 1915 was very
crucial for both black history in general and black religious history in particular. The year 1880 represents the culmination of mission-movement
activities among black Baptists at the local and state levels with the formation of the regional Baptist Foreign Mission Convention (BFMC) in
Montgomery, Alabama. The program of this group was carried over into
the Foreign Mission Board of the National Baptist Convention in 1895. In
1915 disagreement within the National Baptist Convention would lead to
an official division one year later between the National Baptist Convention, Incorporated, and the unincorporated National Baptist Convention of
America. I should emphasize that by 1915 the African mission movement
had been firmly institutionalized among black Christians, including black
Baptists, and that the black church itself went through further stages of institutionalization during the era.

From a broader perspective, the period 1880–1915 represents an increasingly difficult time for Afro-Americans. The political rights that recently emancipated Southern blacks had enjoyed during Reconstruction
were gradually eliminated as reactionary Southern governments assumed
control. Just as dangerous to blacks as these "legal" structures that fostered segregation and poll taxes was the rise of illegal, secret vigilante
groups that openly harassed and murdered their victims. These factors

---

[2]Two very good sources for the study of black American Christians' attempt to evangelize Africa are Sylvia M. Jacobs, ed., *Black Americans and the Missionary Movement
in Africa* (Westport CT: Greenwood Press, 1982), and Walter L. Williams, *Black Americans and the Evangelization of Africa, 1877-1900* (Madison: University of Wisconsin Press,
1982). Unlike the above works, this present study concentrates upon African missions as
a movement among black Americans, devoting less attention to missionaries in Africa per
se. Furthermore, this study traces the development of the movement in one body of black
Christians and therefore should provide a more intimate understanding of significant theological ideas and trends. In addition to the studies by Jacobs and Williams, the reader might
be interested in a general account of Afro-American settlers in Liberia during the nineteenth century. See Tom W. Shick, *Behold the Promised Land: A History of Afro-American Settler Society in Nineteenth-Century Liberia* (Baltimore: Johns Hopkins University
Press, 1977).

combined with the shocking indifference of the United States government, crop failures, and the possibility for enhanced employment elsewhere occasioned by the First World War led to the migration of Afro-Americans to the urban areas, a transition that brought a whole different set of experiences for the masses.

This study focuses on the states of Virginia, North Carolina, South Carolina, Georgia, Florida, Mississippi, and Alabama, though attention will be given to Baptists in other regions. It was in the South, particularly Virginia and the Carolinas, that consistent missionary interest in Africa, especially in West Africa, had its origins in the antebellum period. It was also in this region that African missions received the most sustained support during the period under study. The Southern region also had the largest concentration of black Baptists in the years 1880–1915 and therefore is representative of mission interest among Afro-American Baptists. The designation "West Africa," unless otherwise indicated, refers principally to the nation of Liberia and secondarily to the area we know as Nigeria. It is in these areas that the above-mentioned Baptists concentrated their earliest activities and in which they maintained a presence throughout the 1880–1915 period.

## PROCEDURAL METHODOLOGY

The present study chronicles the development of African mission support from the founding of the largely regional Baptist Foreign Mission Convention in 1880 to the beginning of the division in the national successor, the National Baptist Convention, in 1915. As stated previously, I am working from the central thesis that black Baptists' African mission movement was specifically conscious of race and that it developed in the theological context of securing the spiritual and material uplift of African peoples throughout the world. Black Baptists, along with other black Christians, came to view the destinies of Afro-Americans and Africans as inextricably bound. They operated from the conviction that God was acting in history to effect spiritual and material salvation of all peoples of African descent and that the divine One would use them to present true Christianity and civilization to a world of injustice. Furthermore, this understanding of missiology contributed significantly to the denominational growth and institutionalization of black Baptists.

The mission movement thus can be seen as developing through several distinct but overlapping phases. First, the basic theological understanding and rationale for the movements developed in the context of slavery. The remainder of this introduction outlines the major themes and movements that provided the setting for early black missionary interest in Africa: the rise of foreign mission societies in the U.S., the development of both black and white Baptist missionary interest in Africa, the blending of Protestant Christianity and Western culture in the missiology of black and white mission groups, and the relationship between African colonization and African missions among Afro-Americans.

Chapters 1, 2, and 3 focus on the second stage in the growth of the mission movement: activities at the state and regional levels. The postwar rise of mission sentiment in the Southern states, especially in Virginia and the Carolinas, could easily be discussed, chronologically speaking, right here. But as we shall see, state activities and those of the regional BFMC overlapped in terms of development and thus logically can be discussed in the three chapters of part one. In this section, we observe that the BFMC, though it intended to act as a national organization, still remained for the most part a Southern organization, in terms of both its participants as well as its capacity to influence the growth of African mission sentiment.

In part two, chapters 4 and 5, we witness the third stage in the growth of African missions among black Baptists when the movement becomes truly national. As black Baptists saw the need for structural unity in one organic body, the mission activities of the BFMC were incorporated into the Foreign Mission Board of the newly formed National Baptist Convention. As movements become more organized, structured, and institutionalized, conflicts and divisions often arise between those who prize the new order of things and those who believe firmly that something of paramount importance in the tradition is being lost or seriously compromised. The African mission movement is no exception to this phenomenon. And thus we see conflicts leading to the formation of a new regional group, the Lott Carey Baptist Foreign Mission Convention (LCC) in 1897, because of different approaches to the work of African missions and cooperation with white Baptists.

Part three, chapter 6 covers the entire period under study and focuses its attention on the whole issue of mission ideology, especially on how black

Baptists viewed concerns such as African religions and customs, colonialism, education for the mission field, and the relationship between Africans and Afro-Americans. Chapter 7 concludes the study.

## FOREIGN MISSIONS
## IN NINETEENTH-CENTURY AMERICA

As previously indicated, in order to understand better the foreign mission movement among black Baptists in the years 1880–1915, it would be helpful to place it in the historical background of American Protestant theology of the nineteenth century. It would also be helpful to examine briefly white Protestant missiology and the establishment of black and white missionary presence in West Africa. An ardent proponent of mission enterprises, I question most of these missionaries for not exhibiting more receptive attitudes toward the positive aspects of African religions, cultures, and history.

Beginning in the final decade of the eighteenth century, Protestants throughout the world, mainly Euro-Americans, began a crusade to evangelize the non-Christian world (for the most part, nonwhite peoples in North and South America, Africa, Asia, and Australia).[3] Great Britain—the political, cultural, and religious parent country to the U.S.—set patterns in missionary work for the Americans to follow. During this time Baptists were often in the forefront with other denominations in the pioneering of foreign mission work. In Britain the Baptist Society for the Propagation of the Gospel among the Heathen was organized in 1792 as a result of the missionary concerns of William Carey, the famous British Baptist minister and missionary to India. This society was followed three years later by an interdenominational group, the London Missionary Society. The concern for foreign missionary work was concretized in the U.S. very early in its history by the formation of missionary societies: the New York Missionary Society in 1796 supported by Presbyterian, Reformed, and Baptist church

---

[3]For a good historical treatment of these missionary endeavors, see Kenneth Scott Latourette, *A History of the Expansion of Christianity*. Vol. 5: *The Great Century in the Americas, Australia, and Africa, A.D. 1800–A.D. 1914* (New York: Harper & Row, 1943; rpt., Grand Rapids MI: Zondervan Publishing House, 1970). Chapter 11 provides a good overview of European and American endeavors in "black" Africa during the years 1800–1914. See 435-60 for a treatment of missionary enterprises in West Africa.

people; the Missionary Society of Connecticut in 1798; and the predominantly Congregational American Board of Commissioners for Foreign Missions in 1810.

As two American Board missionaries—Adoniram Judson and Luther Rice—headed for their missionary field in India, they became persuaded that baptism by immersion, a central tenet of Baptist Christianity, was the only legitimate form of the rite. Logically, they then sought support for their missionary labors from Baptists in the U.S. In 1814 the first national denominational organization among Baptists was formed as a fruition of this quest, the General Missionary Convention of the Baptist Denomination of the United States of America for Foreign Missions (often referred to as the Triennial Convention).[4]

With the heavy concentration of Afro-Americans in the South because of enslavement, black Baptist missionary interest developed most strongly in that region in relation to the white Baptist churches there. Because of these racial interconnections, it is important to note several characteristics of nineteenth-century American missions. First, to a great extent, the foreign mission movement—like the temperance, Sabbath-observance, tract, and Sunday school movements—was an outgrowth of the revivals of the Second Great Awakening. These revivals fostered the enthusiasm to share the gospel with all of those outside the Christian faith, in the U.S. and abroad. In line with this, the First Great Awakening (1720–1750), but more especially the Second Great Awakening in the early nineteenth century, brought many blacks into the folds of the Baptist and Methodist churches. Prior to these revivals, blacks had been largely ignored by the white churches.

In terms of foreign missions, many white Christians viewed themselves as people chosen of God to spread the one, true religion of Protestant Christianity. White Americans, following examples of Christian history (and their interpretation of the Scriptures), looked upon themselves as a chosen people—both in terms of their religion and their nation. Other religions might be sincere human efforts to find God, in contrast to the Christian religion in which God sought humans. Some religions might be

---

[4]Robert T. Handy, *A History of the Churches in the United States and Canada* (New York: Oxford University Press, 1977) 176-77.

considered to have contained specific revelations of God. But Christianity was seen as the one true faith in which God spoke supremely through the mediator between God and humanity, Jesus of Nazareth.

This belief in the superiority and perfection of Christianity accompanied a firm belief in the superiority of Euro-American culture. The European form of Christianity, as is true with any form, was firmly linked with and influenced by its culture. In other words, because Euro-Americans professed Christianity or at least granted that it or some branch of it—Protestantism or Catholicism—was the only true church, they believed that theirs was a Christian civilization. One result of this identification of Protestantism with culture and nation was the belief that a people being missionized should take not only the particular religious beliefs, practices, and rituals of the American or European Christians, but that the whole society should be retrieved from ''backwardness.'' Hence ''heathenistic'' and ''superstitious'' influences and customs should be brought into conformity with Western standards.

Beginning with colonial times, even Americans not commonly associated with traditional structures of Christianity regarded their nation as a particularly favored one. For example, a committee of the Continental Congress composed of notable revolutionary heroes such as Benjamin Franklin, John Adams, and Thomas Jefferson felt enough confidence in the ideals of the War of Independence that they could liken the American people with the chosen people of the Bible.[5] It is not surprising, therefore, that persons of more theologically orthodox persuasion could also hold up the U.S. as an ideal to be emulated. Lyman Beecher, the nineteenth-century social reformer and revivalist, thought that the U.S. could teach all of humankind to rise to its highest capacities. Already, the example of the American Revolution had ignited fires of revolution across Europe in Portugal, Spain, Greece, and France. These types of revolutions would bring humankind closer to the goal of true democracy. Beecher expected that in the future this passion for democracy would encircle the globe so that all the world would bathe in the fresh waters of freedom.[6]

---

[5]Lester B. Scherer, *Slavery and the Churches in Early America, 1619–1819* (Grand Rapids MI: William B. Erdmans Publishing Company, 1975) 118.

[6]Winthrop S. Hudson, *Religion in America: An Historical Account of the Development of American Religious Life,* 2d ed. (New York: Charles Scribner's Sons, 1973) 112-13.

Horace Bushnell, the New England theologian and pastor, saw a connection between the levels of civilization and religion. Americans, unlike other peoples, had not allowed sinfulness to replace true religion. As a result, they retained their high levels of civilization while those people who had turned from God sank deep into primitivism. Bushnell believed that as possessors of Christian civilization, white Americans had an obligation to assist "primitive" groups such as the American Indians and African peoples to rise above their low level of social, economic, and religious existence. In fact, he claimed, the Western hemisphere had been preserved as a stage upon which God would enact a divine plan for all of humankind.[7]

When most American whites spoke of this nation and the churches as instruments of the Lord, however, they thought from a Caucasian frame of reference. For example, Harriet Beecher Stowe, author of the renowned *Uncle Tom's Cabin,* could envision a time when the world would require a peace-loving, patient, and humble race of men and women to teach it these values. That would be the day of the African race. She believed that the Anglo-Saxons, particularly the Americans, had been chosen to subdue the world for Christ. This race—or branch of a race—more than any other exhibited the requisite inner qualities for such a task: aggressiveness, the pioneering spirit, and a willingness to engage in struggle.[8] Thus, many white Christians (and not-so-orthodox religious people) viewed our nation as a Christian civilization or, at least, on its way to becoming one. As possessors of both Protestant Christianity and Western culture, they felt it was their responsibility to spread these values to other parts of the world.

Clearly, within white Christendom there was optimism with regard to evangelism and missions. Not only did white Christians expect Christian civilization to subdue the U.S.; they also expected it to engulf the world. Most Protestants, in other words, looked forward to a millennial period on earth. For many, this period in which the world would be ruled by Christian principles in all aspects of life—politically, economically, socially, and religiously—would precede and pave the way for the Second Coming of Christ (postmillennialism). Other Christians expected that their evan-

---

[7]Ernest Lee Tuveson, *Redeemer Nation: The Idea of America's Millennial Role* (Chicago: University of Chicago Press, 1969) 149-50, 154-55.

[8]Ibid., 152-53.

gelistic activities would hasten the Second Coming, and Christ would rule before the millennium (premillennialism). In either case, many white Christians considered their task of eternal significance. By the promulgation of Protestantism and various aspects of Western culture, politics, and customs throughout the world, they believed that they were moving humankind closer to the day when God's reign would be supreme over the earth.[9]

## BLACK PROTESTANTS

Black Christian theology and practice operated out of this milieu.[10] This is not to suggest that Afro-American Christians were mere imitators of white Christians. Prominent scholars such as Albert Raboteau, Lawrence Levine, Donald Mathews, and Milton C. Sernett have amply researched and demonstrated the distinctiveness, creativity, and innovation of black Christianity even during the time of slavery.[11] But it is imperative to point

---

[9]For a full treatment of this millennial theme, see ibid. Other church historians have demonstrated the influence of millennialism in American religions, including Robert T. Handy, *A Christian America: Protestant Hopes and Historical Realities* (New York: Oxford University Press, 1971) and Martin E. Marty, *Righteous Empire: The Protestant Experience in America* (New York: Dial Press, 1970).

[10]For an examination of the relationship between Western culture and Christianity in the thought of nineteenth-century black leaders, see the following: Howard Brotz, ed., *Negro Social and Political Thought, 1850–1920: Representative Texts* (New York: Basic Books, 1966); Floyd J. Miller, *The Search for a Black Nationality: Black Emigration and Colonization, 1787–1863* (Urbana: University of Illinois Press, 1975); and especially Leonard I. Sweet, *Black Images of America, 1784–1870* (New York: W. W. Norton & Company, 1976). Melville J. Herskovits and E. Franklin Frazier are often cited as proponent and opponent, respectively, in the debate over the elements of African beliefs and practices in the Afro-American church. See Frazier, *The Negro Church in America* (New York: Schocken Books, 1974) and Herskovits, *The Myths of the Negro Past* (Boston: Beacon Press, 1958).

[11]For insightful treatments of Afro-American religious history, see Albert Raboteau, *Slave Religion: The Invisible Institution in the Antebellum South* (New York: Oxford University Press, 1978), and Donald G. Mathews, *Religion in the Old South* (Chicago: University of Chicago Press, 1977). Milton C. Sernett has a fine collection of articles in his edited work *Afro-American Religious History: A Documentary Witness* (Durham: Duke University Press, 1985). Gayraud S. Wilmore in his finely written, classic work *Black Religion and Black Radicalism*, 2d ed. (Maryknoll NY: Orbis Books, 1983) has done an excellent job demonstrating the historical connections between black religion and social change in the U.S. Lawrence Levine also provides an in-depth treatment of Afro-American religion in his *Black Culture and Black Consciousness: Afro-American Folk Thought from*

out that black Christians joined their white counterparts in heralding Protestantism as the ideal form of religious belief and practice. A case can be
made for the presence of African elements in the practice and worship of
black religion, particularly in the invisible institution (the religion of black
slaves).

Nevertheless, to a large extent black Baptist and black Methodist
churches that were organized outside white ecclesiastical structures or that
broke from those structures carried identical beliefs, rituals, and theology
of corresponding white bodies. Blacks too considered Western culture superior to non-Western cultures. They also prayed and expected that a period in history would arrive when Protestantism and Western civilization
would be established throughout the world. It makes no difference whether
one speaks of Paul Cuffee, the black merchant and member of the Society of
Friends who provided for thirty-eight Afro-Americans to return to Africa; or Daniel Coker, the African Methodist Episcopal missionary to Sierra
Leone; or James T. Holly, the Episcopal priest, missionary to Haiti, and
exponent of black emigration—most black church people took for granted
that non-Western and non-Christian peoples must come under the purview
of the American Christian's understanding of Christian theology.

Again, black Christians adapted the Christian faith to their circumstances.
Using Scripture and their own experience in America, they modified the av-
erage white interpretation of the faith because they had to deal in a very press-
ing manner with theodicy—the challenge of reconciling faith in an all-
powerful, loving God with the existence of human suffering. They rejected
both racism and slavery as inconsistent with Christian faith and the dignity
and worth of their person. But certain questions had to be faced. For instance,
if God is a god of mercy and love, and if God is no respecter of persons between whites and blacks, then why did God permit blacks to undergo the ordeal of slavery, which threatened familial ties, dignity, and self-respect? Black
Christians generally accepted the faith of St. Paul in Romans 8 and other biblical statements which asserted that, from the worst of circumstances, God
works to bring forth good for divine pleasure and glory. Beneath all sufferings

---

*Slavery to Freedom* (New York: Oxford University Press, 1977). Of course, these are only
several examples of recent critical works by general and religious historians who are ex-
ploring this vital area of study.

were a purpose and a blessing. Hence, blacks, while not condoning the institution of slavery, could interpret it (as did some whites) as a part of a divine provision for blacks to acquire Christianity and Western civilization.

Having acquired these blessings, blacks could become special instruments of God for the salvation of the African peoples who were non-Christian and without Western culture. Many blacks felt that they, not whites, were more loyal to the religion of Jesus. Despite the limitations blacks encountered, their churches provided them with one golden opportunity to express their ultimate commitment to the Christian faith. In church and lay activities, black Christians were free to express their sense of personhood and racial pride. Though deprived of all the world, they had Jesus. Particularly in the area of foreign missions, black Christians had instances to demonstrate solidarity with their African kin. Believing along with white Christians in the efficacy of the gospel, they longed (and worked) for the day when Christian civilization would lift Africans from degradation. Ethiopia would stretch her hands to God in worship; and as evidences of political and material progress, princes would come forth from Egypt (Ps. 68:31). The lure of foreign missions for blacks, therefore, has always included the cause of racial progress.

## THE ESTABLISHMENT OF THE
## BAPTIST PRESENCE IN AFRICA, 1814–1880

Let us turn our attention now from a general discussion of Protestant missiology to that of Baptist missiology. Between 1814 and 1880 Baptists, black and white, took an aggressive interest in missionizing the African continent. Their theologies and philosophies mirrored the general beliefs and attitudes of American Christendom in regard to foreign missions. Baptists carried out their missionary program with the cooperation of three agencies: the American Colonization Society (ACS), the black Baptist churches, and the white Baptist churches.

## THE AMERICAN COLONIZATION SOCIETY
## AND THE PHILOSOPHY OF EMIGRATION

The ACS was certainly dedicated to the dubious goal of repatriating blacks to Africa. It is equally significant, however, that the organization was heavily imbued with an aura of Christian missions. In the late eighteenth century, Samuel Hopkins, the New England theologian, proposed that blacks be trained as Christian ministers and sent to Africa as missionaries. Hopkins envisioned the creation of Christian civilization by Westernized blacks who would be instruments for lifting Africans from their paganism and darkness. The colonization scheme, he thought, would also serve the meritorious function of removing the moral blight of slavery from the U.S., thus allowing this nation to answer fully its calling to be a true Christian commonwealth.[12]

The American Society for the Colonizing of Free People of Color, or the American Colonization Society (founded in 1816–1817, chiefly under the leadership of Robert S. Finley, a Presbyterian minister),[13] and its child, the colony of Liberia, should be viewed in the context of this theology rather than in mere political terms. True, colonization was supported for political and economic purposes. Some persons held out hope that with the knowledge that blacks would be repatriated, slaveholders and other Americans would be more willing to accept emancipation of the slaves. Others supported the colonization because they believed that it offered no threat to the slave system, since only free blacks were being colonized or blacks who were emancipated under the condition that they would be repatriated.

Yet colonization from the very beginning was linked closely with the concept of African missionary work. Many missionaries were transported to Africa at the full or partial expense of the society. Many blacks colonized by the society in Liberia were Christians. But most of all, the philosophy of the Colonization Society carried, as stated above, a strong missionizing theme that was accepted by many Christians, white and black. Indeed, the organization was an outgrowth, in part, of benevolent concern for blacks. W. B. Johnson, the first president of the Southern Baptist Convention and a lifelong Baptist denominational leader, was an ardent defender of the slave system. But Johnson symbolizes those persons who viewed colonization and African missions as working in a harmonious relationship. By supporting the colonization of blacks in Africa, specifically

---

[12]For an analysis of Samuel Hopkins's relationship with the African colonization movement, see Sweet, *Black Images of America*, 23-24.

[13]For a description of the American Colonization Society, see P. J. Staudenraus, *The African Colonization Movement, 1816–1865* (New York: Columbia University Press, 1961).

Liberia, white Baptists and other Christians could see that they were alleviating the conditions of blacks in this country and, by means of the black emigrants, performing their missionary responsibility of spreading Christian religion and Western culture to Africans.

The colonization scheme never received an overwhelming, sustained amount of popular support from either white or black Americans. While some proslavery people felt comfortable with the plan, other Southern slaveholders basically distrusted the organization as an antislavery device that constituted a threat to their economic interests. Many Northern antislavery people after 1830 gravitated gradually to the position of abolitionism, insisting that the process for dismantling the slave system should begin immediately with no compensation to the slaveholder for his/her loss of "property." Black and white foes of slavery viewed the society with a deep suspicion, to say the least, believing that its purpose was the maintenance of the slavery apparatus and the forced removal of blacks. Blacks particularly resented the underlying assumption of many colonization supporters that Afro-Americans were inferior to whites and unable to compete successfully in American society.

Notwithstanding, a number of prominent blacks endorsed the idea of black emigration, if not the American Colonization Society,[14] and coupled it with their belief that Afro-Americans bear the duty of passing on to their African kin the blessings of civilization and Christianity. In the late 1700s Samuel Hopkins was not the only person concerned with African colonization. Groups of Afro-Americans in Boston and Rhode Island were established for the purpose of providing blacks with means to return to Africa. The longtime interests of Paul Cuffee, a prosperous black Quaker merchant, materialized in 1815 when he provided thirty-eight Afro-Americans

---

[14]See Floyd J. Miller, *Black Nationality,* and Benjamin Quarles, *Black Abolitionists* (New York: Oxford University Press, 1975). Throughout American history, Afro-Americans have expressed interest and identification with Africa. See Okon Edet Uya's edited work *Black Brotherhood: Afro-Americans and Africa* (Lexington MA: D. C. Heath and Company, 1971); especially for the purposes of this study, see Louis Mehlinger's "The Attitude of the Free Negro toward African Colonization," 24-40, in the aforementioned volume. Canadian blacks also took part in the emigration schemes of the eighteenth and nineteenth centuries; see James W. St. G. Walker, *The Black Loyalists: The Search for a Promised Land in Nova Scotia and Sierra Leone, 1783–1870* (New York: Africana Publishing Company, 1976).

with passage to the British colony of Sierra Leone in West Africa. During the nineteenth century black spokespersons such as Martin R. Delany, Alexander Crummell, Edward W. Blyden, James Theodore Holly, and Henry McNeil Turner either advocated that blacks emigrate to the African continent or to some destination in the New World.

After 1850 black community members made strong appeals for Afro-Americans to make a general, mass exodus from the United States because increasingly they believed that material and political liberation and equality were hopeless and unfounded aspirations for blacks in the American context. The Southern slave system appeared more unshakably entrenched than ever. Blacks in so-called free states continued to encounter severe forms of discrimination, rejection, hostility, and the deprivation of political rights. In addition, the 1850s brought disheartening political setbacks such as the passage of the Fugitive Slave Law in 1850 and the Dred Scott Decision by the U.S. Supreme Court in 1857. The law of 1850 made any free black person vulnerable to kidnapping if accused of being a runaway. The Dred Scott Decision not only ruled that slaves were not entitled to freedom upon entry onto ''free'' soil, but it also virtually declared blacks to be noncitizens in the country of their birth. The advent of the Civil War, followed by the passage of the Thirteenth, Fourteenth, and Fifteenth amendments and the era of Reconstruction, would smother the fires of emigration for a while. But with the collapse of Reconstruction and the gradual takeover of political control by reactionary whites in the South, this interest in emigration would blossom again in the late 1870s and the 1880s. As we shall see in the next chapter, this post–Civil War period was a time of renewed interest in African evangelization as well.

## BLACK BAPTIST ORGANIZATIONS PRIOR TO 1880

Though our focus is the period 1880–1915, it is useful to note that prior to 1880 black Baptists took keen interest in the Christianization and material improvement of black peoples, foreign and domestic. Indeed, it was during this period that the seeds of missiological themes were firmly planted. This interest blossomed in the organization of a number of pre-1880 black Baptist denominational organizations. Racism in the church resulted in blacks generally withdrawing from predominantly white or white-controlled churches and denominations and forming black institutions in which they could worship God in the manner most compatible with their temperament and circumstances. A number of independent black Baptist organizations[15] were founded, including the Providence Baptist Association formed in 1835 and based in Ohio; the Wood River Baptist Association (1838) in Illinois; the Northwestern and Southern Baptist Convention (1864); the General Association of Western States and Territories (1873); and the New England Baptist Missionary Convention (1874).

Most of these early black Baptist organizations were regional rather than national in character. Understandably, slaveholders in the South, in an effort to ensure the stability of the slave system against ideas of freedom gained from association in independent black organizations, discouraged black Baptist denominational unity. If we exclude the South, the first all-black national organization formed to serve Baptists was the American Baptist Missionary Convention founded in 1840 at the Abyssinian Baptist Church in New York City. It seemed that black Baptists were on the verge of having a truly national organization in 1866 when they gathered in Richmond, Virginia, to establish the Consolidated American Baptist Missionary Convention, a merger of the American Baptist Missionary Convention and the Northwestern and Southern Baptist Convention.

For the most part, these organizations concerned themselves primarily with domestic concerns, especially prior to the eradication of American slavery. After the Civil War, however, there appeared to be a decided interest in foreign mission work among black Baptists, North and South. As early as 1869, the Consolidated American Educational Association, a subsidiary of the Consolidated Convention, described itself as an organization "officered and managed principally by colored persons, and laboring for the education and evangelization of their race in the south, in Africa, and wherever found unimproved."[16]

<hr>

[15]Carter G. Woodson, *The History of the Negro Church*, 3d ed. (Washington, D.C.: Associated Publishers, 1972) 107. William H. Moses, *The Colored Baptist Family Tree: A Compendium of Organized Negro Baptist Church History* (Nashville: Sunday School Publishing Board, National Baptist Convention, U.S.A., 1925) 11-12. Also see Lewis Garnett Jordan, *Negro Baptist History U.S.A., 1750–1930* (Nashville: Sunday School Publishing Board, National Baptist Convention, 1936).

[16]An appended booklet, "An Appeal," Minutes of the Consolidated American Education Association (CAEA), 1869.

At the 1877 meeting of the Consolidated American Baptist Convention[17] in Richmond, the Committee on Fields submitted a report, subsequently accepted by the larger convention, that four traveling agents be appointed to gather a total sum of thirty thousand dollars. One third of the money was to be expended on each of the following categories: home missions, publishing and educational aspects of the convention, and foreign missions. Another recommendation of the committee called for the support of a missionary in the black republic of Haiti.

The convention was presented with a report which acknowledged that domestic responsibilities practically exhausted its financial resources. Nevertheless, the organization was bound to respond favorably to the needs of foreign missions. Besides concern for Haiti, the demands of Africa were loud and clear. The Consolidated Baptists were in a precarious position. While white Baptists in both the North and South could make claims for rendering service to the continent, the Consolidated Baptists had made no appreciable efforts in that direction. The convention was urged either to establish its own Board of Foreign Missions or to enter into cooperative arrangements with other groups actively engaged in African mission work.

The minutes of this convention highlight not only a religious obligation of Afro-American Baptists, but a racial responsibility as well. This can be assumed from the fact that the Consolidated Baptists targeted the two black lands of the Haitian republic and the African continent. But at least some Baptist members of this convention spoke of the racial motivations for Africa in explicit and unequivocal terms: "Though of American birth and education, we are nevertheless sons of Africa. God has ordained it. He has written it on our faces, and on the tablets of our hearts, and no political changes, nor no social amalgamation, or [rhetoric] can blot it out."[18]

Within a decade the scramble for Africa among European nations had begun. Already the Consolidated Baptists were voicing their concern for the future existence of Africa as an independent continent. Noting British interest in and entrenchment upon the continent, the report calls upon blacks to awaken to a providential bidding for them to maintain the integrity of

---

[17]Annual Minutes, Consolidated American Baptist Convention (CABC), 1877, 20-21, 30-31.

[18]Ibid., 31.

their homeland from any imperial designs of England. This meant that black Christians had a special obligation to their racial brothers not only in regard to their spiritual development, but in regard to their political security as well: "God signals the intelligent men of our race, to begin to occupy the land, lest the African soon become a wandering Jew, without Judea, and without Jerusalem."[19]

Meanwhile, black Baptists in the South were also cultivating a foreign missionary program. In the 1870s the black Baptists in the states of Virginia, North Carolina, and South Carolina commissioned missionaries for service in West Africa. The foundation of a substantial Baptist presence in West Africa, however, began much earlier with three men—William Crane, Lott Carey, and Colin Teague—and the 1815 founding of the Richmond African Baptist Missionary Society in Virginia.[20] William Crane, a white Baptist from New Jersey, moved with his wife to Richmond in 1811. Crane's entire life was marked by a strong missionary interest and a benevolent, though not abolitionist, concern for Afro-Americans. While a member of the First Baptist Church under the supervision of the Reverend John Courtney, Deacon Crane organized a night school for young black men. Among those students were two black Baptists, Colin Teague and Lott Carey. The Richmond African Baptist Missionary Society grew out of Crane's informing the students about African missions and about the work of the American missions and the American Colonization Society.

Lott Carey assumed leadership in enlisting moral and financial support for African missions among his fellow Afro-American Baptists in the area. Crane was elected president (probably ceremonial and to legitimate the organization in the slave society of Virginia) and corresponding secretary. But Carey, elected recording secretary, played the larger role in making the missionary program a success. As a matter of fact, both Carey and Tea-

---

[19]Ibid.

[20]For accounts of these three men and the Richmond African Baptist Missionary Society, see Miles Mark Fisher, "Lott Carey, the Colonizing Missionary," *Journal of Negro History* 7 (October 1922): 380-418; William A. Poe, "Lott Carey: Man of Purchased Freedom," *Church History* 39 (March 1970): 49-61; and the chapter on Lott Carey in James B. Taylor, *Virginia Baptist Ministers*, vol. 2 (Philadelphia: J. B. Lippincott & Co., 1859). The reader might also be interested in Leroy Fitts, *Lott Carey: First Black Missionary to Africa* (Valley Forge PA: Judson Press, 1978).

gue present remarkable examples of black leadership in a church and in a society ruled by whites in the antebellum South. Both were ministers of the gospel. Born slaves, both purchased their freedom and the freedom of their families. Both exhibited a strong interest in African missions, becoming missionaries to Africa. Carey died in Liberia, and Teague eventually settled in the British colony of Sierra Leone. But it appears that Carey exercised the greater gifts for leadership in preaching style as well as in intellectual capacity.

The Richmond Society and Southern black Baptists played a crucial role in the development of missionary interest and support among Baptists in the U.S. Through the agency of the Richmond Society, black Baptists demonstrated their concern for African missions by generous financial donations, which exceeded those of their white counterparts. With the intercession of Crane, the society became an auxiliary of the Triennial Convention (which had been formed in 1814). After hearing the reports of agents sent to Africa by the Colonization Society (again, through Crane as intermediary), Carey and Teague determined that they would go to Africa as missionaries. Crane in 1819 appealed to both the Triennial Convention and the Colonization Society on their behalf. Both organizations agreed to support the two Baptist clergymen: the society, as colonists; the convention, as missionaries.

Most of Teague's and Carey's financial support, however, came through the medium of the Richmond Society.[21] In 1819 the General Convention of Baptists listed only two dollars for African missions. In 1820, the year of the men's departure, the Richmond Society deposited $438.25 of the $500.25 that the Triennial Board of Foreign Missions gave to them. The American Colonization Society aided them with $200 in monies and another $100 in books. By 1840 the Richmond Society had paid the Baptist denomination $700 for African missions. For a number of years after 1840, the Richmond group would donate annual sums ranging from $100 to $150.

## WHITE BAPTISTS IN AFRICA

For many years white Baptists generally left the work in African missions to Afro-American missionaries. For several possible reasons most

[21]Fisher, "Lott Carey," 388.

whites chose missionary fields in Burma, China, and other Asian fields
rather than in West Africa. (1) The negative and racist concepts about Africa and its people perhaps played a role in deterring missionaries from the
field. (2) Significant Baptist forerunners of foreign missions, William Carey
in England and Luther Rice and Adoniram Judson in America, had set
precedents for work in Asia. (3) Most whites operated from the unscien-
tific and racist assumptions that (a) climate caused the death of white missionaries in West Africa, and (b) Afro-Americans, as African descendants,
could more ably survive there. Actually, it was malaria carried by mos-
quitoes that caused the death, as was discovered at the turn of the century.
Second, blacks from the U.S. succumbed to the fever in the same proportions as their white missionary counterparts. Because of these misconcep-
tions about the climate, white and black Baptists alike felt that the
evangelization of the continent must be achieved through the instrumentality of Afro-Americans.

Baptist involvement in African missions would have its ups and downs,
with the great bulk of missionary responsibility falling on the shoulders of
Afro-American and Liberian Baptists. The first white Baptist missionaries
journeyed to Africa in 1835: William Mylne, a resident of Richmond and
native to Scotland, and William G. Crocker, a native of Newburyport,
Massachusetts. In April 1841 Mylne's health compelled his return to the
U.S. After losing his wife and returning to Africa for his second trip in
1844, Crocker died of malaria.[22] During this period the Reverend and Mrs.
John Clarke also served as missionaries in West Africa. Upon their departure, Baptist work rested exclusively in the hands of the indigenous
converts.[23]

In 1843 there was a significant division in the Triennial Convention,
the Baptist group founded in 1814, when a group of abolitionist Baptists
broke away over the question of the convention's stand on the issue of
slavery. The more important and devastating rupture, however, came in

---

[22]Baker J. Cauthen, ed., *Advance: A History of Southern Baptist Missions in Foreign
Lands* (Nashville: Broadman Press, 1970) 14; G. Winfred Hervey, *The Story of Baptist
Missions in Foreign Lands: From the Time of Carey to the Present Date* (St. Louis: Chancy
R. Barns, 1886) 487-92.

[23]J. DuPlessis, *The Evangelisation of Pagan Africa: A History of Christian Missions to
the Pagan Tribes of Central Africa* (Cape Town, South Africa: J. C. Juta & Co., 1929) 96.

1845 when the convention divided over the propriety of commissioning slaveholding missionaries. The Southern Baptist Convention (SBC) organized in the South and the American Baptist Missionary Union (ABMU) made its base in the North. Northern Baptists' missionary endeavors in Africa withered gradually until 1856 when the American Baptists withdrew support altogether and sold their mission field to the SBC. The Southern Convention, perhaps to demonstrate that their strong theological defense of slavery did not exclude all benevolent and missionary concern for black people, appears to have turned to Africa with renewed attention. In 1846 the SBC Foreign Mission Board appointed two black Baptists, A. L. Jones and John Day, for missionary labors in Africa (though Jones, currently in Liberia, died before he had been informed of the appointment). By 1849 all missionary personnel in the African mission field were black, and this staff included thirteen missionaries, seven ministers, and six teachers. There were mission posts at eight locations.[24]

Beginning with the appointment of Thomas J. Bowen of Georgia in 1849, two significant trends emerged. One, there was a greater involvement of whites in African mission work. Two, the SBC Foreign Board gradually shifted the focus of its concern from Liberia to Nigeria. Thomas Bowen was the first white American Baptist missionary to explore the land of the Yoruba people in Nigeria. Bowen published a book on Yoruba grammar that was a revision of a work by the African bishop Samuel Crowther. Bowen also wrote extensively on Africa, his most memorable and major work being *Adventures and Missionary Labours*. . . . His work does carry the mark of racism and an ethnocentric view toward African societies. Nevertheless, in writing about a territory hitherto unexplored by American missionaries, Bowen does exhibit a tolerance and understanding

---

[24]H. Cornell Goerner, ''Africa,'' in Cauthen, *Advance*, 138. Also consult the following for an examination of Southern Baptist missionary involvement in Africa: C. Sylvester Green, *New Nigeria: Southern Baptists at Work in Africa* (Richmond: Foreign Mission Board, Southern Baptist Convention, 1936); H. A. Tupper, *The Foreign Missions of the Southern Baptist Convention* (Philadelphia: American Baptist Publication Society, 1880); Nan F. Weeks, comp., *Builders of a New Africa* (Nashville: Broadman Press, 1944); Mary Emily Wright, *The Missionary Work of the Southern Baptist Convention* (Philadelphia: American Baptist Publication Society, 1902).

of African peoples, customs, religions, and land that were often lacking in the writings of missionaries before and after his stay in Africa.[25]

Other missionaries entered Nigeria in the decade of the 1850s, which added to the shift of Southern Baptist missionaries from Liberia to Nigeria. They include J. S. Dennard and John H. Lacy, 1853; Mr. and Mrs. A. D. Phillips, 1855; J. F Beaumont, a layperson, 1855; the two couples of J. A. Reid and R. H. Stone, 1858. Joseph M. Harden, a black Baptist, in 1855 transferred from the Liberian mission to the Lagos mission.

Though these persons and others began the Nigerian mission work for Southern Baptists, other factors hindered mission growth. First, in the 1860s intertribal wars among the Yoruba considerably stifled the movement of all Christian missionaries in that portion of Africa. Second, the American Civil War diverted missionary interest as well as financial and, perhaps, human resources from the African mission fields to the domestic front. Third, the death of many missionaries, including Joseph Harden, and the breakdown in the health of others took their toll on the missionary program. When R. H. Stone left Nigeria for health reasons in 1869, the full responsibility of maintaining the Baptist church in that area devolved upon Mrs. Sarah M. Harden, the widow of Joseph Harden. It was not until 1875 that Baptist missionaries from the U.S. returned to Africa: W. J. David, a white missionary from Mississippi, and William W. Colley, an Afro-American from the Richmond Institute in Virginia.

To the credit of the SBC, they refused to allow these setbacks and hardships to deter them from continuing African mission work. At the 1869 meeting of the SBC Convention, the Committee on African Missions advised the convention to view the contemporary circumstances as challenges to advance to greater faith rather than as opportunities to retreat from the mission field. The board, referring to the New Testament, argued that the imprisonment of Peter and the murder of James spurred the growth of Christianity. Likewise, difficult working conditions in Burma during the inception of missionary work there did not halt the activities of U.S. Bap-

---

[25]*Adventures and Missionary Labours in Several Countries in the Interior of Africa from 1849 to 1856*, 2d ed., with a new introduction by E. A. Ayandele (London: Frank Cass & Co., 1968). Ayandele's introduction (vii-L) is quite informative of the missionary and his theology.

tists. Besides, with the increase in baptisms, Baptists should see clear signs of God's work in Africa.[26]

This type of reasoning obviously held sway. In 1871 A. D. Phillips, who had left the continent a few years earlier for health reasons, returned to Africa. The purpose of his return was to explore the coast and report his findings to the SBC. He visited sites in both Liberia and Nigeria. Though whites at the time of this exploratory expedition still were basically barred from re-entry into the lands of the Yoruba, Phillips's report to the 1872 meeting of the SBC advised the Baptists to maintain readiness in the event the opportunity presented itself.[27]

There appears to have been serious thought within the SBC of discontinuing African missions during these post–Civil War years of economic hardship for the South. But the African Committee of the Foreign Mission Board in 1872 recommended that the African field remain open for several reasons. One, Baptists should not retreat from an enterprise that had already cost many lives and much money. Two, judging from past experiences "and the opinions of our returned missionaries," the committee felt that "this mission will be useful." Three, the committee members reasoned that it is always helpful to have a variety of missions for "interest" and as a stronger premise for mission fund raising. Perhaps on the basis of this third proposition, the committee listed a fourth reason: only African missionary work received the active support of black Baptists in the South.[28]

During this period the prevailing view would remain that Afro-Americans should be utilized for African mission work. For example, the African Committee report of 1872 recommended that *most* of the mission work be carried out by black missionaries. The reasons offered were basically the same as those of the pre–Civil War period: "They would be more acceptable to their own race; they would be more likely to live in Africa, and could be more cheaply sustained."[29] Actually, white Baptists, perhaps because of a shortage of personnel and resources, desired to turn as much

---

[26]Annual Minutes of the Southern Baptist Convention, 1869, 28-29.

[27]Ibid., 1872, 36-37.

[28]Ibid.

[29]Ibid., 36.

responsibility over to the Afro-Americans as possible. The committee requested that special appeals be directed to black Baptists in search of missionary support. In the event that black churches would be able to sustain
the expenses, the SBC could channel all of their resources to the European
and Asian mission fields. Besides, "the reflex influence would be most
blessed in developing the Christian character of these churches."[30] The
committee members felt confident that qualified black candidates could be
found if "earnestly" sought. Yet, the committee demonstrated their lack
of full confidence that Afro-Americans could or should bear full responsibility for the direction of mission work when they added that "in organizing this mission, and establishing it upon a permanent basis, at least one
white man should be employed as Superintendent."[31]

Though Southerners appeared to dominate in African missions during
the pre–Civil War period, the post–Civil War era would witness a rebirth of
missionary zeal among Northern Baptists. As early as 1867 the American Baptist Foreign Missionary Union's Executive Committee was seriously considering a renewal of assistance to Baptists in Liberia who had
formerly received such aid.[32] By 1871 J. T. Richardson, the Liberia Baptist leader, was serving in a crucial position as a missionary agent of the
union.[33] Moreover, in 1871, Northern Baptists could claim to support
fourteen Baptist preachers and teachers at various locations in West Africa.[34] At the General Conference meeting in Philadelphia in 1875, a report
was adopted whereby the number of members of the Liberian affiliate of
the Executive Committee of the Missionary Union would be increased from
three members to seven with at least three of the committee members being
laypersons. The conference also set the goal of five thousand dollars to be
collected to aid African mission work during the next year.[35] Records show
that a year later the missionary zeal for Africa was still gaining momen-

---

[30]Ibid.

[31]Ibid.

[32]*African Repository* 42 (August 1867): 253.

[33]Ibid., 47 (June 1871): 189.

[34]Ibid., 47 (August 1871): 265.

[35]Ibid., 51 (October 1875): 116.

tum. The 1876 conference regretted that it had ever abandoned the African field and sought to pursue its interest in missions through cooperation with the Southern Baptist Convention and black Baptists.[36] Like their Southern counterparts, however, Northern Baptists during this period devoted most of their limited financial resources for foreign missions to the missionary fields in Europe and Asia.

## AFRICAN MISSIOLOGY OF WHITE BAPTISTS

As whites entered Africa they carried with them certain basic theological and social assumptions of most missionary-minded American Protestants. Baptists, too, believed that they had a mission to speak not only a "spiritual" message, but also to spread Christian civilization to non-Christian lands. For the most part, Baptists regarded African societies as degraded ones needing redemption of both individual souls and the corporate communities. Colonization was looked upon as a great means through which to foster the Protestant faith and Western civilization.

At the meeting of the Triennial Convention of Baptists in 1835, the delegates assembled received a report expounding the necessity for African missions and expressing faith that Christianity would play a crucial role in the development of African culture. First, the Committee on the African Mission urged the convention to attach as great a significance and dedication to work in Africa as to any other location of missionary service. True, African societies have been degraded through "heathenism." But equally certain, the Scripture has given a prophecy that Ethiopia shall stretch forth her hands to God. As Africans would turn to accept the one and only gospel, their material situations would improve simultaneously. In the midst of controversy over the abolition of American slavery, persons north and south could agree that the slave trade was un-Christian. The extension of Christianity would have the effect of ridding the continent of the slave trade. As erroneous beliefs, customs, and practices were eliminated, Africans would no longer interest themselves in selling each other for gain.[37] "Prophecy must be fulfilled, in the stretching forth of Ethiopia's hand unto

---

[36]Ibid., 53 (January 1877): 30-31.

[37]Annual Minutes, Triennial Convention of Baptists, 1835, 72-73.

the Lord. Ours is the work of helping Ethiopia to stretch out this hand to the Lord for deliverance; not for using it for her own subjugation. Important, indeed, must be the mission, whose unmixed object it is to assist in the accomplishment of a prophecy so clear."[38]

This concern for African mission work followed the founding of the Southern Baptist Convention in 1845, as I have noted previously in this chapter. After the ecclesiastical division in the ranks, the Southern Baptists saw the South as maintaining the missionary legacy of Adoniram Judson—just as their political counterparts at the time of secession would view themselves as persevering in the tradition of Washington and Jefferson. William B. Johnson, president-elect of the SBC, exemplified this viewpoint in his address to the convention in 1845. Consistent with the Judson tradition, Baptists of the South had the obligation to go around the world, into every "wilderness and desolate place," to preach the gospel. Africa, presumably, was to be included in this field ripe for harvest.[39]

As a matter of fact, many missionaries would see the huge black presence in the South as one reason why Southern Baptists would look upon themselves as the most qualified for the evangelizing of Africa. For example, Eli Ball, writing to several clergymen of Savannah, Georgia, in a letter dated 21 June 1852, expresses this opinion: "I believe that God has reserved for the Southern states chiefly the honor of spreading through benighted Africa the light of the blessed gospel, by means of their free colored people, and such slaves as they may see fit to liberate for the purpose of going to Africa."[40] This statement reveals that Ball also favored colonization and the Colonization Society as agents of mission work.

William H. Clark, SBC missionary to Nigeria, viewed Christianity as going beyond personal acceptance of the gospel. He believed that Africans must accept Christianity on a mass level. If one African village would renounce its traditions, beliefs, and customs and turn to Christianity, then other towns would follow suit. Clark stressed that a high price would be asked of anyone who sought to share the gospel in Africa: self-sacrifice;

---

[38]Ibid., 72.

[39]Cauthen, *Advance*, 21-22.

[40]*African Repository* 28 (October 1852): 344.

perseverance; the ability to live among the people and to share their ac-
commodations and foods; dedication to preaching; and firm regularity in
prayer.[41]

Clark supported colonization as an instrument to foster Christianity and
Western civilization. He, however, agreed with Bowen that the best place
would be in the Niger Valley of West Africa. Clark felt that Afro-Americans played a significant role in God's providential plan to lift Africa from
barbarism. He believed that Liberia had done much to advance the cause
of Christianity and held out hope that it might eventually play a crucial role
in the elevation of West Africa. But he doubted that the influence of the
American colony of Liberia could ever permeate the interior of the continent. In the interior of the continent, in a sparsely populated area of the
Nufi kingdom along the Niger River, there was an ideal, providential spot
for an Afro-American colony in Africa.[42] Clark writes: "*A colony we shall
have,* that shall prove Heaven's blessing to the kingdom of the Soudan. Let
Liberia go on and prosper; but we must have, we shall have, God will place
a colony for his own purposes, in the valley of the Niger."[43]

Thomas Jefferson Bowen of Georgia represents both traditional and novel
approaches to missionary work. Undoubtedly, Bowen held racist notions of
black inferiority. The missionary believed that blacks would never equal whites
in terms of innate capabilities. Equally repulsive is Bowen's opinion that blacks
left to themselves never made any significant advances in civilization. In line
with many white contemporaries, Bowen viewed pure blacks on the western
coast of Africa as a contemptible and degraded lot of people. But what is really
unfortunate was the foundation he provided for that observation. According
to Bowen, one would find greater, superior societies as one ventured inland
because these peoples—for example, the Yoruba, Ibo, and the Hausas—sup-
posedly had white ancestry.[44]

Nevertheless, in Bowen's writings one can discern a degree of sympathy, understanding, and toleration of African peoples, beliefs, and cus-

---

[41]Ibid., 32 (April 1856): 122.

[42]Ibid., 34 (April 1858): 105-107.

[43]Ibid., 107.

[44]See E. A. Ayandele's introduction to Bowen, *Adventures and Missionary Labours,*
xxxii-xxxiv.

toms often lacking in many other missionaries, white or black, during that time and since. In a letter to the Foreign Mission Board of the SBC written in January 1852, Bowen revealed his plan to record a firsthand account of his experience of African societies. Such a project is necessary given that "the social life and real character of the Africans have seldom been studied. We have looked at them through other and much less favorable mediums. For my own part, I respect them far more than I did, and I am convinced that they are capable of being Christianized and civilized."[45]

In chapter 25 of *Adventures and Missionary Labours*,[46] Bowen demonstrated an unusual degree of comprehension and perhaps some appreciation for Yoruba religion. He pointed out that the Yorubas worship only one supreme god in theory. He explains that "idols" are not worshiped, but are merely symbols or representations of the lesser gods. Bowen compared the veneration of the lesser gods by the Yorubas to the homage paid by Roman Catholics to their saints. He did grant that the masses of people might fail to comprehend the role of the idols. But Bowen wrote: "The Guinea man who bows before idols, and trusts in the amulet called a fetish, is certainly very stupid, but he does nothing which is not imitated by half the people of Christendom."[47]

Bowen appears to have articulated better than any other pre-1880 white Baptist missionary the necessity of allowing an indigenous African civilization to develop, albeit along Christian foundations. In other words, he endorses in some sense the idea of permitting Christianity to adapt to the cultural needs, aspirations, and concerns of African people rather than attempting to pass on a Euro-American Christian civilization based upon the uncritical assumption that it was immaculate and ideal for all peoples. Missionaries, he urged, should avoid committing "the too common mistake of supposing that our form of civilization is the exemplar of the whole earth. It is not the best for ourselves, and is not adapted to Africa at all. The climate and the moral constitution of the people are unanimous in demanding an African civilization for Africa."[48]

[45]*African Repository* 28 (October 1852): 201.

[46]Bowen, *Adventures and Missionary Labours,* 310-20.

[47]Ibid., 312.

[48]Ibid., 327.

Notwithstanding, these things should not be taken to suggest that Bowen was either a cultural or religious relativist. This SBC missionary firmly believed that Christianity was *the* true religion.[49] However much of the truth any other religious system possessed, people still required the intercession of Jesus of Nazareth as mediator between God and themselves. Despite Bowen's advocating some indigenous form of African civilization, he also was an ardent exponent of colonization even after the close of the Civil War in the U.S. Bowen, despite his abhorrence of the slave trade, believed—as many nineteenth-century religious people—that God had chosen the white race as a tutor for the African race. Even from the unfortunate institution of American slavery came some good. Namely, blacks gained civilization and Christianity. In emigrating to Africa free blacks would not only avoid harsh economic competition with American whites in the future, but they would also play a providential function in carrying the blessings of Christian civilization.[50] As Bowen wrote, "The God of all the earth, without whose directing influence not even a sparrow falls to the ground, has not located so many Africans in America without a purpose."[51] Along with missionary endeavors and commerce, African colonization was one instrument that would operate to redeem Africa.

Bowen's belief that American Christians were in the process of spreading civilization and Christianity to African people can be seen in his attitude toward the Liberian republic. Certainly, as an outpost of Christianity and civilization, Liberia was a providential instrument for bringing these blessings to the continent. He believed that Liberia possessed great potential to be a strong nation. Liberians had gotten off to a good start in 1847 when they patterned their government after that of the United States.[52] Far

---

[49]See ibid., 321-45, as support for this thought. Bowen writes, for example,

But our designs and hopes in regard to Africa, are not simply to bring as many individuals as possible to the knowledge of Christ. We desire to establish the Gospel in the hearts and minds and social life of the people, so that truth and righteousness may remain and flourish among them, without the instrumentality of foreign missionaries. This cannot be done without civilization. (321-22)

[50]Ibid., 58-60, and Bowen's letter in the *African Repository* 30 (October 1854): 292.

[51]Bowen, *Adventures and Missionary Labours,* 59.

[52]Ibid., 57-66.

from being a relativist at this point, Bowen's concern was that Liberians could have made greater efforts to spread their influence to other peoples in Africa. Though churches and schools were open for indigenous Africans who chose to make use of these institutions, more "special efforts" must be made to bring Africans into these institutions. Making allowance for the social distance between the Liberians and the Africans, Bowen nevertheless refused to excuse the underlying contempt with which Liberians regarded Africans.[53]

Bowen believed that a new colonization venture should be made in the state of Nigeria. Both in terms of geography and climate, he felt that the land of the Yorubas would be an ideal area to lay foundations of a new colony. The people there showed signs of being more receptive to Christianity and Westernization than those in Liberia.[54]

Surely he envisioned that this new society would contain a variety of benevolent influences that no non-Christian tribe in Africa had experienced. With these benefits patiently, painstakingly, and fully applied, any group of people would be able to escape completely the ills of heathenism.[55] Describing the prerequisites for progress, Bowen wrote:

> There must be a somewhat extensive diffusion of correct science, a knowledge of the world and its history, just notions of civil government, some proficiency in the arts which are indispensable to enlightened men, commerce, and above all, the sanctifying influence of Christianity, all cooperating before we can reasonably hope for the conversion and elevation of any people.[56]

## BLACK PRESENCE AND MISSIOLOGY

Thus, black Baptists' missionary endeavors began in cooperation with the foreign mission activities of their white counterparts. Lott Carey, the black Baptist missionary from Virginia, to a great extent laid a foundation for practice and theology of both white and black Baptists in Africa. Carey

---

[53]Ibid., 33.

[54]*African Repository* 33 (September 1857): 280-81.

[55]Ibid., 30 (October 1854): 290-92.

[56]Ibid., 291.

journeyed to Africa as both a colonizer and missionary whose mission was to bear Christianity and civilization. It is clear that he shared the theological assumptions of his white Baptist counterparts. In answering the needs of the colonists, Carey, shortly after his arrival, found himself moving beyond the "spiritual" realm of mission work. For a time he practiced self-taught medicine. Though he led a rebellion of the colonists against certain policies of the Colonization Society agent, the issues were eventually resolved and he continued in the role of a colonist. By 1828 he had risen to the vice-governorship and even served once as acting governor in the absence of the governor. In a war between the Afro-American colonists and the indigenous Africans, Carey lost his life while preparing to defend the colony.[57]

Hilary Teague was the son of Colin Teague (Carey's associate), and eloquent minister, politician, and newspaper editor. He would be among those Baptists who would carry on the Carey tradition. His conception of Liberia as an outpost of Christian civilization in a barbarian wilderness survives in a hymn he wrote to celebrate the victory of the colonists over indigenous Africans who had attacked Liberian settlements.[58] Teague begins by praising God for divine power and sovereignty. In speaking of his African enemies, Teague characterized them as a people craving the blood of the colonists, possessing limitless hatred and malice, and having hearts devoid of love. The barbarians trusted in idol gods, while in contrast the Christian and civilized colonists relied on the one, true God to whom alone belongs credit for their victory over the Africans.

Furthermore, colonization, in Carey's view and that of Baptists, was seen as a significant apparatus for "redeeming and regenerating" the continent. Just as the British people rose from savagery to the status of the most powerful people in the world, the Africans too were "swiftly rising into the light and comforts of civilization." Almost twenty years after the arrival of his father in Africa, Teague was expounding a belief in 1840 that would be reiterated by T. J. Bowen, the white Baptist missionary, a decade or so later: the African continent would be redeemed principally

---

[57]See n. 2.

[58]*African Repository* 12 (July 1837): 231.

through the three agencies of Christian colonies, missionary stations, and commerce. Colonies were especially helpful in that they stood as concrete, lasting examples for Africans to imitate. Whether colonization resulted in the elimination of American slavery, Teague claimed not to know. His primary reason for supporting the colonization scheme was the redemption of Africa from barbarism.[59]

Teague, however, loathed American slavery as well as racial prejudice and discrimination. Writing from the Liberian capital of Monrovia on 2 January 1851, Teague hailed the colony of Liberia as a haven for Afro-Americans seeking freedom and equality. He actually appealed for Afro-American emigration, since one of the major needs of the young republic was a larger population. The black race possessed all the capacities of any other race. But if any people were to be perfected, they must exist in an atmosphere where their cravings for freedom, justice, and equality can be realized. The acquisition of classical training would not save blacks from the harshness of racial discrimination in the U.S. Teague granted that there were certain shortcomings to living in Liberia. Still, by far it was a much better place for blacks than the U.S.[60] Noting the marginal existence of even free blacks in the antebellum U.S., Teague wrote: "But it's so much more pleasing to be voting for one's own representatives, than to be peeping round the corner at those who are voting—so much more pleasant to clean one's own farm, than to clean another's boots, especially when he is conscious that it is the *ne plus ultra* of his accent."[61]

In examining the Baptist missionaries' concern for colonization and the establishment of Christian societies, one must not overlook the strong belief in the personal dimension of evangelism that characterized the missionaries' theology. Men and women must have a personal confrontation with Jesus, be forgiven of their sins, and thereafter live new lives of personal piety and holiness. John Day was one of the first black missionaries appointed for work in Liberia in 1845 by the newly organized SBC, and he served for a time as the superintendent for Baptist missionary work in

---

[59]Ibid., 15 (October 1840): 316-17.

[60]Ibid., 27 (July 1851): 199-200.

[61]Ibid., 200.

Liberia and Sierra Leone. His letter dated 17 November 1853 is an example of the evangelical missionary theology and method. It was imperative, according to Day, that the unconverted admit that he/she is a lost
sinner and become "a penitent seeker after salvation." Day praised God
that he had preached to the "heathen." He encouraged other missionaries
to rely upon the preached word rather than trying to "prepare it by a little
education; a little civilization." It was vanity to rely upon one's own judgment rather than to trust the explicit command of God. It was preaching
that destroyed Satan's kingdom and builds the kingdom of Christ.[62]

Day is a prime example of how black Baptists' emphasis upon personal
evangelism and personal piety coincided with their advocating African
colonization and its offspring, Liberia, as a means by which to uplift black
people. Three months prior to his letter discussed above, he had addressed
correspondence to free blacks in the U.S., urging them to support colonization. That letter was written in the decade of the 1850s, a time when
a resurgence of interest in colonization was taking place among black
Americans. Day wondered how blacks could live in a land that placed such
a number of restraints upon their activities and stifled their aspirations for
progress. How could their human spirits still manage to escape the harmful
consequences of this racial containment? Unlike blacks in the U.S., Liberians did not have to relegate themselves to servile positions. Quite the
contrary, they were exposed to an environment that nourished, sustained,
and encouraged the fullest development of the human spirit. As a result,
blacks in time would be second to no other people. This was not a fantastic
dream, he argued, when one recalled that African civilization once had
blossomed in grandeur while Europeans were immersed in barbarism.[63]
"May not a reversion take place, and Africa again be the garden of the
earth?"[64] Given the freedom and equality afforded blacks in Liberia, Day
contended that Liberia was already a paradise in comparison to other places
where blacks lived, places where they were "pointed out as a distinct and
inferior class."[65]

[62]Ibid., 30 (November 1854): 341-42.
[63]Ibid., 30 (May 1854): 144-46.
[64]Ibid., 146.
[65]Ibid.

Of course, many blacks in the antebellum U.S. refused to embrace colonization and emigration programs even during the difficult decade of the 1850s. They continued in their antislavery activities and struggles against racism, believing, hoping, and praying that their efforts and those of sympathetic whites would eventually result in the elimination of slavery and the nation's recognition of its black inhabitants as full and equal partners in the democratic experiment.

Day, in his letter, dealt with the major objections that these colonization opponents advanced. First, he discarded the notion that blacks should remain in the U.S. to wage an antislavery battle out of a feeling of obligation to their brothers and sisters in slavery. He pointed out that free blacks' presence in the country so far had not had the effect of dismantling slavery, and he believed that it never would. Besides, African brothers and sisters were held in a bondage much more devastating than the physical slavery in America. They were lost in the realm of barbarism, in the grips of Satan.

Second, Day addressed the concern raised by whites and blacks that because the Colonization Society was a racist organization founded upon the principle of black inferiority, its objectives could not include the true well-being of Afro-Americans. The missionary repudiated the racism of some proponents of colonization, but he maintained that the society was the most benevolent activity being conducted on behalf of black liberation. Day believed that God was involved in the work and goal of the society for the good of blacks. And, regardless of whether human motives were mainly evil or chiefly good, all things worked under the sovereignty of God's plan for the freedom and development of black people. Rather than strive against this God-approved enterprise, blacks should rise and assist the Lord in this work of colonization. "Come to the land of true liberty, where you and your children may not only be happy yourselves, but where you can assist in making Africa the praise of the whole earth."[66]

Five years later Day still defended the close relationship between colonization and evangelism, viewing the task of Afro-Americans as a providential one to bring Christian civilization to a backward and lost continent. Writing on 13 November 1858, John Day reflected on his many years of

---

[66]Ibid.

missionary service in Africa and expressed the belief that he now stood "on the verge of Jordan." He continued to view Liberia as a nation chosen by God. The economic woes of the country were interpreted to mean that God lovingly "rebukes and chastens" the country.[67] He linked Afro-Americans, Liberians, and Africans as objects in a providential plan: "Ethiopia is to stretch out its hands in prayer and praise; its inhabitants are to be exalted. And American slavery, emancipation and colonization, are to perform their part in the great work. If the present colonists are recreant to their trust, God will nevertheless accomplish His purpose through them."[68] Africa, depopulated by wars and the slave trade, now stood beckoning black Americans to return to the land of their forefathers.

Notwithstanding the assistance of white Baptists north and south, the major responsibility for carrying on the work of missions rested in the hands of black Baptists in Liberia. When small amounts of aid or none at all came from Baptists in the United States, particularly during the period of the American Civil War, Liberians continued to evangelize and erect churches. Also, just as black Baptists in the Southern states served as vanguardists for African missions, likewise black Baptists in Liberia, especially during the years 1868–1880, played a leading role in influencing white and black Baptists in the U.S. to renew or inaugurate systematic mission programs.

Most missionary efforts for the first forty or fifty years of black Baptist presence in Liberia were directed toward the colonists rather than to the indigenous inhabitants. One factor contributing to this situation was the language and cultural differences between the two groups. In both groups religion and culture were so closely allied that giving up on one meant surrendering the other. In addition, the Colonization Society had acquired the land by questionable means at best and by fraudulent methods most probably. The Africans understandably resented the presence of the colonists, and the superior attitude on the part of the latter served to exacerbate conditions. One must bear in mind also that much of the time and energy of the colonists were absorbed in adjusting to a wholly new physical environment.

---

[67]Ibid., 35 (February 1859): 56-57.

[68]Ibid., 56.

At any rate, a more vigorous, concerted effort to reach the indigenous populations was inaugurated in March 1868 when representatives from ten Liberian Baptist congregations convened in Marshall, Liberia, to organize the Liberia Baptist Missionary Union. Planning to direct its attention to the evangelization of non-Christian indigenous Africans, the group designated twelve areas for missionary activities, with each church responsible for the area(s) closest to it. But this organization also had significant ramifications for the African missionary movement in the U.S. To gain American support, the Liberian Union appointed their corresponding secretary, J. T. Richardson, as an agent to the American Baptist Missionary Union in the U.S.[69]

Richardson made a special appeal to black Baptists in the United States.[70] The Liberian Baptist leader urged young black Baptists to come to Africa as missionaries. Like many other black Baptists in the U.S. and Liberia, Richardson saw a link between evangelization and racial progress and also a link between the experiences of blacks in the U.S. and those of Africans on the continent. He considered black Baptist active involvement in African missions a factor in the redemption of Africa, the fulfillment of a great promise made by God for the entire black race. He wrote: "She [Africa] has long been shrouded in moral night, and her sons abroad have had to pass through a fiery ordeal, crying unto God to deliver them and their heathen brethren of this land. And it seems that Providence says their prayers are being answered, and they shall be redeemed, despite the ragings of men and devils."[71]

Besides Richardson, other black Baptists in Africa expressed concern for the evangelization of indigenous Africans. The Reverend Jacob W. Vonbrunn, an indigenous Bassa, lived with his people and conveyed the Christian message in that language. He also traveled to the U.S. in search of funds to erect a chapel and two or three schools for Africans.[72] Robert F. Hill, a native of Virginia, journeyed to Africa with Thomas J. Bowen

---

[69]Ibid., 44 (July 1868): 219.

[70]See Richardson's letter, ibid., 46 (January 1870): 16-18.

[71]Ibid., 16.

[72]Ibid., 47 (August 1871). 267.

and Harvey Goodale in 1849. Hill chose to remain in Liberia while Bowen proceeded to Nigeria. In 1867 Hill returned to the U.S., where he visited old friends in the South and conversed with potential emigrants to Liberia. In Philadelphia, he addressed the convention of the American Baptist Missionary Union. His delivery was well received; in fact, his presence and appeals count in large measure for the renewal of vigorous missionary interest in Africa among Northern Baptists.[73]

Finally, Beverly Page Yates (also an emigrant from the South) wrote in 1873 that he had served with the Southern Baptist Convention for twenty years. In his letter to Afro-American Baptists dated May 1873, Page expresses elation at the news that missionary interest in Africa among black Baptists was growing.[74] Clearly, black Baptists took pride in the tradition of Carey and Teague, the initiators of Baptist missionary work in Africa. But Yates advanced to draw a connection between blackness and the evangelization of Africa. He placed blacks under *racial* as well as spiritual obligations to their African kin. Whether black Baptists would come themselves—bringing their "culture and experience"—or would finance others, they must pay their obligation to Africa so that it might "be elevated, enlightened, and saved." In cooperating with missionary efforts to uplift Africa, religiously and culturally, black Americans were performing a providential role, one for which they would be held accountable on the Day of Judgment. Thus, Page bade Afro-Americans to turn their attention to Africa:

> You will not come [to Africa] as the prodigal son, wasted, weary, and wretched; but like the Jews, hastening from the land of Egypt, laden with precious and valuable spoils. You are one in origin with us, and with the benighted tribes in whose behalf we plead—one in interest, and one in worldly destiny. Come and help to make them with us one in our most precious faith and glorious hope, that they may be one with us throughout eternity.[75]

---

[73]Ibid., 44 (September 1868): 278-80; and 43 (September 1867): 285.

[74]Ibid., 49 (August 1873): 251-53.

[75]Ibid., 252.

## CONCLUSION

As indicated, the goal of this project is to trace the growth of Christian missionary interest in Africa among black Baptists from 1880 to 1915. As such, the intent of this work is to focus more upon the activities, ideas, and plans supporting the growth of the missionary movement among Afro-American Baptists rather than the activities of particular Baptist missionaries in Africa.

Understandably, the missionary program of black Baptists in the years 1880 to 1915 was influenced by the thinking of Baptists prior to 1880. In the preceding pages I have shown that black and white Baptists—indeed, most missionary-minded Christians of nineteenth-century America—believed that their efforts of foreign mission work would result in the spread of Christian civilization throughout the world. That is, the objectives of Baptists in Africa passed beyond the attempt to evangelize individuals and included the transformation of entire societies. These Christian societies were to be products of two influences—Protestant Christianity and Western culture. For the most part, neither white nor black missionaries stressed very much any indigenization of Christianity that sought radically to divorce the faith from Western culture.

Among black Baptists a theology developed, influenced by this context, that was concerned with a providential plan for the black race. Afro-Americans and Liberians were supposed to join hands with their indigenous African counterparts, and under the guidance of God they were to erect a Christian civilization that would loose Africa from all bonds—political, economic, and religious. In reaction to two expressions of American reality, racism and racial slavery, Afro-American Baptists developed a missionary program designed to save individuals and redeem whole societies of African peoples. In this missionary movement, from Carey to Yates, one detects a sense of racial pride and at least a theoretical concern for Africa despite the circumscribing circumstances in which blacks found themselves.

Herein can be seen an emerging theology that transcended a concern for individual piety and raised significant questions for the social applications of the faith. Always being reminded of their marginal and unwanted presence in the U.S., black Baptists developed an approach to the faith that sought to make it useful for the elevation of the entire race. In the following pages we will see that this concept of a people chosen to spread Christian civilization, begun in the pre-1880 years, was sustained during the 1880–1915 period, the era that witnessed further organization of black Baptist forces and the growth of European colonialism in Africa. This dedication to the spiritual and material redemption of Africa would serve as a vital catalyst uniting black Baptists at the state, regional, and eventually national levels. By focusing on the Baptists, we are able to case-study the significant impact that this missiology had upon the self-concept of Afro-American Christians and their understanding of the faith.

## PART 1

# THE BAPTIST FOREIGN MISSION CONVENTION, 1880–1894

This section focuses upon the organizational activities of black Baptists in the period 1880–1894. Again, major emphasis falls upon Baptists in the states of Virginia, North Carolina, South Carolina, Georgia, Florida, Alabama, and Mississippi. Part one proceeds as follows: chapter one records the context, formation, and early growth of the Baptist Foreign Mission Convention (BFMC), 1880–1893; chapter two examines the growth and decline of the BFMC in the years 1883–1894; chapter three analyzes the rise of the African mission movement on the state level and comments upon the support of Baptist women for the cause. Before proceeding with this section, some comments should be made about the organizational structures characteristic of Baptists during this period and how they affected the growth of African missions begun by black Baptists. Baptists, generally speaking, placed great emphasis upon ecclesiastical authority on the local level as opposed to the regional or national levels. In the following chapters, the reader should bear in mind that this decentralized, congregational church structure had an effect upon the African missionary movement. In most instances support for the mission program began at the local or state level and spread to the regional and national levels. On the one hand, this stress on ecclesiastical decentralization caused Baptists to feel closer to their missionaries, who were supported initially by their local associations, missionary societies, or state conventions. Therefore, they were often prone to support the movement financially. On the other hand, the absence of overarching, binding church structures and directives could hamper mission support and organization in an area without a locally sponsored missionary or one where the missionary withdrew or died in the field.

# CHAPTER 1

# AFRICAN MISSION MOVEMENT AND THE FORMATION AND EARLY GROWTH OF THE BFMC, 1880–1883

In the introduction, I outlined the beginnings of the African mission movement pursued by black Baptists during the antebellum years. It is during the aftermath of Emancipation, however, that black Baptists made their greatest strides in this area of church work. What had been primarily local efforts at organizing mission endeavors for Africa developed into statewide programs. The state Baptist conventions organized in the 1860s and the 1870s witnessed the increased rise of concern for the evangelization of Africa—particularly conventions in Virginia, South Carolina, and North Carolina.

In the 1880–1894 period the missionary concern on the part of black Baptists for the uplift of African peoples—religiously and materially—continued to be a significant part of the religious and denominational endeavors as it had been in the pre-1880 years. During the 1880–1894 era this missionary concern at the local and state levels culminated in the organization of a regional convention, the Baptist Foreign Mission Convention (BFMC), founded in 1880 in Montgomery, Alabama. Though this group purported to be national in scope, it remained in a practical sense a regional (and Southern) organization. To be sure, black Baptist organizations in other sections of the country expressed sentiment for mission work in Africa. Indeed, the Baptist General Association of Western States and Territories, founded in 1873, actually sent missionaries to Central Africa. But the BFMC undoubtedly played the leading role in this mission work. In chapters 2 and 3 we shall examine its role in sending missionaries to Africa and its struggles to remain a viable, financially stable, independent black Baptist group. In this chapter, we shall study the roots of the organization among Southern black Baptists and its formation and early growth during the 1880–1883 years.

In order to understand fully the organization and growth of this convention, one must grasp several historical contextual factors. Remember that the period 1880–1894 was one in which the political situation of both Afro-Americans and Africans sharply declined in the face of white domination. The 1870s and 1880s were decades of increased European intervention in and penetration of the African continent—politically, economically, and religiously (by means of missionary endeavors). The new dynamic role—colonialism—that the European nations played in Africa is symbolized by the international Berlin Conference of 1884. This conference sought to arrange terms by which European nations would recognize each other's sphere of interest on the continent of Africa and thus lessen the possibilities of armed conflict among themselves.

If Africans gradually lost sovereignty over their lands, black Americans experienced the loss of the political rights acquired and practiced by them in the late 1860s and 1870s. By the turn of the century, white supremacists had captured control of the Southern governments of the former Confederacy and had effectively purged blacks and liberal whites from active political life in the South. The oppression of both black peoples was aggravated by an intensification of unreserved and "scientific" concepts of white supremacy and black inferiority among Europeans and white Americans in the latter quarter of the nineteenth century.

It is in this context that blacks renewed their interest in the motherland. In some instances black ministers and laypeople emigrated to the continent—especially the former American colony of Liberia—seeking both to spread the gospel among their "benighted" African siblings and to find a new home and more authentic political and economic liberties. Most blacks, however, refused to abandon the land of their birth even in the face of mounting restrictions on their civil liberties. Instead, they migrated from the rural areas to the cities in the North and South; and they journeyed north and west attempting to escape the vindictiveness and brutality of a resurgent, revitalized racism on the part of many whites. Just as in antebellum times, these blacks still cherished a seemingly foolish hope that the sunlight of perfect freedom and equity would, with the furtherance of the gospel and their own industry, eclipse their night of oppression.

But the memories of Africa had not disappeared from their collective consciousness. Indeed, in a society where blacks were constantly looked upon as pariahs, racial consciousness could not die. So, they remembered Africa, as in the antebellum period, in both religious and racial terms. With the increasingly visible reminders that they were still an outcast people, they had even more reason to return to the African dream, the biblical "prophecy" that God would one day bless all peoples of African descent both materially and spiritually, forever freeing them from oppression and any ungodliness (Ps. 68:31). Black Christians, after Emancipation and Reconstruction, once again began to emphasize the belief that their presence in the United States was a part of God's plan to equip them with Christian civilization so that they might carry or send tidings of these blessings to their African kin. Once African peoples embraced Christianity and Western civilization through the instrumentality of American black Christians, a new state of affairs would be inaugurated. Then they would be elevated to positions of freedom and equity alongside other peoples. This missionary concern among black Baptists was most dramatically manifested in the movements to develop African mission programs within recently organized black state Baptist conventions in the South.

## INDEPENDENT STATE ACTIVITIES, 1878–1880

The formation of the Foreign Mission Convention and the rise of a regional-national interest among black Baptists in African missions grew more directly from the organizing efforts of Southern black Baptists. The black Baptists of the Southeastern states of South Carolina, North Carolina, and Virginia moved in forcefully to fill the gap in American Baptist support of Liberian mission work caused by the withdrawal of the American Baptist Missionary Union and the shift of mission support of the Southern Baptist Convention (SBC) from Liberia to Nigeria.

In 1878 the Baptist Educational, Missionary, and Sunday-School Convention of South Carolina decided that despite the infancy of the organization founded only twelve years earlier, South Carolinian black Baptists

needed to become more actively involved in foreign missions because all
Christians had to look beyond their immediate vicinities and to respect the
Great Commission of Jesus to spread the gospel message throughout the
earth. Africa seemed to most a logical place, demanding their immediate
attention for a number of reasons. First, the South Carolinians stated, most
Baptists in the U.S. directed their foreign mission program to unsaved
people of the Far East while only two Baptist missionaries were engaged
in African mission work. This appeared as a particular imbalance in the
distribution of mission stations since one-fourth, or 500,000, of the
2,000,000 Baptists in the U.S. were of African ancestry. A large portion
(70,000) of those half million black Baptists lived in South Carolina. Finally, pointing more explicitly to the racial kinship between Afro-Americans and Africans, the Board of Managers stated, "And, then, Africa is
the land of our forefathers."[1]

The convention moved beyond merely advocating African mission work
and actually resolved unanimously to send a missionary to Africa. The
group selected the Reverend Harrison N. Bouey as its missionary ap-
pointee. A native of Columbia County, Georgia, Bouey grew up in Augusta and served as a public school teacher. After his conversion in 1870,
he attended the Atlanta Baptist Seminary.[2] The Reverend Bouey set sail
for his African mission post aboard the *Azor* along with the newly organized Shiloh Baptist Church. The black Baptists of South Carolina considered it their duty to provide the infant church pastoral oversight until the
group became self-sufficient in its new environment.[3] Unlike many em-
issaries to foreign fields, the missionary was placed in a friendly and sup-
portive environment. Liberia had been colonized by his fellow black
Southerners, many of them Baptists. Though the church that journeyed with
Bouey settled at two different places, this did not prevent "several worthy
brethren" from providing him with adequate support to make ends meet.[4]

---

[1] Annual Minutes, the Baptist Educational, Missionary, and Sunday-School Convention
of South Carolina (BCSC), 1878, p. 17, and appendix, p. vi.

[2] For a biography of Harrison N.Bouey, see William J. Simmons, *Men of Mark: Eminent, Progressive and Rising* (New York: George M. Revell & Co., 1887; rpt., Chicago:
Johnson Publishing Company, Inc., 1970) 675-76.

[3] Ibid.

[4] Annual Minutes, BCSC, 1880, p. 3.

Furthermore, the Liberians extended a warm greeting to Bouey, which was symbolized by the acceptance of his two churches into the Liberia Baptist Association on 3 December 1879—within seven months of their arrival in the country. As a matter of fact, the association adopted a resolution giving thanks to the black Baptist convention in South Carolina for commissioning Bouey ''to cooperate with us in the grand mission work in Liberia.''[5] Indeed, Bouey did cooperate with the Liberians to the fullest. ''The minutes of this Association [in Liberia] give evidence not only of the generous reception Brother Bouey received, but also of his energy and activity. His name appears in connection with several movements which seem to indicate advance movement on the part of the Liberian brethren.''[6]

Since the above quote comes from a meeting of the Baptist Educational, Missionary, and Sunday-School Convention of South Carolina that took place 5-9 May 1880, the association minutes mentioned therein might refer in part to Bouey's participation in a convention of Liberian churches meeting 15-18 April 1880. On those dates, Baptist churches assembled in the Good Hope Baptist Church in Marshall to organize the Liberia Baptist Missionary Convention.[7] This convention represented a move on the part of Americo-Liberian Baptists to cease limiting their missions to the colonized elements of Liberia and to take a more aggressive posture toward evangelizing the entire world, particularly Africa. This convention was expressly founded to provide a more effective means to accomplish that goal. According to the minutes of this first meeting, Bouey's active contribution to the work of the new organization fell into three main areas. He was elected corresponding secretary of the new organization, was a member of the Board of Managers, and a member of the Committee on Constitution and By Laws. But particularly significant in terms of the relationship between black Baptists and Americo-Liberians was the resolution proposed by the Afro-American missionary and subsequently adopted by the body stating that the president of the new body, J. J. Cheeseman,

---

[5]Ibid., 4.

[6]Ibid.

[7]Minutes, founding session of the Liberia Baptist Missionary Convention, 1880, pp. 3-4, 6.

would have authority to appoint foreign agents for both England and the United States.

Though it appears that Bouey moved to Liberia with an intent to take up permanent residence, it is significant that both he and his South Carolinian Baptists envisioned his work as fulfilling a missionary role—that is, helping that state convention to fulfill its obligation to carry out the Great Commission. In addition, Bouey's active participation in the newly organized Liberia Baptist Missionary Convention signaled his commitment to extend the gospel beyond the Americo-Liberian settlers and their descendants to the indigenous African peoples.

In 1879, the black Baptist State Convention of North Carolina followed the lead of their Southern neighbors and appointed a missionary to Liberia. It appears that James O. Hayes journeyed to Africa in the missionary-emigrant tradition of Lott Carey and H. N. Bouey. Not only did he plan to work under the auspices of his state convention to evangelize the Africans, but Hayes seemingly intended his move to be a permanent one. The *African Repository* noted that he would be "accompanied by his parents and others."[8] Hayes's appointment indicated the upsurge of interest in African missions among black Baptists in North Carolina. In 1880 J. O. Crosby, the convention's corresponding secretary, noted this growth of interest: "I have visited some of our largest churches and associations, both in the east and the west, and find the people both ready and willing to aid both foreign and home mission work. They seem to feel a deep interest in the evangelization of the heathen, and especially those of Africa."[9]

But those Baptists in Virginia (Lott Carey's and Colin Teague's home state as well as the home of the still-active Richmond African Baptist Missionary Society) played the major, if not the key, role in stimulating this new interest in African missions. Article I, Section II of the Constitution of the Virginia Baptist State Convention outlined as its objective the spread of Christianity and churches throughout Virginia and Africa. To wit, black Virginia Baptists considered Africa second only to their own state as an object of missionary concern, though undoubtedly blacks in other parts of

---

[8]*African Repository* 55 (July 1897): 81.

[9]Annual Minutes, Baptist State Convention of North Carolina (BCNC), 1880, p. 13.

the South were unchurched and in need of material and educational assistance.[10]

Apparently, the most influential promoter and organizer of this movement was William W. Colley, a black Baptist Virginian, who went out under the appointment of the SBC Foreign Mission Board in 1875 as an assistant of W. J. David, a white Mississippi Baptist. The SBC minutes of 1876 reported that as of 14 October 1875, Colley and David had advanced from Liberia to their original preference, the land of the Yorubas in Nigeria.[11] The arrangement with the white missions board failed to satisfy Colley, and very soon he called for the involvement of black Baptists in the African mission program. He wrote in 1876: "I hope the colored brethren will begin their work in Africa this year, either by sending a man or supporting one. This is *their* field of labor. I ask when will they obey their Saviour's commission?"[12]

In 1878 the Foreign Mission Board of the Virginia Convention commissioned Solomon Cosby, a Virginian, for service in Africa. Cosby was jointly supported by the SBC and the convention in Virginia. He journeyed to Lagos while Colley traveled from there to Abeokuta to replace David, who had been called back to the States because of serious sickness.[13]

In November 1879 Colley returned to the United States and shortly thereafter began to canvass the South for the formation of a national black Baptist foreign mission convention. Why Colley and the black Virginia Baptists urged black Baptists to take an independent course in mission work can be explained by one or a combination of the following. (1) The post-Reconstruction period was one in which blacks sought to assert themselves in an independent fashion from whites. The Virginians shared the belief of other American blacks that it was necessary for blacks to make a unique contribution as a group of people. This idea had a profound impact in the

[10]Annual Minutes, Virginia Baptist State Convention (VBSC), 1878, p. 3.

[11]Annual Minutes, Southern Baptist Convention (SBC), 1876, p. 35. Unfortunately, I have been unable to locate biographical material on Colley's prior life and background. But as chapters 1 and 2 will reveal, Colley played a very significant role in the mission field and as a vigorous proponent of the African movement among black Baptists.

[12]Ibid., 36.

[13]Ibid., 1878, 38.

1880s when black Baptists had to decide under what conditions they would enter cooperative ventures with white Baptists. (2) Popular beliefs among both white and black Baptists were that blacks were most suitable for missionary work in Africa because of climatic conditions there; that they had the ability to communicate more effectively with Africans than whites could; and that Afro-American Christians owed a special debt to their cousins.

But these factors alone do not reveal the whole story. Racial parochialism among white missionaries and missionary-minded counterparts in the States also helped spark interest in forming a separate black Baptist missionary organization. Certainly it would not be surprising for blacks to abandon a venture where they were continually placed in subordinate positions. Since they had taken similar courses in relation to postemancipation churches, such a step in the area of African missions was merely a logical consequence of the general movement toward independence and control over their own institutions.

Conflicts between the black missionary on one hand and his white counterparts and/or white mission boards on the other did arise. Solomon Cosby indicated some degree of conflict between himself and the Southern Baptist missionaries in a letter to E. G. Corprew, the corresponding secretary of the Virginia Convention. In a letter dated 11 March 1880, Cosby outlined that he had no money with which to execute the kind of mission work he would have liked. As such, no serious effort had been made to found a mission to the Africans on behalf of the black Virginia Baptists. Instead, Cosby reported, ''I have to the present been laboring upon another man's foundation.''[14] He indicated that very little, if any, financial support had been granted him by the SBC. Cosby wrote:

> My work as you know has been confined to Lagos, which is the mission [of the] Southern [Baptist Convention] U.S.A.; while I have endeavored to do all within power here for the cause of Christ[,] I have met with not little inconvenience in laboring upon the field of another Society. I deem it not necessary to give particulars why it has been so; but let it suffice to say that this people knew before I left America that I was not coming out

---

[14]Annual Minutes, VBSC, 1880, 37.

under their board, but of another Board, and as such they have ever looked upon me.[15]

Though Cosby considered such restrictions by the SBC a result of his nonaffiliation with their Foreign Mission Board, his problems probably were connected with the missionary operating methods of many Southern Baptists and other white Christians—methods founded upon the assumption that blacks, even fellow Christians, should not be accorded equal treatment. This narrow attitude certainly was apparent in the behavior of Cosby's and Colley's colleague in the Nigerian mission field, W. J. David. While many Southern Baptists were advocating cooperation with black Baptists, the 1881 SBC minutes reveal that David felt strongly that white men should manage the mission field. He encouraged the SBC to follow the example of European traders, colonial governments, and missionaries: whites should supervise the work over Africans. Though it was clear that indigenously trained Africans must be the ones to evangelize the continent, they must be under the supervision of whites. As for black American Baptists assisting in the enterprise, the Southern Baptist missionary explained his position with painful lucidity: ''I wish to divert the minds of the Board from depending upon colored laborers from the South too much. In equal proportion, it will do well, I hope, but it will not do to let the colored force preponderate.''[16]

In the 1882 SBC minutes David expressed his sorrow upon the death of Cosby in April 1881. But, he added, ''Send if possible, two healthy, *energetic* God-fearing *white* men, this year.''[17] Given this attitude, two developments were bound to occur. First, many African Christians broke away from the mission church of the SBC to establish the Native Baptist Church in the mid-1880s.[18] African church members compared David's

---

[15]Ibid.

[16]Annual Minutes, SBC, 1881, 45.

[17]Ibid., 1882, 70.

[18]For accounts of the controversy in the Lagos Church involving David, consult James Bertin Webster, *The African Churches among the Yoruba, 1888–1922* (Oxford: Clarendon Press, 1964) 49-58; and E. A. Ayandele, *The Missionary Impact on Modern Nigeria, 1842–1914: A Political and Social Analysis* (London: Longmans, Green and Company, 1966) 198-201.

church in Lagos to slave depots. James Bertin Webster wrote concerning the turmoil that David's behavior caused in the Lagos church: "It is relevant to point out that David's attitude towards Africans left much to be desired. There are frequent references to 'flogging' and 'clubbing' not only of mission personnel but also of tradesmen who serviced the mission."[19] Second, Colley led a movement among black Virginia Baptists to organize a separate mission program. Many of the acts cited above occurred during the 1870s and apparently served as a strong impetus for Colley and others to organize separate black Baptist mission activities in Africa. But even more significant than these individual acts and atrocities, David represented a conception of African mission work which contradicted that of black Christians. This white missionary envisioned American blacks even on the mission field as playing a secondary role to the white missionaries in the evangelization of Africa. Black Christians, on the other hand, saw themselves as God's major instruments to save their African kin, a responsibility they dared not shirk in deference to others.

But this expression of racial chauvinism on the part of white Baptists went beyond the ideas and activities of one missionary. The Foreign Mission Board of the SBC initially supported David in the Lagos controversy. Even subsequent to David's recall, the SBC never overtly condemned his racist behavior.[20] From the viewpoint of many black Baptists, such actions and inactions raised a negative implication for the whole role of the denomination in West Africa.

There is evidence, however, which more firmly posits that racial discrimination played a vital role in the decision of American black Baptists to form a national foreign mission movement. Edward Freeman, a Baptist historian, linked the formation of the Baptist Foreign Mission Convention with the treatment accorded indigenous Africans by mission authorities.[21] Referring to Colley's experiences in the field, Jordan said that white missionaries set certain restrictions upon Afro-Americans that hindered them in their work with African peoples. According to Jordan, such limitations

---

[19]Webster, *African Churches*, n. 1.

[20]Ayandele, *Missionary Impact*, 198-201.

[21]Edward Freeman, *The Epoch of Negro Baptists and the Foreign Mission Board* (Kansas City: Central Seminary Press, 1953) 69.

greatly accelerated the move for black organization and independence in foreign missions. "So graphically did he [Colley] present the situation that when he issued a general call for a meeting of pastors and leaders there was no hesitation or evidence of reluctance to undertake the sacrificial task of foreign mission work by Negroes, most of whom had been recently set free from slavery."[22]

## VIRGINIA BAPTISTS AND THE
## BAPTIST FOREIGN MISSION CONVENTION

However significant the role of racial parochialism, it is quite obvious that the BFMC to a great extent represents an outgrowth of the Virginia Baptist State Convention. In his book *Africa in Brief*, John J. Coles, one of the first missionaries appointed by the Foreign Mission Convention, said as much. "Be it ever remembered that out of the Virginia Baptist State Convention came the 'B.F.M. Convention of the U.S.A.' " This convention must carry serious historical validity since, according to Coles, his manuscript was read by Colley himself, examined for "its accuracy," and verified by the missionary.[23]

Endeavoring to pursue the goal of evangelizing and uplifting their racial kin, Virginians early realized that the lack of sufficient funds greatly hampered their missionary work. At the 1879 meeting of the Virginia Convention, E. G. Corprew, the corresponding secretary, cited the lack of sufficient funds as an obvious factor that had hindered both domestic and African mission work for many years running. Corprew suggested that the appointment of a general agent to travel the state and to solicit support among Baptist leaders and organizations might go a long way in solving the financial crisis facing the convention. In order to pursue more successfully the mission enterprise in Nigeria, West Africa, a total of $1000 had to be raised for the establishment of mission facilities.[24]

Correspondence from Solomon Cosby, the missionary in Lagos, further dramatized this financial problem. As Colley before him, Cosby found

---

[22]Lewis G. Jordan, *Negro Baptist History, U.S.A., 1750–1930* (Nashville: Sunday School Publishing Board, National Baptist Convention, 1930) 89.

[23]John J. Coles, *Africa in Brief* (New York: New York Freeman Steam Printing Establishment, 1886) xiii.

[24]Annual Minutes, VBSC, 1879, 34-36.

living in Africa very expensive. He reported that he would leave the field unless the Foreign Mission Board would raise his salary. Cosby, speaking personally, wrote that he would not shrink from suffering, "sickness or anything else," but he must have adequate means with which to survive.[25] In March 1880 the missionary wrote that he was unable to give "a favorable report" on mission work because, for want of money, little had been done.[26]

Faced with these shortages in funds, black Virginia Baptists sought support from their racial siblings in other states, particularly in the South. In January 1880 the Foreign Mission Board in Virginia passed a resolution calling upon Colley to journey through the South in an attempt to interest black Baptists in the foreign mission enterprise. Significantly for the Carey-Teague missionary tradition, Jordan reported that even prior to this meeting of the board, Colley had already conferred (in November 1879) with the leaders and pastors of Richmond Missionary Society. As a result of that meeting, an invitation was extended for Baptists to assemble in November of the following year in Montgomery, Alabama.[27]

Possibly, the Richmond group passed an official resolution and then reported the same by way of Colley to the Board of Foreign Missions of the state convention. After all, the latter body dealt with missionary societies throughout the state and had corresponding relationships with other black Baptist organizations such as the New England Missionary Convention and the Baptist General Association of Western States and Territories. Thus, the resolution passed by the state board might have been a mere appropriation of an original motion from the Richmond Society. Furthermore, the whole procedure before the board might have been simply ceremonial, given that many of the most ardent supporters of African missions were members of the Richmond community and could have been members of the society—for example, Joseph E. Jones, William Troy, James A. Taylor, W. W. Colley, J. H. Holmes, and Deacon H. H. Osborne.

---

[25]Ibid., 38.

[26]Ibid., 1880, 37.

[27]Lewis G. Jordan, *Pebbles from an African Beach* (Philadelphia: Lisle-Carey Press, 1918?) 33.

Again, there is a question as to whether the original purpose of Colley's trip through the South was one of securing financial support for the mission program of Virginia or of testing people's sentiments about organizing a national Baptist missionary convention. With the resolution adopted by the board, Colley traveled to all of the states of the Southeast except Mississippi. Although Colley was authorized to visit all states, he elected to concentrate an overwhelming amount of his attention upon the southeastern section of the country. He visited no New England, Middle Atlantic, Midwestern, or Western state.

Again, we must bear in mind that the bulk of blacks lived in the South during this time. Also, Colley's itinerary might simply have been occasioned by the accessibility of nearby states. He returned to the convention meeting in Hampton, Virginia, in May 1880 with news of a successful journey.[28] The convention made the following resolution: "*Resolved*, that this Convention feels assured that the time has come when we should make a grand move for foreign mission by the united efforts of all of the states of the Union."[29] It was further resolved that a committee of fifteen members would establish a time and place for the formation of the convention.

Colley became the most active individual responsible for organizing the BFMC, whose founding session was set for Montgomery, Alabama, in November 1880. He campaigned both by letters and personal appearances. His energy, earnestness, and sincerity seem to have been more significant ingredients for his success than any special gifts of oratory. Jordan, the Baptist historian, described him in the following manner:

> Elder Colley, as far as can be learned from the few surviving friends who met and knew him personally, seems not to have been endowed with any special gifts or eloquence, but he was deeply imbued with the desire to serve by giving the Word of God to "Darkest Africa." He insisted that those who had received the light had a sacred duty to pass on the message to their brethren still in the darkness of that benighted land.[30]

As indicated above, Colley, according to Jordan, also deeply impressed his listeners with the knowledge that black missionaries of the white SBC

---

[28]Annual Minutes, VBSC, 1880, 14.

[29]Ibid., 15.

[30]Jordan, *Negro Baptist History*, 89.

Board did not have complete freedom to pursue vigorously their missionary obligations.

In addition to his personal qualities, Colley also had concrete examples of the African mission tradition upon which to build a new, more comprehensive black organization. Black Baptists in three states—South Carolina, North Carolina, and Virginia—were at that time involved in missionary work in Africa. Though black Baptists in other states[31] had not made such pragmatic moves in the direction of foreign missions, awareness of the need for such had been mounting in all parts of the United States in black Baptist organizations such as the New England Baptist Convention, founded in 1875, and the Consolidated American Baptist Missionary Convention, organized in 1866. Many of the Baptists in these organizations, limited by their financial resources and by what they saw as a huge field of responsibility in the U.S., felt an obligation to carry out the Great Commission.

## THE GATHERING IN MONTGOMERY—1880:
## THE PARTICIPANTS

On a beautiful, sunny Wednesday, 24 November 1880, 151 ministers and active laypersons from eleven different states met in the First Baptist Church in Montgomery, Alabama, as the founding assembly of the Foreign Convention. Jordan's account from eyewitnesses of that first convention reveals a meeting characterized by a sacred, solemn mood—an occasion marked by a "warmth and intensity of feeling." Rather than "the usual spirit of levity and the jovial greetings of friend to friend," there was the feeling of heavy responsibility for the momentous and serious task of foreign missions that confronted them. Also, there was a mood of "harmony and unanimity in their actions" during the entire session.[32]

In another section of Jordan's account, he remarked that there was a joyful anticipation on the parts of the men and women who attended the session. This was an opportunity for church leaders in various sections of the South to gather and to share experiences, hopes, and expectations. The

---

[31]C. C. Adams and Marshall A. Talley, *Negro Baptists and Foreign Missions* (Philadelphia: Foreign Missions Board of the National Baptist Convention, U.S.A., 1944) 32.

[32]Jordan, *Negro Baptist History*, 89.

preceding is of special significance in that the persons who assembled in Montgomery were leaders in their local churches, associations, and state conventions. This event takes on added importance because the Consolidated American Baptist Missionary Convention, the first truly national organization among black Baptists, had collapsed the previous year. Jordan wrote of this occasion:

> The meeting was hailed with much joy and delight because here the men hoped and expected to meet the representative men of the denomination from all the states, to become better acquainted with one another as of one household faith. They hoped to know more of each other's work, each other's plans, and each other's views and desires; and by counselling one with the other to better carry forth the work of their common Savior and Lord.[33]

Interestingly, Southern states were the best represented at the session, and these included Alabama, North Carolina, Georgia, Florida, Mississippi, Tennessee, Virginia, Louisiana, Arkansas, and Texas. Only one state delegation came from outside the South: Ohio, represented by P. H. Williams of Middleport.

There were at least two notable absences from this first meeting of the Foreign Mission Convention. Georgia Baptists were present only as "unofficial" delegates, more as observers than participants. Such a stance did not originate out of unconcern for foreign missions or a lack of appreciation for the African missionary tradition among the Baptists of that state. At the 1880 session of the Georgia Baptist State Convention meeting six months prior to the formation of the BFMC, the Committee on Mission reported: "While we are anxious to do all in our power to advance our home work, we would not forget the claims of the foreign field, and hope that something will be done to send missionaries to the heathen."[34] The corresponding secretary of the convention, W. J. White, remarked that he was in agreement with the thinking of "some of our most intelligent brethren" that the mission work of black Georgia Baptists should be extended to foreign fields while not neglecting domestic responsibilities. He urged the convention to move in this direction, since the entire earth should be given

[33]Ibid., 115.

[34]Annual Minutes, Missionary Baptist Convention of Georgia (MBCG), 1880, p. 25.

the gospel. But, White more specifically called upon black Georgia Baptists to realize a special missionary obligation to those lands predominated by peoples of African descent: ''Africa, Hayti, San Domingo, have special claims upon us, and no doubt God will bless any effort we may make to send these benighted countries the pure Gospel of the blessed Jesus.''[35]

White turned the attention of this convention to the invitation of the Virginia Convention, which asked Georgia to lend its cooperation in the attempt to establish and maintain African mission work. Initially, he approved of the idea, believing that one state convention would not be able to accomplish very much in foreign missions in the near future.[36] But the minutes of the Georgia Convention one year later reveal an uncertainty among Georgians concerning the wisdom of Georgia's aligning with the organization, even though White had given his endorsement of the enterprise. The Committee on Missions reported that the corresponding secretary, White, did not attend the 1880 assembly in Montgomery and that the committee ''knows but little about his movements.'' White reported that the convention had authorized him to go, but that contrary to earlier plans, the convention organizers chose to meet in Alabama rather than Atlanta. After the 1880 meeting of the Georgia Baptist State Convention, White corresponded with Colley, the leader of the foreign-mission convention movement, and prominent Baptists outside Georgia in an effort to decide the proper course of action for him to take. He decided in the negative because it was not clear to persons in certain states that the coming meeting was to be fairly representative of any views but those of the Virginia delegation. ''As the result of this correspondence, I decided not to attend the Montgomery meeting, because no other State except Virginia had taken such action as to make the meeting a Convention really representing their views.''[37]

Apparently, White felt that either the Virginians would attempt to monopolize the proceedings or that the participation of Georgia and other delegations would serve only to rubber-stamp the programmatic objectives of

---

[35]Ibid., 29.

[36]Ibid., 30.

[37]Ibid., 1881, 26.

Virginians. Other members of the Georgia Convention elected to go, observed White, but only as voluntary, nonofficial representatives. At this point he offered no recommendation concerning the course of action Georgia should take; he left the matter entirely in the hands of the convention. No single opinion, White noted, could be ascertained within the convention itself since "there is considerable diversity of opinion among our wisest and best brethren in reference to the wisdom of the movement."[38]

In assessing the situation, the corresponding secretary brought the convention's attention to the stances of two neighboring states. Florida, White claimed, had taken no official action regarding the Foreign Mission Convention; and the South Carolina Baptists had decided to continue their foreign mission work through the Foreign Mission Board of the American Baptist Missionary Union rather than through the organ of the black Foreign Mission Convention.[39] In sum, it appears that Georgia Baptists adopted a wait-and-see attitude, predicated upon a concern that the proposed organization be truly representative of the sentiments of *all* states, not merely Virginia.

The position of South Carolina black Baptists requires a different explanation than that offered for Baptists in Florida. Florida, like many other states, was overwhelmed with its domestic programs; and having no missionary in a foreign field, the growth of African mission sentiment there was understandably slower than in Virginia or North Carolina. But prior to 1880 South Carolina, like Virginia, had placed missionaries in West Africa. The commissioning of a missionary to Africa was aided by a powerful missionary sentiment in that state which was as strong in 1880 as the few previous years.[40]

Furthermore, unlike Georgia Baptists, South Carolina Baptists apparently never raised any question concerning the role of Virginians in the organization of the convention. The 1881 minutes of the South Carolina Convention suggest that these Baptists were unconcerned that the interests of Baptists in other states would be subordinated to those of the Virginians.

---

[38]Ibid.

[39]Ibid., 26-27.

[40]Annual Minutes, American Baptist Missionary Union, 1880, p. xv.

As a matter of fact, South Carolina Baptists envisioned the interest in African missions as a "movement on the part of a large number of our brethren all over the South." The minutes described the movement as one that "claimed and received the attention and sympathy" of the Board of Managers of the convention.[41]

The answer to South Carolina's absence lies in the simple fact that the black Baptists of this state elected to cooperate with the white, northern American Baptist Missionary Union (ABMU) rather than the Foreign Mission Convention. Invitations for cooperation with the black Baptists and the union arrived at roughly the same time. The Board of Managers outlined three basic reasons why South Carolina chose to work with the Missionary Union. One, they recognized this group as the appropriate Baptist organ for conducting foreign mission work: "That body is the regular organization of the denomination for that kind of work." It is likely that this statement meant to convey that the Missionary Union was the most appropriate Baptist body through which either foreign missions generally or African missions in particular should be executed. A careful reading of the minutes indicates that South Carolina black Baptists regarded the body in this light because they thought of it—not the SBC or any other body—as the extension of the original Baptist body, the Triennial Convention, founded in 1814. This view is underscored by the fact that the South Carolinians noted in their minutes that the African mission field, particularly Liberia, was among the first areas of activity for foreign mission work by the union.[42]

The second chief reason why the Board of Managers listed the ABMU as their choice was the necessity to do mission work as cheaply as possible. The union, it was argued, was an established organization. This fact guaranteed that all funds raised would be channeled directly to the field. On the other hand, the board feared that the operating expenses of a new organization would deprive the mission field of a great amount of the financial contributions.

The third argument advanced by the board is, like the first, subject to differing interpretations. The board stated that "a permanent separation

---

[41]Annual Minutes, BCSC, 1881, 5.

[42]Ibid.

from the denomination Missionary Union in our foreign work is unwise in view of the fact that we are connected with it in both branches of the home work—the work as done by the Publication and Home Missions Societies.''[43] The key word is ''unwise.'' Would the severing of foreign mission ties with the union constitute an ''unwise'' course of action because the religious work of South Carolinians would be awkwardly divided and thus cause a waste in time, money, and energy? Or, did the above statement mean to convey subtly that the convention's refusal to cooperate with the union in the area of African missions would open South Carolinians to the risk of forfeiting vital financial support for domestic religious programs from offended Northern white Baptists? Last, did the board intend to convey both of the above interpretations?

Two additional considerations present themselves. First, there were still many black Baptists in the postwar South who eschewed very strong positions of black ecclesiastical independency, believing that the best course of action lay in close cooperative ventures with white Baptists. (This theme is treated in greater detail in chapter 4.) Second, the position of South Carolina black Baptists is related somewhat to the relative ease that their missionary, Harrison N. Bouey, felt on the mission field. As stated previously, Bouey's assimilation was a simple one; he was a black American missionary who worked in cooperation with other black (Americo-Liberian) missionary workers. Indeed, his mission field, Liberia, was one founded by blacks from the U.S. Colley, of Virginia, on the other hand, worked in a new mission field alongside a white missionary and for a white board that placed restrictions on his activities. Clearly, then, Colley and the Virginians had a greater impetus to organize a separate *black* mission program than the South Carolinians.

## VIRGINIA BAPTISTS AND THE FOUNDING CONVENTION

Symbolized by Colley's officiating as temporary chairperson, the Virginia Baptists led the assembled Baptists in organizing the first black Baptist *national* foreign mission convention. The constitution adopted at this founding assembly illustrates the dedication of these Baptists to the evan-

---

[43]Ibid., 5-6.

gelization of Africa. The preamble states that although the delegates believed that they had been called to serve other areas of the world, Africa enlisted their "most profound attention." In Article 2, the delegates left themselves open to God's commandment to pursue missions in other lands, but it was the African continent that is specified and first named.[44]

Official representation was held out to practically all Baptist organizations: Sunday schools, churches, women's missionary groups, associations, and so forth. Each church was guaranteed one representative plus another for each "1000 members or a fraction of the first 1000." Realizing the financial strain that many blacks faced, the constitution permitted the organizations to contribute by ability rather than setting a fixed amount. Nonetheless, individual Baptists could become annual members with the payment of five dollars. Persons attained life membership by paying fifty dollars over a period of ten years or by paying five dollars each year for a period of "ten consecutive years."[45]

The constitution provided for representation from all states by assuring that the president of any state convention which participated in the work of the convention would become a vice president of the convention. This document placed much of the operating procedures of the organization in the hands of a fifteen-member Executive Board. From within this body, a five-member committee would have the full authority to carry on the work of the convention during recess. Article 8 outlined that a majority of the Executive Board would "be located at some central point." This board would have the responsibility of securing the cooperation and support of appropriate Baptist organizations.[46] Article 15 of the constitution points out the flexible nature of the document. It was described as "only provisional," designed to meet the particular needs and demands of the organization and could be amended by a majority vote "at any regular meeting of this Convention."[47]

These founding members had no intention of limiting membership and participation to Southern black conventions. But the BFMC for the dura-

---

[44]Annual Minutes, Baptist Foreign Mission Convention (BFMC), 1880, in Jordan, *Baptist History,* 157.

[45]Ibid., 155.

[46]Ibid., 155-56.

[47]Ibid., 157.

tion of its struggling existence would mainly be Southern-based. Some results of this founding assembly adumbrated that regional emphasis. First, the selection of officers indicated the strength of the Southern states, particularly Virginia. Besides the vice presidents, which included the president from each state represented in the convention, all officers came from these states. For the forthcoming year, the convention chose W. H. McAlpine from Alabama as president; J. M. Armistead of Tennessee and G. H. Dwelle of Georgia as secretaries; and E. G. Corprew of Virginia as treasurer. Of the thirteen members of the Executive Board that Jordan listed, nine of those came from the Southern section. They were: W. A. Burch of Salem, Alabama, selected as chairperson; G. H. Dwelle of Americus, Georgia; T. L. Jordan of Mississippi; and C. P. Hughes of Shelbyville, Tennessee. Only two states were represented on the Executive Board with more than one person. From North Carolina came Caesar Johnson of Raleigh and A. N. Nuck of Halifax. Interestingly, three members of this group were Virginians: C. H. Carey, Abington; J. W. Patterson, Danville; and D. King, Norfolk. Also, two Virginians held offices on the board—Carey as secretary and Colley as corresponding secretary. According to the constitution, these officers were to be "judicious and experienced brethren."[48] Although the convention organizers made plans for two separate boards, foreign missions and executive, as years passed the work of the former merged into the duties of the Executive Board.

Second, the composition of the twenty-seven-member Foreign Mission Board illustrated the impact that Southern Baptists, most particularly the Virginians, were to play in foreign mission programs. The board had one representative for the following states: Mississippi, Arkansas, Texas, Louisiana, Florida, Alabama, Tennessee, South Carolina, North Carolina, and Georgia. Sixteen of the twenty-seven members were from the state of Virginia and it was headed by a Virginian, Anthony Binga, Jr. of Manchester. Furthermore, one-third of these Virginians were from the region of Richmond, the site chosen by the convention as the headquarters for the board and the home of the pioneering Richmond Missionary Society.[49]

---

[48]Ibid., 154.

[49]Ibid., 168.

The Foreign Mission Convention laid plans for the extension and growth of its work. The Ways and Means Committee gave the Executive Board the authority to appoint a corresponding secretary (W. W. Colley) to do interstate travel in an effort to secure funds for support of African mission work. The board was urged to collect the sum of $5,000 as soon as it could. The Executive Committee of that board was to negotiate with the Virginia Convention for the transfer of Solomon Cosby, the African missionary, from the exclusive control of the Foreign Mission Board of the state convention to the auspices of the Foreign Mission Convention. The vice presidents of the convention were entrusted with the responsibility of having their state denominational papers publish the work of the organization, "when it can be done free of charge." In the event that a state had no foreign mission convention, the vice president to the Foreign Mission Convention (a representative from that state), along with his fellow officers and the state executive committee, would organize and carry on the foreign mission work for that state.[50] Additionally, the convention's Executive Board had the task of sending circular letters to announce the program of the convention and relevant data about the continent of Africa.[51]

These Baptists were breaking new organizational ground, both from the perspective of other black Baptists and in the sense that they worked separately from their white counterparts in the Northern ABMU and the Southern SBC. But they still embraced the belief that all Christians, particularly Baptists, should maintain fellowship and communication with other Christians as situations allowed. They also realized that the African mission program was a costly project requiring the support of as many friends as they could find. For these reasons, the convention appointed messengers to other Baptist groups. T. L. Jordan and R. Ramsey of Mississippi were to represent the convention with the Southern Baptist Convention. All three divisions of the Northern white Baptists received fraternal delegates: American Baptist Publication Society, J. W. Patterson of Virginia and C. O. Booth of Alabama; the American and Foreign Bible Society, C. Johnson of North Carolina; the Missionary Union, W. H. Mc-

---

[50]Ibid., 161.

[51]Ibid., 162.

Alpine, president-elect of the convention from Alabama. Black Baptist groups were also included: the New England Baptist Missionary Convention, W. W. Colley; and the Virginia Baptist Sunday-School State Convention, C. H. Carey, also from Virginia.[52]

At their first meeting, Foreign Mission Convention delegates collected $317.06 for the operation of the organization. The predominant portion came from Alabama, which gave a sum of $211, including $25 from the Alabama Baptist State Convention. So far the Alabama Baptists, who had not engaged in African mission work heretofore, were the perfect hosts and kept their earlier pledge to support the work of the convention. Virginia, already supporting a missionary in the field, reported a sum of $35.90, the next-largest amount. Alabama and Virginia were followed by: Tennessee, $20; Mississippi, $18.60; Arkansas, $12; North Carolina, $10; Louisiana, $8; and the First Baptist Church of Tallahassee, Florida, $1. Presumably Texas and Ohio did not make a report to the Finance Committee.[53]

## FOREIGN MISSION CONVENTION'S GROWTH, 1880–1883

The years 1880–1883 were those in which convention supporters laid the foundation for the future missionary operations of their organization. Perhaps one of the best ways to note this growth is by examining the annual minutes of the convention. By 1881 the convention had indeed made progress; but with only one year having elapsed since its founding, it still had a distance to go in rallying support in all the states. Two events since the last meeting could have caused some delay and concern for the progress of the convention. The first event was the deaths of two prominent Baptists, E. G. Corprew, elected treasurer during the last session, and Solomon Cosby, the Virginia Convention missionary whom the convention had sought to have enrolled as its missionary. Second, all official delegates were from Southern states, which at first notice might represent a setback for the convention in its attempt to become a truly national body drawing support from black Baptists north and south. The state delegations present at this first meeting since the establishment of the convention

---

[52]Ibid.
[53]Ibid., 163.

were: Alabama, Arkansas, Florida, Louisiana, Mississippi, North Carolina, Tennessee, Texas, and Virginia. Georgia still withheld its official
support and South Carolina withheld its representation totally.[54]

Southern states, particularly Virginia, continued to exert the major influence in terms of policy-making decisions and the structuring of the organization. Virginia had the largest number of delegates at the convention,
followed by Tennessee. The Finance Committee reported a similar listing
in terms of contributions for foreign missions. But this time Tennessee led
with $301.86, and Virginia came in second with $121.58. Alabama, which
had out distanced all of the states in contributions during the previous year,
fell to third place with a sum of $62.25.[55] The Foreign Mission Board fea-
tured pretty much the same state representation as it had the previous year.
All members of the newly elected board were from the Southern states:
Virginia, North Carolina, South Carolina, Georgia, Alabama, Mississippi, Tennessee, Louisiana, Texas, and Arkansas. Alabama had two
members on the board. Virginia, on the other hand, retained the majority
share of the members; sixteen board members hailed from the Old Dominion state.[56]

Colley, elected corresponding secretary, was active in this meeting, as
he had been in the 1800 convention. In fact, he was a life member. He
served on at least two committees: (1) "On Missionaries and Mission Fields
in Africa," and (2) "On Foreign Mission Board." The minutes also show
that Colley delivered a missionary sermon on 24 November 1881, at the
evening session. It was taken from Isaiah 54:5 and entitled "The God of
the Whole Earth Shall He Be Called."[57] More than any other individual,
Colley, in his annual corresponding secretary report, informed the delegates of the progress and activities of the organization. In seeking support
for the convention, Colley had traveled as far south as Georgia and as far
north as Rhode Island. He had come in touch with the black Baptists of the
New England Baptist Missionary Convention. But, according to Colley,

[54]Annual Minutes, BFMC, 1881, 5.

[55]Ibid., 28-29.

[56]Ibid., 7-8.

[57]Ibid., 10, 12, 16.

he had also visited white as well as black Christian churches. In his journeys, the secretary said, he had been in "some of the best white pulpits" and had been successful in securing white interest, confidence, and financial contributions for the work of the convention. Some white ministers had pledged their aid for the organization if it collected insufficient funds.[58]

This support from white pastors and congregations illustrates two significant points. First, W. W. Colley had the respect of many white as well as black Baptists for his tireless dedication to African missions. Second, some whites agreed that black Baptists should become active in their own separate institutions in pursuit of the evangelization of Africa. This second point comes as no surprise when we remember, for example, that many Southern Methodists welcomed, not discouraged, their black members to organize a separate Colored (Christian) Methodist Church after Emancipation.

Colley reported that it was too soon to assess adequately how successful the effort of the convention had been in enlisting support among Baptist people, but that definite plans had been set in motion to place missionaries in Africa. The Virginia Baptists had agreed to a request that they transfer Cosby from their board to that of the Foreign Mission Convention. But in May, shortly after things had been arranged, Cosby died in the field in Africa. Colley reported that the convention had wanted to place two missionaries in the African field during the past year. The nearest that the Foreign Mission Board came to sending a missionary, however, was its endorsement of the idea of North Carolina black Baptists to cosponsor their missionary, James O. Hayes. The board contributed $400 to the support of Hayes.[59]

In his report, the corresponding secretary urged the convention to make a missionary appointment as soon as possible. Nonetheless, the former missionary did see the necessity of all missionaries being sufficiently trained for service in Africa, which would include an apprenticeship under his direction "for a few months." Colley reasoned that once the people became acquainted with designated mission workers, they would more freely support them. Traditionally, mission boards have set high standards for those

---

[58]Ibid., 24-25.
[59]Ibid.

who would represent the respective denomination and Christianity on foreign soil. Colley, as spokesperson and leader of missionary recruitment for the BFMC, insisted on cherished, personal virtues and commitment to the faith. According to Colley, the prospective missionaries should "have given themselves to study and preparation." Furthermore, they should be persons of "a pre-eminent Christian character." Only persons of such caliber could hope to carry out the noble intents of the convention. As for a possible site in Africa, the board, in agreement with Cosby and W. J. David, recommended Dahomey in West Africa "where Cannibalism and idolitry [sic] of the darkest nature predominate."[60]

William Troy of Virginia prepared a series of resolutions at the 1881 assembly that aimed toward greater national support for the new organization. Troy prefaced his resolutions by saying that "the spirit of the Gospel destroys all geographical and sectional [lines]." In his resolutions, Troy drew attention to the need to gather support from Baptists throughout the country. Since "all regular Baptists" were "New Testament churches," Troy saw no reason why they should fail to unite in spreading the gospel among non-Christians. Furthermore, this Virginian envisioned a high place in the new movement for "our old and experienced ministers." Their "wisdom and zeal" were vitally needed in order to carry out missions in Africa more effectively.

Troy suggested that a circular letter be sent to all appropriate Baptist organizations throughout the country requesting that they cooperate with the convention. The delegates approved this idea and commissioned Troy and two other Virginians—Joseph Endom Jones and P. F. Morris—to draft the letter.[61] The motto of the letter was "Africa for Christ." The letter outlined three basic principles for foreign mission work. (1) It called upon Baptists to realize that God commanded Christians to seek the salvation of all peoples. This commandment included seeking the salvation of Africans, many of whom were without the gospel. (2) The letter stressed that "human instrumentalities" play a role in bringing the gospel message to non-Christians. (3) The letter pointed out that missionaries must come from the

---

[60]Ibid., 24.

[61]Ibid., 31.

churches and that the latter had an obligation to support them. The churches could not use home mission work as an excuse to avoid their responsibilities in the area of foreign missions. And perhaps directing themselves most pointedly to the black Baptists in South Carolina and Georgia, the authors of the letter concluded the third point by objecting to a wait-and-see attitude. Rather than follow such a line, the letter said, Baptists should join actively in the movement to ensure that the organization would be a success.

The letter also pointed out that by conducting foreign mission work, black Baptists were carrying out their religious and material obligation to their race. The letter sought to balance the universalist claims of Christianity, which transcend racial and ethnic bounds, with the particularist aim of trying to apply the faith to the specific needs of a given people. While maintaining that Christian mission work in a given area is not to be uniquely reserved for any one race of Christian people, the letter does point out the "peculiar" link between Afro-Americans and Americans, thus indicating a special religious responsibility on the part of black Americans for their racial kinspeople on the continent. The letter reads:

> Because of peculiar relations existing between the Africo-Americans and the Africans in our Fatherland we regard this work pre-eminently [as] the work of the American Negro. We do not hold or argue that this work is SOLELY the work of the Negro, to do so would be doing wrong because of the fact that it would be contrary to the genius of Christianity, still we hold that the circumstances surrounding the Negro point to him as the leader in this work.[62]

Since it was made clear that black Baptists must take the leadership in African missions, the authors of the letter called upon Baptist support throughout the nation.

The Committee on Ways and Means also echoed the call of Colley and Troy for national support of African missions. Believing that the success of the missionary program depended upon securing the interest of Baptists throughout the nation, the committee resolved that executive committees should be established in all the churches participating in the Foreign Mis-

---

[62]Ibid., 34.

sion Convention. These committees should have seven members and include women. Each state was requested to raise the sum of $500 to support one missionary. The committee agreed that the Foreign Mission Board should appoint James O. Hayes of North Carolina and move to establish other mission stations as early as it was feasible to do so.[63]

Undoubtedly, the BFMC leaders were somewhat impatient with what had been accomplished during the past year. They yearned to accomplish quickly tasks that the SBC and the ABMU, their white Baptist counterparts, had worked on for decades. But despite their reasonable impatience, they managed to establish firm, clear foundations for the work of a multistate convention organized only one year earlier. This success points to the character, qualifications, and experience of W. W. Colley and black Baptists throughout the South who had taken leadership in the formation and growth of independent black congregations and conventions in the postwar period.

When the convention assembled in June 1882, the movement for African missions among Southern black Baptists was still gaining momentum. Emmanuel K. Love, of Georgia, welcomed the delegates and reasserted the African missionary tradition: the responsibility for the evangelization of Africa must rest predominantly, if not completely, in the hands of black Baptists.[64] "Every pulsation of our heart beat for the teeming millions of Africa groping in ignorance dark as the night." The recorder for the convention summed up Love's Annual Sermon (delivered on the first day of the session) as one that in part "made us see the importance of sending the gospel as the *chief* means of the redemption of Africa."[65] Obviously, "redemption" conveyed more than simply Christianizing the inhabitants. Love, as others before him, was calling for racial uplift in all areas of concern, material and spiritual.

In addressing the convention, Colley noted both the growth in missionary interest and that many white Baptists were delighted that blacks were being led by God to do foreign mission work. Later in the report of

---

[63]Ibid., 27-28.
[64]Ibid., 1882, 8-9.
[65]Ibid., 9.

the corresponding secretary, he more specifically outlined the growth of African mission work. Within the past six months, the secretary had traveled a total of 4,792 miles. In many places drought had hurt the financial contributions of the churches. Thus, he had to give many free lectures on African missions, which deprived the program of much-needed funds. The secretary pointed to signs of great interest and organization for missions in "Texas, Louisiana, and Tennessee." Mission interest in Georgia and Mississippi also grew considerably. Colley expected that the state of Texas would soon support a missionary. Throughout the country, he reported, at least 154 missionary societies had been formed. If each society donated seven dollars, the convention could possibly support two missionaries on the sum of $1,778.[66]

At its January meeting, the board had selected Joseph H. Presley to serve for the summer as Colley's assistant corresponding secretary. The Foreign Mission Board agreed to use the rules of the SBC for its own governance procedures, which symbolizes the historical genius of Afro-American Christianity: willingness to use structures of white-controlled institutions to foster the goals of its own agenda. The board at that meeting directed Hayes, the missionary from North Carolina, to go to the Dahomey kingdom in West Africa. The board mailed him a total of $175 for quarterly salary and living expenses. Yet on 4 April 1882, Hayes remained in Brewerville, Liberia, contrary to the previous instruction, living in a house of "leaves, poles, and logs." The board needed money, Colley urged, with which to furnish a house and church for the missionary in spite of the fact that the Sisters' Missionary Societies of North Carolina had forwarded $100 for Hayes's support.[67]

Realizing the difficulty of supporting a missionary and remembering the historic and religious tie between American-Liberians and black Baptists of the South, the Foreign Mission Board made a move toward cooperation with the Liberian Baptists at this meeting on 1 July 1882 in Macon, Georgia. The resolutions adopted at that session noted that Liberia would be a vital gateway to other West African countries. Of the 30,000 black

---

[66]Ibid., 7-8.

[67]Ibid., 12-13.

American emigrants, Liberians, and West Indian emigrants, the Baptist church by far represented the "aggressive and ruling factor." Perhaps referring to the Liberia Baptist Missionary Society (founded in 1880), the board noted that Liberians were united in a mission society.[68]

## CONCLUSION

Founded in 1880, the Baptist Foreign Mission Convention was in part an outgrowth of the African mission program of three states: South Carolina, North Carolina, and Virginia. Of the three, Virginia played the largest role in organizing and maintaining this convention. In line with much of the racial thinking among blacks of that period, black Baptists in the years 1880–1883 organized a racially independent organization and laid plans to pursue actively the Lott Carey tradition that began more than a half century earlier.

In a context of increasing racial restrictions in the U.S. and in Africa, tensions between black missionaries and white boards and missionaries, and the growth of that perennial tradition among black Christians to form and govern their own institutions, black Baptists—mainly of the South— organized the BFMC. Its purpose was spiritually and materially to redeem the mother continent and so hasten the day when African descendants all over the world would share in and promote Christian civilization in true freedom and equity with other peoples. This chapter has demonstrated that these black Baptists, principally under the leadership of William W. Colley of Virginia, faced their task with sincere resolve and dedication, and so set the work of the convention upon firm footing.

---

[68]Ibid., 21.

# CHAPTER 2

# BFMC: THE NATIONAL PERSPECTIVE IN FOREIGN MISSIONS, 1883–1894

The BFMC's debut upon the ecclesiastical horizon was a good one. The enterprise had the support of religious leaders dedicated to African missions who approached their task with earnestness and professionalism. This chapter demonstrates two paradoxical situations in the remaining years of the BFMC's existence, 1883–1894. First, despite the eagerness of black Baptist leaders such as William Colley and William Troy, and the self-sacrificing efforts of missionaries such as John J. and Lucy Coles, the early successes of the BFMC were gradually eclipsed by the organization's inability to establish a financial base of operations commensurate to the task that it envisioned for itself.

Second, black Baptists' dedication to missionizing their African kin did not dissipate even during a financial crisis so severe as to threaten the very survival of the organization. Indeed, in the midst of these woes, African mission stalwarts reaffirmed their commitment to the idea of racial separatism in religious structures, preferring to ''go it alone'' rather than accept an ''integrated'' arrangement that would have rendered them second-class followers. After all, it was an enterprise in which they felt that God had especially prepared them to be first-class leaders. The African missionary tradition still survived and buttressed these black Christians' dedication to the development and growth of their own institutions.

It is in this sense that we speak of ''the national perspective in foreign missions.'' They sought to triumph over the financial adversities confronting them, not by submerging themselves in a white-controlled organization, but by continuing in their efforts to expand their membership and influence throughout the communities of American black Baptists. Though this latter aim remained unrealized, as we shall see, their strivings nevertheless prepared them for the true national phase that arrived with the founding of the National Baptist Convention in 1895. Let us now turn to the successes, failures, and the persistence of the BFMC Baptists during the 1883–1894 period.

## EARLY SUCCESSES

From 1883 to 1886, the African missions movement of the Foreign Mission Convention experienced remarkable success, but declined during the years 1887–1894. Foreign Mission Board and corresponding secretary reports at the 1883 convention described support for African missions among black Baptists as continually growing. Two assistant agents had been appointed to assist in the work of securing support among black Baptists: Joseph H. Presley and John J. Coles, two future missionaries to West Africa. According to the report, the states of "Louisiana, Mississippi, North Carolina, West Virginia, and Virginia"[1] had organized foreign mission boards and were making significant progress so that only three more years would be required for proper organization of mission work in these states. The report observed that in Louisiana and Mississippi the local ministers—obviously a very significant class of Christians for success in any enterprise—stood ready to conduct missionary work in Africa. The Foreign Mission Convention's news organ, *African Missions,* which solicited contributions from black Baptists, was an obvious success. Seven hundred to 1500 copies of this paper came from the press each month.[2]

An examination of the minutes of the following year yields proof that the convention was having some considerable success in gaining the support of black Baptists nationwide and that the Baptists of Virginia still retained the predominant influence. Of the fourteen vice presidents, six were from areas outside the South. As noted earlier, the president of each black Baptist state convention was represented in the national convention as a vice president. Thus, Southerners continued to dominate in terms of sheer number of vice presidents, although the states represented indicate that the movement was indeed becoming national. The six vice presidents were:

---

[1]Annual Minutes, BFMC, 1883, pp. 17-18.

[2]Ibid.

W. T. Dixon of Brooklyn, New York; T. D. Miller of Philadelphia, Pennsylvania; W. H. Brooks of Washington, D.C.; Harvey Johnson of Baltimore, Maryland; H. N. Jeter of Newport, Rhode Island; and J. W. Muse of Columbia, Missouri. It is also significant that except for Muse, all members of this list were supporters of the New England Missionary Convention, which since its formation in 1874 had exhibited a strong interest in foreign missions, particularly in the Caribbean. This is further proof that the BFMC was beginning to have an impact beyond the South.

Yet, Virginia Baptists were so situated as to retain essential control over the missionary policy. Other states had influential representation in the operation of the convention, to be sure: W. A. Brinkley of Memphis, Tennessee, served as president; Harrison N. Bouey, the former South Carolina missionary in Liberia, had returned (in 1882), and as a resident of Selma he represented Alabama as the first vice president of the convention; and A. A. Powell of Charlotte, North Carolina, served as assistant secretary. But Virginia Baptists filled all other significant offices: H. H. Mitchell of Richmond, Virginia, recording secretary; Richard Spiller of Norfolk, treasurer; and Joseph Endom Jones of Richmond, corresponding secretary. It seems that the Foreign Mission Board had evolved into the official title and function of the Executive Board. Anthony Binga, Jr. still held the chairpersonship. Most of the board members represented states east of the Mississippi River: North Carolina, South Carolina, Mississippi, and Tennessee each had one delegate; Alabama, two; and Georgia, three. Arkansas had one, and Texas had two delegates on the Executive Board. Fifteen Executive Board members—a clear, if slim, majority—hailed from Virginia.[3] The above picture remains essentially the same until 1895: a growth of national interest in African missions, with the most policy-making power being wielded by Southern, especially Virginia, Baptists.

The success of the new organization is evident in that it gained the attention of W. J. David, the SBC missionary who only a couple of years previous to the 1884 meeting of the Foreign Mission Convention had vigorously called for the appointment of *white* missionaries to Africa and a lessening of the SBC's reliance on black Southern missionaries. Accord-

---

[3]Ibid., 1884, 2, 4.

ing to the 1884 minutes, David was present at the meeting and gave a
"glowing account" of African missionary work. The convention made him
a life member, which suggests that any animosity between him and Colley, and other black Virginia Baptists had either decreased or did not play
a very crucial role in the convention. Of course, this action simply could
have been a means of indicating that the BFMC's racial role in Africa was
not to preclude ties with nonblack Christians, ties that could prove very
helpful financially. Whatever we make of the white missionary's presence, it symbolized that the African mission movement, fostered and promoted mainly among Southern black Baptists, had gained the attention of
whites as well as blacks.[4]

The outreach of the BFMC to other Baptist bodies, black and white, is
exemplified in the minutes of the 1886 convention meeting. A movement
was in progress to unite this organization and the Western black Baptists
of the Baptist General Association of Western States and Territories, which
had successfully placed missionaries in central Africa, as we shall later observe. The American Baptist Missionary Union was also making overt
gestures for cooperation in the field of missionary work. The recently organized black group, the American National Baptist Convention, was
represented by five delegates.[5]

## THE COMMISSIONING OF MISSIONARIES

But the achievement that brought most national attention to the Foreign Mission Convention was its sending six missionaries to West Africa
in 1883–1884. Interestingly, most of the missionaries were from Virginia,
and all of them lived in Southern states east of the Mississippi River. There
were two married couples, Joseph H. and Hattie Presley and the Reverend
W. W. Colley and wife. Two bachelors, John J. Coles of Virginia and
Henderson McKinney from Mississippi, were instructed to go to Liberia
College for missionary preparation before embarking for the mission field.
Coles wrote that since Liberia College fell "so far" short of an adequate
preparation, Coles and McKinney elected to begin mission work imme-

[4]Ibid., 13.
[5]Ibid., 1886, 8, 14, 32, 44.

diately. Coles's book *Africa in Brief*, written during his mission work in Liberia, provides a very vital set of facts, observations, and assessments about African customs and habits as well as the theology and methodology of these early black Baptist missionaries.[6]

This commissioning of missionaries obviously brought a great deal of esteem and pride to Southern black Baptists. For the first time in American history, a separate and "national," black, Southern-based Christian organization had sponsored the placement of missionaries in African fields solely *as missionaries,* rather than as missionary-emigrants. Formerly, black Baptists, such as Carey and Teague, embarked to Africa as emigrants who sought to carve out a Christian civilization in a "heathen" wilderness as a means of converting the indigenous inhabitants. These Foreign Mission Convention appointees, on the other hand, journeyed to Africa solely as missionaries, without abandoning the U.S. as their homeland. At the 1886 meeting, the Executive Board once again approved the sending of missionaries. Four Mississippians—J. J. Diggs and his wife, and E. B. and Mattie Topp—were commissioned for service in Africa. They, joined by the returning J. J. Coles and Lucy, his recent bride, set sail for Africa 3 January 1887 from New York City and landed on its west coast 7 February.[7]

## DECLINE IN MISSION SUPPORT

But even before the last missionary couples sailed for Africa, problems had already begun to emerge. One major set of problems centered on the missionaries themselves. The first was perhaps not a very serious difficulty, but it caused some dismay and slackening of support for African missions by black Baptists and tarnished the record of the newly formed missions organization. James O. Hayes, the North Carolina missionary cosponsored by that state and the Foreign Mission Convention, as early as 1883 informed the Executive Board that he no longer wished to affiliate with the convention, but rather with another board. Hayes promised to return the $125 advanced by the convention, but failed to do so. Shortly

---

[6]John J. Coles, *Africa in Brief* (New York: New York Freeman Steam Printing Establishment, 1886) 15.

[7]Annual Minutes, BFMC, 1887, 9.

thereafter, Hayes wrote that he had changed his mind, realized his mistake, and was now asking for reappointment as a missionary of the convention. For six months in 1883 the board continued its support of Hayes, although he had not sent in the customary missionary field report of his activities. Nevertheless, the board recommended his reappointment.[8]

At the 1884 meeting the convention learned that the *National Baptist* newspaper had printed a letter from James O. Hayes that cast the organization in an unfavorable light.[9] The newspaper quoted an excerpt from a letter by Hayes to the Baptist Missionary Union; it read: "I am a missionary out here from North Carolina, and have not had a cent sent to me since 1882, and am now hard up for bread; but in some way or another the Lord has provided for me."[10]

Whether Hayes was being truthful at the time he wrote this letter or whether he was quoted out of context is unknown, but the effect that such had upon the work of the convention was certainly not beneficial. Indeed, a white proponent of black cooperation with the Baptist Missionary Union used that letter to argue the soundness of that position. The writer claimed that he did not know the society with which Hayes was connected, but one thing was abundantly clear: if Southern blacks would unite their African mission efforts with those of the Missionary Union, money for certain vitals such as food and housing would arrive to its destination in a timely fashion.[11] Thus, missionaries such as Hayes would not have to suffer deprivation on the mission field. The Executive Board was called upon to publicize a reply to the article and to clarify the position Hayes held with the black convention.[12] These Baptists felt an urgent need to clarify the situation because the implication that could be drawn from the statements of the ABMU official concerned the inability of blacks to organize, manage, and support their activities and institutions. If the convention did in fact publish a response to the article, extant materials do not provide a copy.

---

[8]Ibid., 1884, 8.

[9]Ibid., 15.

[10]*National Baptist* (Philadelphia), 11 September 1884, 8.

[11]Ibid.

[12]Annual Minutes, BFMC, 1884, 15.

The appearance of such missionary letters seemingly did not end with the Hayes affair. In 1887, three years later, the Executive Board referred to other correspondence: "These letters have been exceedingly damaging to the cause [in] that they indicated that something was either wrong upon the part of the Board, or that the Missionaries were not keeping the obligations which they had put themselves under to the Board."[13]

Besides the problems connected with missionary correspondence, illness and death of the missionaries sent to the field took a heavy toll on mission activity in Africa and, presumably, foreign mission interest in the States. The first casualty in the field was Mrs. Hattie Presley, who died only seven months after her arrival in West Africa. J. H. Presley had been there for less than half that time before he took seriously ill,[14] "rendered powerless, both body and mind." "For months he knew not night from day."[15] The Executive Board members wanted to recall Presley soon after the seriousness of his illness was apparent, but changed their minds when both Presley and McKinney suggested that he be allowed to stay. Later, however, upon the recommendation of Colley, the board decided to recall Presley for a period of recuperation. On 26 May 1885, Presley departed Africa and landed in Richmond, Virginia, on 13 July. The missionary had spent less than two years in Liberia.[16]

Lewis G. Jordan, future corresponding secretary of the Foreign Mission Board of the National Baptist Convention, wrote an interesting account of Presley's return to the U.S.[17] In 1885 Jordan visited the west coast of Africa because a group of black Texans contemplating emigration to Africa had commissioned him to make a study of the land. While on this assignment, Jordan had the opportunity to meet several convention missionaries in Liberia. According to Jordan, the death of Hattie Presley had a profound and devastating effect upon her husband. "Brother Presley never recovered from the shock of her death and became too weak to even walk

---

[13]Ibid., 1887, 12.

[14]Ibid., 1884, 14.

[15]Coles, *Africa in Brief,* 15.

[16]Ibid.

[17]Lewis G. Jordan, *A Brief Record of Negro Baptist Missionaries* (N.p., n.d.) 7-8.

alone . . . , I had the joy of bringing him home to America leaning on my shoulder on the Barque Monrovia for 29 days."[18]

Presley was present at the 1885 meeting of the convention. He addressed the assembly on subjects such as "Africa in the Bible" and "Africa in the Early History of Christianity." Presley also strongly supported a resolution of Congressman J. W. Pierce of New Orleans. This petition urged Congress to appropriate funds for the establishment of a steamship line between the United States and Liberia. Establishing such a commercial link, it was said, would help both countries economically.[19]

But Presley's health was never to regain its former vigor. The Executive Board reported to the 1886 general convention that they would be unable to recommend Presley's reappointment as general traveling agent. The board had appointed Presley, "thinking that the mental condition of Reverend Presley was much improved." Unfortunately, his performance had not met with their satisfaction.[20] For a number of years Joseph Presley would continue in the work of the pastorate. By 1910 the missionary, having suffered two strokes, was an invalid. Unable to continue in the pastorate and "financially embarrassed," Mr. Presley had to lay his case before the fifteen-year-old National Baptist Convention. The following excerpt from that letter reveals not only his helpless state but also the toll that his missionary sojourn in Africa had exacted from his health: "I am the only living male Missionary of the number that went to Africa in 1883. I have had to fight hard ever since my return to this country, and altho [sic] I have fought a hard battle, I am at last an invalid, no voice left to sing His praise or to preach His word, so I now put my case in your hand."[21]

As the above quote suggests, Presley was not the only convention missionary who suffered from exposure in the field. The Reverend Henderson McKinney of Mississippi met his death in 1886. Traveling with an interpreter and a guide, McKinney set out on a mission tour through the backcountry of Liberia. The party came to a river that had to be crossed by means

---

[18]Ibid., 7-8.

[19]Annual Minutes, BFMC, 1885, 14-15.

[20]Ibid., 1886, 30.

[21]*Mission Herald* 15 (September 1910): 4.

of ferry. After calling for assistance for a period of time, McKinney, in order to protect the lives of the party and the equipment they were transporting, and to rest, buried the other two men, the baggage, and himself in "a great hole of sand . . . , leaving a hole at or near their heads as a means of ventilation."[22] Coles, who described this incident, did not present the complete details, for obvious reasons. Presumably, the space for ventilation that McKinney dug for himself was closed by loose sand and the missionary thus suffocated.

Coles's account and those of the Virginia and the Foreign Mission conventions' minutes contradict each other. First, Coles's narrative leaves the impression that McKinney's death took place in 1886. The copyright of Coles's book and his actual presence in the field seems to authenticate his account. But the Virginia Convention placed McKinney's death in April 1887. The Foreign Mission Convention's account was dated 15 April 1887.[23] Whereas Coles gave a detailed report of McKinney's accidentally killing himself, the Virginia Convention declared, "He died April, 1887, after a severe illness of short duration."[24] Even if for some reason the two conventions, both controlled by Virginians, elected not to relate the actual situation to the people, that still would not satisfactorily explain the year's delay in reporting the accident.

At any rate, by 1887 a combination of illnesses and deaths had halted the mission work of half of the original members sent out by the board in 1883. But that same year, E. B. Topp and his wife Mattie E. had to return because of Mrs. Topp's illness.[25] Mrs. Topp, who was rather "frail in health[,] broke down entirely" laboring in the African field. But Elder Topp, upon his return to the U.S. on 24 June, continued to work for the evangelization of the continent. He was appointed by the Foreign Mission Board to canvass the states of Florida, Mississippi, and Louisiana as a traveling agent. According to the Baptist historian Pegues, Topp's work on the domestic front was highly successful, for he collected more than

---

[22]Coles, *Africa in Brief*, 107.

[23]Annual Minutes, BFMC, 1887, 10.

[24]Annual Minutes, VBSC, 1887, 17.

[25]Annual Minutes, BFMC, 1887, 17.

$1200 on an annual basis.[26] Indeed, the minutes of the Baptist General Convention of the State of Florida indicate that the whole foreign mission enterprise had its great growth in 1888, the year Topp urged that convention to meet the challenge of evangelizing the "fatherland."[27]

The missionaries in the field apparently had questions as early as 1885 about the board's capacity to raise sufficient means to support them in a foreign land. The Executive Board reported at the 1886 meeting that the missionaries had requested that they be able to send John J. Coles to America in an effort to secure support for the African mission work. The board meeting December 1885 disapproved that suggestion, noting that the group had been at their station only a little more than a year. The missionaries disobeyed the directive of the board and sent Coles. Their position was that if the board had sufficiently known all of the facts, they would not have disapproved the missionaries' request.[28] On 3 January 1887, Coles and his bride returned to Africa with Mr. and Mrs. Topp and J. J. Diggs.

But the influential and well-respected W. W. Colley—at the time of Coles's return to America—was becoming a center of attention, in a manner that ill served the work in the mission field. Colley, in Africa for three years with his wife, had been so impaired in his health that he had been advised to leave the continent or face death. It would be one year before he could safely return to the mission field.[29] But during the time Colley was preparing to return to the United States, the Executive Board heard for the first time in March 1886 that Colley had shot and killed an African boy. According to the board, rumors were circulating concerning the incident. On 1 June they decided to issue an order to Colley to turn over his mission station to McKinney and return to America immediately to report to the Executive Board. But before the letter was mailed, Colley was already en route to the States because of illness. He arrived at Richmond 13 September 1886. According to Colley, a mentally ill man went into a house on the

---

[26]Albert W. Pegues, *Our Baptist Ministers and Schools* (Springfield MA: Wiley & Co., 1892) 492.

[27]Annual Minutes, Baptist General Convention and Baptist Sabbath School Convention of Florida (BGCF), 1888, 9.

[28]Annual Minutes, BFMC, 1886, 28.

[29]Ibid., 16.

mission site. Colley ordered the man outside and later discovered that upon firing a gun to frighten the man into compliance, he had inadvertently shot an African boy in the head.[30] There was an inquest by "twelve civilized men." Later, Colley met with two Liberian magistrates "in the presence of the Governor." Both the court and the inquest ruled the killing an accident. "The witnesses were all heathen."[31] The board expressed regret and hoped that such did not hamper African mission work.

Possibly such an incident did cause some slackening of support for the Foreign Mission Convention. It certainly seems to have raised serious questions for some persons involved in the organization. The original Executive Board Report encountered some difficulties and was committed to a committee of seven persons. The revised report seems to have been only a technical correction of the original report, with a concern that "a good literary and industrial school" be established at the Bendoo Mission Station in Liberia. William J. Simmons of Kentucky at that point introduced a resolution expressing satisfaction with the conclusion of the board in the Colley incident and requesting a copy of the proceeding on official record in Liberia. P. H. A. Braxton of Baltimore, however, moved that the adoption of the report be reserved for the following day, Saturday, at eleven o'clock. The motion carried. But on Saturday Braxton moved that the report be recommitted. Simmons's amendment was approved after this motion was tabled.[32] Perhaps many people at the convention felt a great deal of uneasiness with the fact that such an incident had occurred. Maybe many wondered why news of such a serious nature had been withheld from the board for such a long period of time and further wondered if the Virginia-dominated board was seeking to gloss over the matter in favor of their compatriot.

Jordan, who had firsthand contact with Colley around the turn of the century, suggested that the matter did not end here. When Jordan encountered Colley in 1900 and 1901, Colley was working for the United Brethren around Clifton Forge, Virginia. "The Board at Richmond had brought

---

[30] Ibid., 29-30.

[31] Ibid., 30.

[32] Ibid., 10-11, 14-15.

him home and released him in Richmond without work, and with a large family."[33] According to Jordan,

> Elder Colley had been grieving because he had unwittingly caused the death of a native boy, and although the Liberian government fully exonerated him by pronouncing the shooting accidental, yet the Board located at the time [1892] in Richmond, Va., had subjected the faithful missionary to such severe censure that his spirit quailed under the disfavor of some of his brethren and he had withdrawn from the denomination.[34]

The Virginia and Foreign Mission Conventions' minutes do not support Jordan's contention that the Richmond-based board was censorious toward Colley. Rather, it seems that they stood firmly behind Colley. If the Foreign Mission Convention's board did in fact censure the missionary in 1892, it was a matter unrelated to the shooting incident that happened in 1885 and was brought before the convention a year later. It is possible that "the disfavor of some of his brethren"[35] did take its toll upon Colley, but whether that possible disfavor came chiefly from Virginians rather than non-Virginians is highly questionable.

Finally, Jordan's account incorrectly implies that Colley withdrew from the denomination immediately following convention discussion of the shooting incident. The minutes of the organization do not support such a conclusion, unless Solomon T. Clanton of New Orleans, Louisiana, the recording secretary, made an error. His records show that as late as 12 September 1889—three years after the incident had been brought before the convention—Colley delivered "a strong address" to the assembly "which was warmly applauded." Later in the week (Friday, 13 September), Colley made another address to the delegates centering "on the religion, customs, population, and work in Africa." William J. Simmons of Kentucky made a resolution that authorized five persons to develop African mission tracts. Besides such notables as J. E. Jones of Virginia, Harvey

---

[33]Lewis G. Jordan, *On Two Hemispheres: Bits from the Life Story of Lewis G. Jordan as Told by Himself* (N.p., n.d.) 29.

[34]Ibid.

[35]Ibid.

Johnson of Maryland, H. N. Bouey from South Carolina, and C. O. Boothe
of Alabama, Colley was also listed as a member of the committee.[36]

But perhaps most impressive of all was the decision by the convention to
adopt a resolution proposed by H. J. Europe of Mobile, Alabama, that the
president of the United States appoint William W. Colley as consul to the
Congo Free State. The preamble of the resolution suggested something very
crucial about black Baptists' view of the United States, Africa, and the relationship between Christianity and Western culture. It stated that "such an appointment . . . [aids] the cause of civilization and Christianity and reflects
credit on the United States Government." But Europe's preamble also made
mention of Colley's eight-year missionary service in Africa, expressed the
belief that he knew more about the land and peoples than any other American
black person, and demonstrated confidence that the former missionary was
"in every way qualified" to function as consul.[37]

Finally, the records of the 1889 convention reveal that Colley, having
served as traveling agent for the past year, had been paid a sum of $516.97
as salary as well as an additional $72.20 for traveling and business ex-
penses. The various minutes of the convention proceedings demonstrate
that the board often provided employment of some type for missionaries
returned from the field. So if Colley did become burdened by accusations
from some members and finally withdrew, his withdrawal appears to have
taken place over a much longer period of time than Jordan suggested.[38]

But a problem greater than the difficulties related to missionaries and
mission fields confronting the BFMC was the lack of sufficient funds to
carry out the mission objectives established by the convention. To be sure,
in a sense the "missionary" problem and the financial problems were often
indissolubly linked in a circuitous cause-and-effect relationship. For example, the missionaries in the field wrote letters to Baptists at home com-
plaining about the shortage of funds. Their immediate requests might have
been granted or responded to in some degree. But such letters, as the board
pointed out, also had the paradoxical effect of lessening people's confi-

---

[36]Annual Minutes, BFMC, 1889, 8, 20, 22.

[37]Ibid., 27.

[38]Ibid., 46.

dence in the work of the Foreign Mission Board, the convention, and the ability of the two to conduct foreign mission work. This uncertainty on the part of people, according to the board, might thus lead to decreased financial contributions.

By the mid-1880s economic troubles began to develop for the Foreign Mission Convention. The limitation of financial resources of former slaves and children of former slaves was always evident. Coles's 1886 return to the U.S. from the field for the purpose of raising funds indicates the impending financial crisis that besieged the convention in the 1885-1894 period, a time of nationwide economic difficulty.[39] The Executive Board noted in its 1887 report to the convention that of the $7,000 goal set at the 1886 meeting, less than fifty percent had been received into the treasury. For the ensuing year, the board set a goal of $7,000, a minimum amount needed for the pursuit of mission work. The board also informed the convention of its inability to finance the *African Missions,* the official organ of the organization, and asked the convention to finance the paper, since it would be vital as a medium to promote the mission program. In addition, the board recommended that the fourth Sunday in July be set aside as ''Africa's Day''—an occasion for prayers and contributions to the mission cause.[40]

## THE EXECUTIVE BOARD RESPONDS, 1885–1893

The board advanced several reasons for this lack of financial support, perhaps without giving sufficient attention to the fact that the entire country was passing through economic trouble. First, the Baptist laypeople were quite willing to support African missions. However, their leaders, because of indifference and poor organization, failed to give their firmest support to the cause. Second, the board also mentioned those missionary letters from the field that had the effect of undermining support for foreign mission work.[41] Third, and significantly, the board for the first time seemed to have taken the defensive toward what was perhaps mounting criticism of its managerial work. It admitted that errors had been made, but defended it-

---

[39]Ibid., 1886, 28.

[40]Ibid., 1887, 11.

[41]Ibid., 12.

self on the basis that such mistakes characterized most newly founded organizations: "We have had many drawbacks still the work has gradually gone on. We feel that some mistakes have been made in the management of the affairs of the convention. But these have been such as are common to new enterprises."[42] The board states that it was not interested in placing blame. Perhaps these statements referred to the illness and death of missionaries in the field as well as a veiled criticism of Colley's actions in the shooting incident. This seems probable, since the board later suggested that the convention would use more "propriety" and "some new and better measures" in selection of missionaries "and the character of work that the convention shall, in the future, expect from them."[43]

The economic situation had not changed markedly by 1888. Only a small amount more than the past year had been collected. Because of this fact, the board reported, it had been unable to increase the number of missionaries. Rather, it had had to send present missionaries only a partial amount of their salaries "on two or more occasions" during the past year.[44] At that point the board had accumulated a debt of $1,169.83. Besides the decline in contributions, the board once again placed responsibility in the hands of missionaries in order to explain the debt. First, without the approval of the board, the missionaries had erected and repaired buildings. The board, ever conscious of the financial crisis of the convention, would not have allowed such an undertaking, it reported. Second, the board suggested that the missionaries had not been as frugal as they might have been.[45] Apparently we have here the development of a rift—however subtle—between the Virginia-dominated board and the general class of mission supporters. This rift would eventuate in a significant division in the ranks of black Baptists, as we will see in a later chapter.

The Executive Board report of 1889 reveals further troubles with the execution of missions, but concomitantly there was a tenacious determination to continue the work begun by the Foreign Mission Convention. By

---

[42]Ibid., 115.

[43]Ibid., 11.

[44]Ibid., 1889, 21-22.

[45]Ibid., 23-24.

November 1888 all the missionaries had returned from the African field. Though the convention meeting in 1888 had ordered that the missionaries be sent back to Africa, the board realized that such was impossible due to the financial status of the organization. The missionaries instead were dispatched to the Southern states to raise money, but they had to discontinue their efforts after only a few months. Since no missionaries were in Africa "and the times being close," people were not very responsive with their contributions. According to the board, the missionaries' presence in America rather than in Africa was seen by many supporters as evidence that African mission work had been forsaken by the Executive Board.[46]

Nevertheless, the tenor of the report was optimistic. In February 1889 the board had decided to have an indigenous preacher take charge of the mission field rather than have the country without a Foreign Mission Convention missionary. In reply to a request from the board, E. E. Smith, the U.S. consul-general in Monrovia, informed Joseph E. Jones, the corresponding secretary, that he had hired the Reverend George Bailey. In April 1889 the board determined that they would return two of the three missionaries, Mr. and Mrs. J. J. Coles, on the first of June. The board would pay $700 for the salary of Coles and his wife and insisted that only sickness should occasion their return before three years had passed. Jones, corresponding secretary, persuaded the Cosby Missionary Society of Richmond to contribute funds to build a school in Liberia. The society agreed on the condition that the school be named after the Virginia missionary Solomon Cosby, and it promised to furnish additional money that might be necessary for the completion of the work. J. J. Coles took the funds with him when he and Lucy Coles sailed for Africa with instructions to begin the work as quickly as it would be feasible to do so.[47]

The board also reported that it had paid off or was prepared to pay off all debts owed by the convention. The board members looked forward to increasing the number of missionaries from year to year. Through J. E. Jones the board had been in contact with a physician who wished "to spend his life

---

[46]Ibid., 1889, 36.

[47]Ibid., 36-38.

in Africa as a missionary.'' The appointment of a medical missionary, the board stated, "would be a wise policy and a matter of economy."[48]

For the ensuing year the board requested $6,000 to carry on mission work. They believed that such an amount could be collected and that this lesser amount, if collected by one general agent rather than several, would be expended less on the convention bureaucracy and more on mission work in Africa. They viewed the future with the expectation of much promise and good results if the missionaries would refrain from leaving the fields and if Baptists in the U.S. would continue to support the cause. Of course, the board noted that many Baptists had a much gloomier outlook for the prospects of the work. For these people, the board members engaged in an extended argument encouraging continued support. The board remarked that this despair concerning the success of foreign mission work resulted from "a lack of faith." Since the work of missions was a divine imperative, Baptists had only one alternative: to carry out God's commandments. The board at this point called Baptists' attention to facts that it probably should have stressed more earnestly years earlier. Baptists needed patience while the work was being effectively organized and while other people were becoming increasingly informed about it. These things required time, the board said. Also, to carry out the Great Commission, to preach the gospel throughout the world, mission-minded people must possess "apostolic zeal and endurance."

The board seemed to emphasize most the need for people to see the enterprise as an activity of God and be renewed in their faith. They appealed to the African missionary tradition. It was clear that God intended African-Americans to preach the gospel to the Africans. Expressing an erroneous belief of the times, the board stated that black people were physically more qualified for work in Africa. The recent tragedies in West Africa should have illustrated the falsity of this myth. But the board perpetuated what had been a popular belief among both black and white Christians since antebellum years. The board members pointed to the rapid death of white missionaries in the mission fields and linked that phenomenon with what they understood as the demand "from every hand" for the involvement of

---

[48]Ibid., 39.

black missionary personnel. What they failed to note was that blacks in
Africa were succumbing to illness and death at the same rate as whites.
Also, the board argued, the missionary interest and devotion were growing
"gradually" among black people. Thus, since God was making it so apparent that black Christians should evangelize the continent, Baptist people should have full confidence that they could perform the task.[49]

Contrary to the high expectations expressed in the last meeting, the Executive Board report of 1890 reveals that little progress had been made
during the year. (1) The board refused to appoint a general field agent and
financial secretary on the grounds of "past experience and a knowledge of
the fact that a reaction had come to the work" among black Baptists; but
it did recommend the appointment of such an officer for the upcoming year.
(2) George Bailey, the indigenous minister in Liberia appointed by the
board, had been suspended when the Coles returned to Africa and found
Bailey absent from the station. (3) Because of insufficient funds, no increase in the number of missionaries was possible. (4) The newspaper *African Missions,* though helpful in terms of generating interest and financial
support for foreign missions, did not bring revenue from its sales. Many
persons who were to sell papers simply did not return any money. (5)
Though services had been conducted in the field, no converts were reported for the past year. (6) The sum of $6,000 was not raised during the
past year, as the board had recommended.[50] (7) Finally, the board, responding to a number of letters, had to suspend John J. Coles temporarily.
The board did not specify the nature of the charges leveled against the missionary, only saying "that there were afloat rumors that are damaging to
the moral standards of Rev. Coles, and likely to impair his influence as a
missionary." An investigation by the board later revealed, however, that
the accusations were groundless. "The missionary, therefore, stands in the
highest favor with the entire Board."[51] But the whole affair surely took a
psychological toll on informed mission supporters, especially in light of
the other difficulties faced by the BFMC.

---

[49]Ibid., 37-39.

[50]Ibid., 1890, 29-31.

[51]Ibid., 31.

E. K. Love earlier had delivered his annual presidential address to the convention. In passing, he called attention to the special and privileged nature of the work of African missions. Love said: "We are engaged in a work in which angels would rejoice, and were they commissioned so to do, they would leave their exalted stations and in a moment all Africa would be hearing with Divine accuracy and seraphic eloquence of Jesus, the mighty to save. But they cannot come; they must praise God in heaven, while we worship him on earth."[52] Love, however, went on to make explicit, concrete suggestions as to how to improve the missionary work; some were original, some had been suggested previously. He recommended the appointment of a general financial agent, the selection of a commissioner to visit and report on the African mission field, the organization of foreign mission societies in all the churches, the establishment of scholarships in mission schools, and the formation of a line item in the annual budget that would take care of "all the necessary incidental expenses" incurred by the missionaries.[53]

The response of the delegates to the presidential suggestions demonstrates an emerging rift between the board and the convention-at-large. McAlpine of Alabama moved that the recommendations be sent to the Executive Board for their consideration. A. R. Griggs of Texas, however, amended McAlpine's motion to the effect that the recommendations would be directed to a committee that was constituted of a representative from each of the states officially enrolled at the convention. The motion was adopted as amended. The minutes are not clear at this point, but later during that morning session Anthony Binga, Jr. of Virginia offered a motion, amended by Walter H. Brooks of Washington, D.C., that authorized each state to name one member to a committee that would deliberate on Love's recommendations and confer with the Executive Board before announcing its report to the entire body. This motion, too, was carried.[54]

As noted, the Executive Board recommended the appointment of a general financial agent for the upcoming year, which was not a novel idea.

[52]Ibid., 1890, 10.

[53]Ibid., 9-10.

[54]Ibid., 10-11.

But the board also concurred in Love's recommendation to send a commissioner to Africa. The fact that a commissioner was appointed leads one to suspect that there was a serious question among convention members as to whether missionaries were giving sufficient reports on the status of the mission work in West Africa. The board suggested that "some one be sent to Africa to make a thorough examination of the Mission and its surroundings, and to bring back a carefully prepared report, so that we may be able to give to the public a full and complete statement of the status of the field."[55]

If the move to select a special commissioner for African missions was an expression of dissatisfaction with the leadership of the Virginians, it produced mixed results. For the board selected a fellow Virginian, J. Anderson Taylor, for the position. Taylor, who had represented the Foreign Mission Convention during the foreign missionary conference in London in 1888, was scheduled to leave for Africa the first of November. The members of the board accepted the appointment of the commissioner as a regular procedure of the convention. Besides the appointments of a general agent and a special commissioner, the board also recommended that the number of missionaries be increased, that serious effort be put forth to maintain a school (with an industrial department) linked to the mission, and that more money be collected and sent immediately to the Executive Board for rapid transference to the fields.[56]

In their 1890 report, the Executive Board defended the work of the convention. The board noted that within a single decade, eleven persons had been employed as African missionaries, "day and Sunday-School conducted, three stations and three out-stations operated at, several houses erected;"[57] and at least $25,000 had been collected and spent on the mission program. This was commendable, according to the board, in light of the fact that the people who conducted this work were untrained for such tasks. Furthermore, this newly founded convention had achieved international recognition in foreign mission circles.[58]

---

[55]Ibid., 1890, 31.

[56]Ibid.

[57]Ibid., 32.

[58]Ibid., 31-33.

From a careful reading of this report, it seems that the board was quite conscious of criticisms directed against it. The members appear to have been quite defensive when they wrote:

> The members of the Board, in managing the affairs of the Convention, have not always found the task pleasant and agreeable, but we have always been willing to make a sacrifice of our time, and have endeavored to conscientiously carry out the wishes of the Convention, and to faithfully discharge our duty to God. If we have failed it has been because of want of light. We have had to face embarrassing circumstances but we have trusted in God, and we believe he will cause success to come to the work.[59]

The Executive Board reported at the 1891 convention that it had had mixed success in carrying out the suggestions of the 1890 session. The board did send a commissioner to Africa. Because of the illness of Taylor's wife, he had to decline the appointment. Instead, D. N. Vassar, a professor at Richmond Theological Seminary, was selected. He left for Africa in February and returned in July. A mission school had been conducted in Liberia, but chiefly at the expense of the two missionaries, John and Lucy Coles. Again, the board was unable to report that it had received sufficient means to support a larger number of missionaries in Africa. Indeed, the convention had failed to meet the $6,000 goal set at the last session. Finally, the board admitted that by delaying the minutes in order to clarify certain significant details surrounding the mission work, it had inadvertently contributed to a sense of apathy among some Baptists.[60]

In ensuing years the outlook for the African missions program of the convention continued to decline. I have mentioned in depth the lack of money and disorganization as factors contributing to the decline of the organization. According to Jordan, by 1893 the mission field had been deprived of all missionaries except the Coles husband-and-wife team because of "tribal wars, disease, death and furloughs." In 1893 the last two missionaries, the Coles, returned to America "and the old mission houses were sold for lumber." The Reverend R. A. Jackson of Arkansas journeyed to

---

[59]Ibid., 32.
[60]Ibid., 1891, 36-38.

Africa, but he was for the most part self-supporting. For two years, the Baptist Foreign Mission Convention was inactive in foreign mission work.[61]

## MAINTAINING BLACK IDENTITY, 1885–1893

In order to stem the decline in missionary interest and support, the Foreign Mission Convention had three major alternatives. First, it could continue its efforts to become more national in scope, soliciting the support of black Baptists throughout the country. Second, it could have devised better means of collecting mission contributions. Third, it could engage in a cooperative enterprise in African missions with white Baptist foreign mission societies. It is indicative of the commitment to bring the gospel to Africa that these Baptists followed the first two paths. It is indicative of the racism of the time as well as the sense of their religious mission to their fatherland that they refused the third alternative.

One method to increase financial donations was the attempt to divide the country into seven missionary districts. This sectioning was tried for a while, but proved unsuccessful. Such a district plan was proposed by the Executive Board at the 1886 meeting of the convention and further commented upon at the 1887 convention. Each district was to consist of three or four states, with a general agent to promote the foreign mission enterprise and to collect funds. There would also be a district board that would meet quarterly, supervise the work of the general agent, and act as intermediary with the national Executive Board. In the past the foreign mission boards in the states served as depositories for churches, religious organizations, and individuals to place their contributions. Now the district board, through the general agent of the district, would collect funds and then forward them to the Executive Board of the convention.[62]

Special note should be made of the First Missionary District, which included the states of Maryland, Virginia, North Carolina, and the District of Columbia. This territory, along with some New England states, would

---

[61]Jordan, *Brief Record*, 8; Edward A. Freeman, *The Epoch of Negro Baptists and the Foreign Mission Board, National Convention, U.S.A., Inc.* (Kansas City KS: Central Seminary Press, 1953) 78.

[62]Annual Minutes, VBSC, 1887, 16; BFMC, 1886, 30-31; BFMC, 1887, 9-10.

be the basic component of the Lott Carey Convention formed in 1897 as a splinter group of the National Baptist Convention.

The conventions of individual states do not appear to have moved with great speed toward cooperation in the new system of organization in spite of later refinement and reorganizations. By 1887 only District Three—composed of South Carolina, Georgia, and Alabama—had actually organized. Harrison N. Bouey, the former Liberian missionary from South Carolina, acted as general agent and secretary. The question is why such a plan did not succeed. There is no mention in the minutes of state conventions or the Foreign Mission Convention that the individual state organizations considered it to be a deprivation of their power and authority. The Executive Board itself could provide no satisfactory reason for lack of support for the new plan. The board dismissed the possibility that the people were uninformed of the plan, since sufficient coverage had been placed in the convention minutes, *African Missions,* and other black Baptist newspapers.[63]

The plan, it seems, was simply premature. Only six years had passed since the formation of the convention. Time should have been allowed for more solid organization of missions at the state level, since states such as Florida were only becoming actively concerned on a broad basis by the mid-1880s. In some other states the missionary interest in Africa did not blossom until the 1890s or beyond. Thus, a step toward organization at the regional level could have appeared superfluous in light of the national organization. Many of those involved or deeply interested in African missions may have seen their energies as already sufficiently expended in the development of state mission work (foreign and domestic) and the work of the Foreign Mission Convention. When combined with the facts that the foreign mission enterprise of the organization experienced a decline in interest and contributions, and that there were economic difficulties throughout the country during this period, this reasoning is even more plausible.

The Third District's organizational success can be explained by reasons other than the possibility that the Baptists in the states of Alabama, Georgia, and South Carolina were more committed to African missions than Baptists in other states. H. N. Bouey, an experienced African missionary,

---

[63]Annual Minutes, BFMC, 1887, 9.

was well qualified to garner support for the cause. Other districts lacked this advantage. James Hayes, the North Carolina missionary, was in the field in Africa. In the case of Virginia and Mississippi, missionaries were either in the field, sick, deceased, or preparing to enter the field. Besides, in the leading African missionary state of Virginia, many mission-minded people were heavily involved already in work at the local, state, and national levels.

Another path available to black Baptists was the extension of their organization in an effort to become truly national (in *scope* as well as *intent*). Such an expansion could come by uniting with other black Baptist conventions to carry out African missions. A very significant merger, at least on paper, took place in 1888 between the Foreign Mission Convention and the Baptist General Association of Western States and Territories. Although the Foreign Mission Convention sought to be a national organization in intent and by means of modest representation from non-Southern states, it was basically a Southern group. Indeed, when other missionary societies such as the Baptist Missionary Union and Southern Baptist Convention referred to this group, they often cited it as a black *Southern* group. Furthermore, it has been shown that as far as the policy-forming aspect of the convention and the routine maintenance of mission activity on an interstate basis were concerned, the group was indeed Southern.

Reading the minutes of the convention, it is obvious that the organization constantly sought to open itself to black Baptist individuals, churches, missionary societies, and associations throughout the nation, the above facts notwithstanding. As early as 1886 when financial and other difficulties began to challenge the convention, it received words of greeting from the Baptist General Association stating their well wishes and unity in the effort to evangelize Africa.[64] To be sure, the General Association was founded in part to evangelize foreign lands. During the 1880s and 1890s, the organization succeeded in placing three missionaries in Africa.

The first call for the consolidation of two black Baptist groups seems to have risen from a newly formed black national organization, the American National Baptist Convention, founded under the leadership of Wil-

---

[64]Annual Minutes, Baptist General Association of Western States and Territories (BGAWST), 1886, p. 8.

liam J. Simmons of Kentucky in 1886. On 25 August 1886 the call was issued in the form of a resolution that the foreign mission societies of both conventions would consolidate their efforts in pursuit of the evangelization of the motherland. The preamble of the resolution stated that there was no reason why the two organizations should not unite forces. The resolution noted the harmonious relationship between the two groups in the past. It is not surprising that such a call would come from the National Convention, since the president and founder at that time was William J. Simmons of Kentucky, and the secretary was Solomon T. Clanton of New Orleans. Both of these men were intimately involved with the foreign mission program of the Foreign Mission Convention. Furthermore, Simmons in particular was a great advocate of racial unity and advancement. Understandably, he exhibited these concerns in the religious as well as secular spheres of society. In addition, notable persons such as Thomas L. Johnson of London and Richard DeBaptiste of South Evanston, Illinois, were heavily involved in foreign mission work of the General Association. Johnson and DeBaptiste served as vice president and corresponding secretary, respectively, of the American National Baptist Convention.[65]

But the General Association apparently took the most immediate and direct steps toward consolidation. The Committee on the Consolidation of Our Foreign Mission Work recommended that a five-member committee be selected to meet with a comparable Foreign Mission Convention group to move toward consolidation. The Executive Board of the latter responded positively to the move and recommended to the 1887 meeting of the convention that procedures be established immediately to effect the purpose of consolidation.[66] But by 1888 the General Association appears to have become much more cognizant of inconveniences and difficulties in the plan for consolidation, namely:

(1) The consolidation group would be of such a size that only large cities would be able to host such an organization;
(2) it would be quite expensive for Baptists to travel such great distances in order to attend annual meetings;

---

[65]Ibid., 4-6.
[66]Ibid., 2; BFMC, 1887, 13.

(3) the size of the proposed consolidated group would hinder the group in an efficient execution of its objectives;

(4) "such an organization would be rather enervating";

(5) many General Association members from the northwest section of the country would be deprived of an opportunity to engage deeply in the work of foreign missions.

Thus, the convention adopted a more moderate approach: "unification in purpose, spirit, and action." Rather than consolidation, the two bodies would unite "in complete cooperation." Both organizations would retain their separate identities and activities. An equal number of members from the executive board of both organizations would form " a co-operative board" with a common treasury. That cooperative board would then dispense money to missionary needs and activities as it deemed proper.[67]

The two conventions met in the same city, Nashville, Tennessee, on successive dates in 1888; the General Association met 18 and 19 September, the Foreign Mission Convention, 19-21, 24 September. Therefore, many of the persons actively involved in the one convention were able to attend the proceedings of the other as visitors. The visitor list of the General Association included prominent Southern black Baptists such as James A. Taylor, P. F. Morris, Joseph H. Presley, and Joseph E. Jones of Virginia; H. C. Bailey of Florida; Thomas L. Jordan and E. B. Topp of Mississippi; Emmanuel K. Love and C. T. Walker of Georgia; S. W. Anderson and W. A. Brinkley of Tennessee.[68]

The Foreign Mission Convention agreed to the proposals of the General Association. It further complied with the request for union by reorganizing its district plan to allow for the states of the western convention to be placed in the Sixth District. The new name of the organization was to be the American Baptist Foreign Mission Convention of the United States of America.[69] There is no evidence that this new name was extensively employed, nor is there any available evidence to suggest that such an institutional arrangement actually evolved very far beyond a paper organi-

---

[67]Annual Minutes, BGAWST, 1888, 6.

[68]Ibid., 6-7.

[69]Annual Minutes, BFMC, 1888, 12-13.

zation. The organization did perhaps lay the groundwork for an even greater Baptist unity among blacks that occurred in 1895.

Almost concomitantly with the proposal to merge with the General Association, the Foreign Mission Convention received a plan to cooperate with the white Missionary Union. As I have indicated elsewhere in this chapter, the 1880s were a period of intense interest on the part of the union to cooperate with the black Baptist groups for the evangelization of Africa. Suffice it to say that many white Baptists, North and South, believed that Afro-Americans were the best qualified to evangelize their fatherland because of the climatic conditions, the illness and death of white missionaries, or a belief that black Americans could better relate to their kinspeople in Africa than whites. The union once sought to effect cooperative ventures with blacks on the state level. With the emergence of regional-national associations such as the General Association and the Foreign Mission Convention, the concern for undertaking cooperative foreign missionary ventures shifted to these groups.

But the Foreign Mission Convention also made overtures of cooperation. As early as 1880, representatives were sent to the Missionary Union as fraternal delegates. In 1884—if we trust the Union minutes—P. F. Morris, a Virginia Baptist, appeared at the Baptist Missionary Union convention and appealed, as a delegate from the Foreign Mission Convention, for cooperation between the two groups.[70] Perhaps Morris and the white Baptists meant different things by the term cooperation. Perhaps Morris meant that the union should assist black Baptists in financing their own mission program by way of the Foreign Mission Convention's treasury and missionaries. This explanation would certainly do much to explain the events that followed.

At the 1886 meeting of the Foreign Mission Convention, representatives of the American Baptist Missionary Union were present as fraternal delegates to the assembly. A committee of the Foreign Mission Convention noted that the union had indicated a wish to cooperate with the group, but that this desire had been expressed "in general terms." The committee recommended waiting for specific plans before making an agreement; meanwhile the Union's

---

[70]Annual Minutes, AMBU, 1884, 23-24.

delegates were received in love. The Executive Board, however, was more explicit. Even at the height of wavering financial support, the board rejected cooperation on the grounds that only black Baptists did what others could not and would not do: evangelize Africa. The board termed Africa the "most neglected country" on earth with regard to American missions. In the mood of rising black unity and pride that characterized the post-Reconstruction era, the board made clear that African mission work served the needs of Afro-Americans as well as Africans. According to the board, by joining forces with white missionary societies, black Baptists would not develop to their highest missionary potentials.[71]

> We believe . . . that to continue our work as an organization will develop qualities and powers in us as a people that will not be developed if we go into another organization. The people connected with the churches are just beginning to see this work in the proper light—in the light of duty. We are endeavoring to train them to give systematically, as regularly as becomes Christians. Now to give up our organization will be to throw a cloak upon our efforts, and to a large degree to hinder the work of evangelizing Africa.[72]

The board obviously believed that cooperation with whites meant submerging black identity in the religious sphere. Besides the loss of identity within a white organization, racism and paternalism might hamper blacks in an arena in which ever since the Civil War they had had a great degree of autonomy. The black church (and the black denomination) remained as the one viable institution in and through which blacks could assert their full sense of humanity, develop leadership qualities, and learn to provide for themselves. It deserves reiterating that the African mission movement represented both an opportunity for black Christians to affirm the meaning of their existence as well as the chance to contribute to the spiritual and material uplift of their African kinspeople. Thus, it is not surprising that in the midst of financial troubles, the Foreign Mission Convention "consolidated" with other black Baptists while simultaneously rejecting cooperation with white Baptists. As the board reasoned, "There is no reason, in our mind, why we should cooperate, but many why we should not—we

---

[71]Annual Minutes, BFMC, 1886, 4, 14.

[72]Ibid., 32.

need experience, we need self-reliance, we need those blessings that come to those who discharge their duty to God and man."[73] These Baptists felt that just as black Christians had a unique role in the redemption of Africa, so did black Baptists in America have the ability to accomplish *among and for themselves* those things white Baptists could not.

Notwithstanding this explicit position on cooperation, the Baptist Missionary Union persisted in its efforts to arrange cooperation. One of the union's representatives at the black convention reported on the 1887 Foreign Mission Convention meeting. He pointed out that the union delegates were received warmly and were given ample opportunity to present their case for cooperation. But "they seemed from the first to be fully determined upon separate organization and independent missions." This representative questioned the ability of black groups to do efficient missionary work in Africa, since they had such limited financial resources. But he believed that the two black denominations, the Foreign Mission Convention and the General Association, must assume the major responsibility for evangelizing Africa, demonstrating that many white Christians still embraced the notion of the providential role of Afro-Americans in the task of redeeming Africa.[74]

By the time the Foreign Mission Convention met in 1888, the union had developed a detailed plan of agreement as a basis for cooperation. The union proposals were as follows:

(1) The Foreign Mission Convention, with the approval of the union, would appoint missionary personnel and set salaries. In case a disagreement arose, both boards would discuss the matter.

(2) The Foreign Mission Convention would be able to select the area for the mission field.

(3) The Foreign Mission Convention would collect funds and deliver them to the treasury of the union. In the event that the black Baptists fell short in raising the necessary amount, the union would provide the additional support. This money from the union would be considered a loan, however, with the understanding that the convention would have to replace the amount.

---

[73]Ibid.

[74]Annual Minutes, AMBU, 1887, in *The American Baptist Missionary Magazine* (July 1887): 197-98.

(4) The Foreign Mission Convention would be free to follow its own methods in the collection of missionary funds.

(5) All transaction of business with missionaries would be done through the executive officers of the union.

(6) Missionaries appointed would be dually aligned and thus obligated to both groups in terms of preparing reports concerning mission activities.

(7) The Foreign Mission Convention had assurance that it would be represented on the Union Executive Board beginning with the first regular meeting after approval of the plan.[75]

The Executive Board of the Foreign Mission Convention recommended that the plan be rejected "unless some material changes are made by the Union." Since it has already been pointed out that these black Baptists were most concerned that an inordinate degree of power and responsibility would be taken from them and placed in the hands of whites, it seems safe to assume that points 3 and 5 placed the most serious obstacles in the path of cooperation. The independent spirit among these black Baptists categorically forbade them from allowing themselves to be "errand boys" for the white-dominated Missionary Union or from accepting the premise that they were incapable of efficiently and effectively transacting their own business. It is not surprising, therefore, that at this same session the convention, though rejecting cooperation with white Baptists, finalized consolidation plans with the black General Association.[76]

The 1889 meeting of the Foreign Mission Convention witnessed the final death blow to the union's plans for cooperation and signaled conclusively that the bulk of black Baptists would follow a separate, independent course in pursuit of African evangelization. The Committee on Resolutions refused the proposal on the grounds that it was premature and impractical.[77] As though to indicate that the convention was issuing its final words on the matter, the committee said that they "firmly but respectfully declined" to accept the plan. Three reasons similar to, but more specific than, the 1888 premises were advanced.

---

[75]Annual Minutes, BFMC, 1888, 13.

[76]Ibid., 20.

[77]Ibid., 1889, 24.

(1) Black Baptists—who at this point were only beginning to grasp the significance of African missions—would abdicate their responsibility for missions in the face of a "strong financial body like the Union."
(2) The black convention needed the occasion "to get the rich experience that grows out of personal management of our mission fields through our Board." The success of even the union, the committee asserted, was predicated in part upon this management experience.
(3) Finally, the committee reasoned that such a plan would call into question the accomplishments of the Foreign Mission Convention in the foreign field and would hamper "the future prosperity" of the mission program.

The committee at this point expressed what was the basic issue underlying all of these points—the belief that they would not hold a truly equal relationship with the union in such an arrangement.[78] To accept such a plan would be to admit that black Baptists were unable to perform the missionary task in Africa.

> For the consolidation is not in the form of a union of equal constituents, but the superior absorbing the inferior in point of prominence, though both the object and the intention are good; again, it is an implied admission that we are incapable of taking the control of such a work, an implication which we are not prepared to admit or let our people think.[79]

The fears of these black Baptists were surely aggravated by the tension between the union and the General Association in 1888, which clearly illustrated to most black Baptists that an equal partnership with their white counterparts was practically impossible albeit theologically palatable. Nearly coincident with its offer of cooperation to the Foreign Mission Convention in the mid-1880s, the union successfully arranged terms of cooperation with the General Association. But in 1888 the association's Executive Board reported a matter to the general convention that raised serious questions as to whether the cooperative venture with the union should be continued. According to Dr. T. E. S. Scholes, a missionary in the field, he had received correspondence from the union informing him that he had been transferred to the mission staff of that body because the General As-

---

[78]Ibid., 23.
[79]Ibid.

sociation had given very little to his support in Africa. But the board members and officers of the association had known of no such change and had thought that they were maintaining their position as managers of the missionary staff in Africa. To be informed otherwise, and by circuitous means, obviously angered members of the association's Executive Board.[80] Thus, they directed the following question to the convention-at-large:

> Is it wise to continue the cooperation of this body with the Union in our work for Africa when such evidence comes to us that the Union or its Corresponding Secretary, very lightly esteems what we have done in the interest of this common work, and disparages, rather than encourages confidence in our endeavors? Such is not the result sought, and certainly not what was expected from cooperation[.][81]

The union, of course, informed the board at a later date that they had not intended to convey such an impression. Whether Theophilus Scholes interpreted the original letter correctly was not resolved. But for the long list of visitors from the Foreign Mission Convention at the 1888 gathering of the General Association, such friction must have contributed to anti-cooperation leanings they already held.

The second item in the Executive Board's report that might have influenced the BFMC against cooperation was Thomas L. Johnson's report from the mission field. Johnson's 1887 report, containing correspondence from Scholes, arrived too late to be included in that year's minutes. Writing on 24 December 1886, Scholes stated his belief that the Executive Board had been correct in accepting terms of cooperation with the union, because black Baptist churches had not been sufficiently interested in and generous to African missions. Apparently, Scholes envisioned cooperation as a temporary arrangement made necessary by financial circumstances, because he warned that such dependence upon the financial help of the union should not obscure the reality of the association's subordinate position. The union, Scholes wrote, had agreed to make up any deficiencies of the association in terms of missionary support, but such monies were to be considered loans, not grants. Thus, the association had two alternatives: to conduct

---

[80]Annual Minutes, BGAWST, 1888, 14.
[81]Ibid.

business in such a way as to gain the respect of others or to allow themselves to fall to the level of "mere automatons, menial." This latter "goal" could be quickly accomplished, Scholes contended, by the association's becoming immersed in debt.[82]

Officials of the Foreign Mission Convention present at the meeting must have feared that such a predicament could befall their group should it become embroiled in cooperation with the union. They evidently believed that their objective must not be cooperation for the sake of acquiring requisite monetary resources, but the development of missionary interest and contributions from black Baptists so that they would never face the prospect of entering into an unequal partnership with the union. Surely the following words of Scholes must have caused some concern or reinforced whatever misgivings Foreign Mission Convention members already held: "I earnestly hope, however, that the temporary relief from embarrassment, the result of cooperation, will not even tend to make us ignore or lessen the fact that we are subordinates, and as such are subject to the over-ruling and dictation of her under whose guardian care we have placed ourselves."[83]

## CONCLUSION

We have observed how the early successes of organization and the commissioning of missionaries during 1880–1883 were soon tempered by some very unfortunate circumstances, including the economic troubles facing the convention and the sickness and death of missionaries in the field. In line with the general mood of independency among black Baptists, the convention refused consolidation with the white Baptist group, the American Baptist Missionary Union, although such a "cooperative" venture might have provided more immediate access to much-needed funds. The convention did assent to a paper agreement on cooperation with another group, the black General Association of Western States and Territories, thus pointing the way to a national union of black Baptist forces in 1895.

The real story about the BFMC during this period was not the financial and other difficulties it faced. Rather, this period severely tested the re-

[82]Ibid., 22.
[83]Ibid.

solve of these black Christians to remain true to their conviction that they, as sons and daughters of Africa, had a religious and historical imperative to take chief responsibility for spreading the gospel in Africa. If they had compromised their separate institution (the BFMC), they would have demonstrated to the world that the people recently freed from bondage were in fact incapable of holding their own in either ecclesiastical or noneccles iastical areas of life: that is, they were unfit for real freedom. Rejecting a merger with their white counterparts while approaching the very brink of dissolution in the African missions enterprise, they maintained their conviction that God, by some divine and inscrutable means—had reserved a mission for them that would not only provide meaning to their own experiences of slavery and discrimination, but lead to the material and spiritual empowerment of African peoples throughout the world.

Furthermore, black Baptists by 1895, despite their organizational problems, had paradoxically moved beyond the local and regional stage in the development of the African missions enterprise and were about to embark upon a truly national effort to redeem the motherland. Before turning attention to this third stage in part two, it will be helpful to consider in the following chapter the impact of two other forces relative to the rise of the missions movement thus far: activities of Baptists at the state level and the role of women. Attention to these two factors contributes to a more insightful and comprehensive account of the events that took place between the years 1880 and 1895.

# CHAPTER 3

# THE AFRICAN MISSION MOVEMENT, THE STATES, AND THE SUPPORT OF WOMEN, 1880–1894

The preceding chapter examined the African mission movement among black Baptists from a regional-national level (the Baptist Foreign Mission Convention). This chapter focuses on two major aspects of the 1880–1894 period: the foreign mission movement at the state level and the role of women. I examine the movement on the state level in order to underscore that the success and failure of the Foreign Mission Convention greatly depended upon the efforts of mission supporters at that level. The participation of women is covered in order to emphasize that although they did not occupy high, visible positions on either the state or regional-national level, they nevertheless contributed substantially to the growth of the African mission program.

I wish to emphasize that the purpose of the latter section is not to provide a comprehensive analysis of the role of black women Baptists in the African mission movement. References to individuals throughout this work indicate the varied roles of women. They served as mission organizers at both the state, regional, and national levels; and they journeyed to the continent both as members of husband-and-wife teams and as single, independent missionaries who in some cases established new mission stations. Elsewhere I have provided an account of black Baptist women's support of African missions, especially as it was channeled through institutions of higher learning.[1] In the present chapter I merely seek to correct any false

[1] See Sandy Dwayne Martin, "Spelman's Emma B. DeLaney and the African Mission," *Journal of Religious Thought* 41 (Spring-Summer 1984): 22-37.

inference that the Baptist Foreign Mission Convention was maintained and supported solely by men, even though male clergy dominated.

## THE STATES

Historically, Baptists have jealously guarded the principle of individual congregational autonomy. They have emphasized that in the final analysis the local church group has ultimate authority over its policies and commitments, and that Baptists' participation in state, regional, or national associations and conventions is not coerced but voluntarily entered into by the local church. Unsurprisingly, then, the black Baptists' commitment to African missions increased as local groups consented to cooperate with each other, as opposed to being forced to do so by a directive handed down from a central authority. Therefore, it is not only interesting but instructive to examine the growth and dynamics of the mission enterprise at the state level.

Two observations emerge from an analysis of foreign mission interest and support among Baptists at the state level. First, as with the general Foreign Mission Convention, the early 1880s was a period of active missionary concern in most of the Southern states, but was followed by a decline in support for African mission work in the late 1880s and the early 1890s. Second, the fact that Baptists of a given state had a representative in the mission field (i.e., a missionary from that state) generally indicated the level of their support for African missions. For example, North Carolina and Virginia maintained missionaries in Liberia throughout this period and thus were, along with Mississippi, the most ardent supporters of the cause. South Carolina supported African mission work enthusiastically between 1878 and 1882. But once Harrison N. Bouey, the state-supported missionary, withdrew from the field, the amount of mission funds collected decreased.

In Mississippi, the reverse of what occurred in South Carolina transpired. Mississippi Baptists had not exhibited deep foreign mission interest prior to the founding of the Foreign Mission Convention in 1880. Once Mississippi missionaries went to Africa, the mission cause grew among the Baptists of this state. Georgia, Alabama, Tennessee, and Florida sponsored no missionaries through the general convention. Though all of these

states supported the mission cause, the materials at my disposal do not indicate that there was ever the degree of African mission support that obtained among the Baptists of Virginia, North Carolina, Mississippi, or, in
the early years, South Carolina. This chapter thus concentrates on the
movement in those four latter states.

## VIRGINIA

In many ways the history of the Foreign Mission Convention is an extended history of the black Baptists of Virginia. No other state contributed
as much to African missions, either financially or in terms of the missionaries' time and labor as Virginia black Baptists. I have illustrated the overwhelming impact that Virginia wielded in terms of policy making for the
convention. To read the minutes of the black Baptist convention in Virginia is like reading the minutes of the Foreign Mission Convention. For
no other state Baptist convention followed missionary matters as closely
on the national level as the Virginia Baptist State Convention.

The commitment of black Virginia Baptists to found a distinctly Afro-
American movement for African missions appears in their refusal to enter
a cooperative arrangement with the Southern Baptist Convention as early
as 1880. While Virginia black Baptists were laying plans for the organization of the Foreign Mission Convention, Anthony Binga, Jr., their corresponding secretary, was in contact with the Southern Baptist Convention
officials in an effort to secure a closer cooperation between the Virginia
Convention and the white group.

The Virginia Baptists had much to boast about in Anthony Binga, Jr.
A native of Amhertsburg, Ontario, Canada, Binga was baptized, licensed,
and ordained to preach in 1867. He surrendered an earlier intention of being
a physician in favor of the ministry. After serving as a school principal for
a number of years in Ohio, Binga journeyed to Manchester, Virginia, in
1872 to pastor the prestigious First Baptist Church. Besides serving as a
school principal in Virginia, this well-known Baptist leader made his imprint on the Baptist church in Virginia, serving as an officer in the Virginia
Baptist State Convention, the Virginia Baptist State Sunday School Con-

vention, moderator of the Shiloh Baptist Association, and a trustee of
Richmond Theological Seminary.[2]

Binga had been informed of the proposal to have the foreign missions
boards of both the SBC and Virginia Convention united into a single standing committee to support the work in Africa. According to the SBC minutes, Binga expected that the Virginia Convention's meeting in Hampton
in May would support the idea heartily.[3] But in a series of meetings between representatives of the SBC and the Virginians, the latter gradually
revealed to the SBC that they would not move closer in the area of cooperation until the Foreign Mission Convention had been organized. Some
SBC officials considered attending the state convention, but declined to do
so on the grounds that they had neither the authority nor invitation to be
official representatives. Perhaps they sensed that they might not be extended the most cordial welcome in light of the growing sense of independency among black Baptists. Instead, the corresponding secretary of the
Virginia Baptists was requested to advocate cooperation with the SBC. But
by the time of the SBC's 1881 meeting, it had become clear to many in
that group that the black Baptist convention had no interest in cooperating
except by the means of "fraternal intercourse and correspondence," as a
letter from Binga was so interpreted. Binga removed any hope that the Virginia Convention would cooperate with the SBC, since it would support
the newly organized BFMC.

But Binga was not the person who evidenced that black Virginia Baptists were preparing to initiate their own, separate venture on behalf of African missions. The president of Richmond Institute, Charles H. Corey,
informed the SBC in a letter dated 2 April 1881 that the missionary Solomon Cosby had been called home from Africa, ostensibly to work under
the auspices of the Foreign Mission Convention. According to the SBC re-
porter, Corey's letter was the first news received by the SBC officials that
Cosby had been called to Virginia. The SBC resigned itself to the obvious
by stating that the committee selected to pursue talks with black Virginians

---

[2]Albert W. Pegues, *Our Baptist Ministers and Schools* (Springfield MA: Wiley & Co.,
1892) 58-61.

[3]Annual Minutes, Southern Baptist Convention (SBC), 1880, pp. 43-44.

had done its utmost to effect cooperation.[4] But it should have been clear to all observers that the Virginia Baptists were doing more than inaugurating separate state mission work in Africa. They were organizing a movement that before long would have regional and national implications—a movement of which they were the proud vanguards.

From the very beginning, Virginians were quite cognizant of the chief influence they were playing in the formation and growth of the Foreign Mission Convention. In the President's Report of 1881, Richard Wells clearly credited Virginians for forming a convention to pursue the evangelization of Africa. The only question remaining was the mechanics by which state foreign mission support was to be conducted—whether directly through the general convention or through the convention via the state convention. Wells recommended the latter approach. He also indicated that Virginia's methods to promote African mission work won the acclaim of Baptists in the North. He looked forward to the day when Baptist foreign mission work would be conducted by the united efforts of black Baptists in the North and South.[5]

The Foreign Mission Board of the state convention in its 1884 report noted that most of the preparation for establishing missions in Africa had been made by Virginians. The board contended that Virginians must bear with this imbalance of responsibility in the conduct of African missions until other states organized much more effectively.[6] The Foreign Mission Board's 1885 report repeated this assertion.[7] This knowledge of their significant role had two impacts upon the Virginians. First, it appealed to a state pride that could be manipulated to maintain active interest and support among the state Baptists. On the other hand, it would be a hindrance to black Virginians to accept a new order of things with the formation of the Foreign Mission Board of the National Baptist Convention in 1895; that body would have fewer Virginian members and thus would be less susceptible to their influence.

---

[4]Ibid., 1881, 43.

[5]Annual Minutes, VSBC, 1881, 34.

[6]Ibid., 1884, 19.

[7]Ibid., 1885, 15-16.

As the major organizers and supporters of the BFMC, the Virginia leaders very early recognized the approaching financial crisis of the convention and felt particular distress because many other Baptist leaders of the state had not adequately supported the fund drive so desperately needed to continue the noble enterprise that the Virginians themselves originated. Richard Spiller, state corresponding secretary, in 1885 noted that there appeared "a lukewarmness" with regard to African missions. He understood that the Virginians could not carry the total responsibility for the convention, but he urged the state convention to uphold its own obligation for African redemption. Spiller wrote: "There seems to be a lukewarmness relative to this work. It is not enough for us to simply pray for the salvation of the heathen, but we are to work for it . . . and while Va. is not expected to do all, we must do our part. . . . four of the missionaries now in Africa are from this State."[8]

At the 1886 convention the State Foreign Mission Board reported that mission work had been "very encouraging." But the board also stressed that Virginia provided almost all of the money for missionary support. Pointing to a developing relationship among the black Baptists of Virginia, Maryland, and the District of Columbia, the board stated that because of the enterprising activities of "our efficient agent" and the contributions of black Baptists in Baltimore and Washington, D.C., the Virginia Convention had been able to meet the task. The board found that when mission leaders came in contact with Baptist people, they gained lay financial support. Therefore, the board claimed that the problem of collecting funds lay not with the willingness of Baptists to give, but with insufficient organization and the nonsupport of pastors.[9]

The board reported on the success of the district plan approved by the Foreign Mission Convention. The Baptists of the District of Columbia and Maryland had agreed to this arrangement of collecting funds by regions and had done African mission work by means of the Foreign Board of the state Baptist convention. The board recommended that the district plan be approved and that Maryland and the District of Columbia be given due rep-

[8]Ibid., 41.
[9]Ibid., 1886, 15-16.

resentation on the state Foreign Mission Board. The board failed to mention that North Carolina was a part of the First Missionary District.[10]

The above plan met the approval of the Virginia Convention. In 1887 the First Foreign Mission District made its first annual report. The board looked ahead with great expectation to the advancing consolidation of the two regional black Baptist groups dedicated to African missions: the Foreign Mission Convention and the General Association. The result of this consolidation would be a tremendous boon for funding missions, though they still hoped that Virginia would continue in the forefront of the movement. The financial report of the District Board revealed that Virginia played a much greater role in collecting funds than either of the other two states and the District of Columbia. North Carolina reported $215.61; Maryland, $231; Washington, D.C., $258.03; and Virginia, $1,327.65. Two significant facts emerged from this financial report. First, and more important, Virginians collected almost double the amount raised by all of the other states combined. Second, all of the monies collected from Maryland came from sources in Baltimore. This suggests that overall Maryland was not very well organized at this point in regard to foreign missions.[11]

At the 1888 session of the state convention, the report of the Foreign Mission Board of the First Foreign Mission District stated that they collected less money for the past year than any previous year, signaling the increasingly difficult task of attracting contributors even in the principal state for black Baptist mission work. They blamed this failure on "hard times and the scarcity of money," but added that wherever the agent, J. Anderson Taylor, went the people had managed to give something, if not very much. A review of the financial report of the board affirms this low level of contribution, especially in Virginia. Whereas the contribution from the District of Columbia climbed from the year 1887 ($376.60), North Carolina's contributions remained roughly the same ($218.74). Maryland's contribution decreased in quantity, with just one church reporting $100 for the entire state. But the most dramatic decrease of all was among Baptists in Virginia ($757.78).[12] Thus, the district plan of the Foreign Mis-

[10]Ibid., 16-17.

[11]Ibid., 1887, 15-19.

[12]Ibid., 1888, 16, 18-20.

sion Convention apparently did not succeed in any of the regional districts
in terms of substantially increasing mission contributions.

Increasingly, two issues cost the state mission efforts valuable revenue: the lack of organization and a growing anti–foreign mission sentiment
in Virginia and other areas of the country. First, the corresponding secretary of the state convention pointed out how the lack of proper and efficient organization handicapped fundraising attempts. Churches and
associations had to unite throughout the state, he contended, in order to
maximize both domestic and foreign mission programs. To effect this
union, the secretary proposed that the convention authorize his office to
communicate with and interest the various Baptist bodies throughout the
state by means of letters and visits.[13]

But the state convention also expressed a strong desire to maintain a
corresponding relationship with other black Baptist bodies outside the state.
Not satisfied to work with other Baptists merely through the Foreign Mission Convention, the secretary reported that minutes of the state convention had been exchanged with "North and South Carolina, Georgia,
Louisiana, Texas, Baptist General Convention of the Western States and
Territories [General Association], and the Wood River Association of Illinois."[14] The secretary expected that some of these exchanges might continue on a year-by-year basis, and perhaps such steps would aid in securing
complete unity of black Baptists throughout the country.[15] It is evident,
then, that the impending financial crisis of the African mission programs
at both the state and local levels convinced the leaders of the need to expand the scope of their domestic organization in order to generate a more
adequate supply of funds. Even the Virginia state minutes reveal a paradoxical situation in which the financial failures of the state and regional
conventions coincided with a growing commitment truly to nationalize the
movement.

With contributions to mission work continually declining or failing to
increase substantially within the Foreign Mission Convention-at-large,

---

[13]Ibid., 63.

[14]Ibid., 64.

[15]Ibid., 63-64.

some Virginians in the late 1880s seriously began to question whether that body was willing to accept the challenge of foreign missions. The Foreign Mission Board of the state convention in 1889 appealed to tradition and state pride by reminding the body that Virginia inaugurated African missions and therefore, the board argued, the responsibility lay upon the state not to allow the program to fail. Black Baptists in Virginia stated that the First District members could do as much for African missions as the entire Foreign Mission Convention was doing. If the pastor in each church would become a firm advocate for the cause of foreign missions among his members, Virginia could support "three or four" persons in Africa with aid from other portions of the district.[16] The board seems to have reasoned that the general Baptist population could still be expected to provide support for the cause. One of the major reasons for the decline in their support was not an aversion to foreign missions. Rather, because all the missionaries had returned from Africa,[17] the people had no visible assurances in terms of personnel that mission work was a genuine or realistic enterprise.

But the lack of proper organization was not the only cause of the state convention's inability to increase missionary support. Apparently, many black Baptists in Virginia feared that engagement in foreign missions would seriously hamper their work in domestic missions. Thus, they did not contribute to the support of the former. The post–Civil War period was one of severe economic hardship for most of the people formerly held in chattel bondage, particularly those still residing in the South. For example, it took the heroic, noble, and sustained efforts of white and black missionaries, North and South, to provide a despised people elementary avenues for basic literacy. Many altruistic persons could, and obviously did, raise the point that the African mission movement drained funding very much needed on the domestic front for their own families and neighbors. Help was especially needed given the steady ebbing of the federal government's promise that blacks would have opportunities for basic rights and material advancement.

The general response to this sentiment was the assertion that foreign mission work would encourage support for domestic missions, not dis-

---

[16]Annual Minutes, BFMC, 1889, 19.

[17]Ibid.

courage it. Pro–African mission sentiment, then, could be phrased in two ways. First, once people were encouraged to give for one cause, this would spiritually (or psychologically) induce them to contribute to the other. In other words, generosity once begun is contagious and thus extends to areas beyond its original object. Second, the command of Christ clearly enjoined every Christian and every church to carry the gospel to every creature throughout the world; obedience to this command, African mission supporters argued, sometimes entailed sacrifices. We must also bear in mind the belief of these supporters that all African peoples had a common destiny and that Afro-American Christians were especially commissioned to work for the realization of this mission via evangelization of the mother continent.

A quote of J. M. Armistead, who once served as president of the VBSC, illustrates the tenacious conviction of African supporters concerning the indissoluble link and harmony between home and foreign mission work: "There are some who seem to entertain great fears that foreign missions will hinder the home schemes. There is about as much reason in this as to fear that a branch will work injury to the spring from which it glows. The God of missions has ordained that the one be in harmony with the other, and the other with the one."[18]

By 1890 revenues for missions throughout Virginia reached an all-time low. The resignation of the general agent, J. Anderson Taylor, meant that no money was collected for that year. The black Baptists of Virginia contributed less than $300 for the fiscal year ending 1 May 1890. The combined contributions from Virginia, West Virginia, North Carolina, and Washington, D.C. netted only $1,303.32. The Foreign Mission Board, however, could report one bright spot. John J. and Lucy Coles of Virginia returned to Liberia as missionaries under the auspices of the Foreign Mission Convention in July 1889 and carried $459 from the Cosby Missionary Society of Richmond for the construction of a mission school.[19] Undoubtedly, the Virginians hoped that the reestablishment of a missionary presence in Africa would serve as a vital stimulus for increased donations to the cause.

---

[18]Annual Minutes, VBSC, 1889, 52.
[19]Ibid., 1890, 29-31.

Yet after several years in the field, the Coles had to return to the U.S. in 1893. War between the Vai and other ethnic groups, as well as J. J. Coles's poor health, precipitated this return. At this point we witness the most desperate moment in the work of black American Baptists; it was almost abandoned entirely. Coles estimated that it would be a year or eighteen months before he and Lucy Coles could resume work there. The state board, however, planned to carry on a missionary program by its continued $300 annual support of J. O. Hayes, the North Carolina missionary who was teaching at Liberia College. Also, the board noted that the Foreign Mission Convention had agreed to cooperate with the Baptists in Liberia. While Liberian Baptists would oversee the work, American Baptists would continue to set the policies. The state board urged the Virginian Convention to overlook all of the obstacles of war and failing health, and to continue working for the redemption of Africa, remembering that sufferings and hardships had characterized all missionary programs in the history of Christianity.[20]

But the mission cause continued to decline. In 1894 the board itself noted that contrary to its predictions a year earlier, there had been an insufficient supply to fill "the great need of money and men." Again, the board urged the convention not to curb its zeal or activities in the face of adversities, arguing that such problems "are common to all Missionary enterprises." But the board expressed in explicit language that African missions confronted a serious crisis: "Our work at present does not present a very encouraging aspect. Missionary interest and zeal seem to be dying from the hearts of the people of our churches and the one great need of the hour is a missionary awakening."[21] Virginia supported only J. O. Hayes of North Carolina in Africa at that time, but the board planned an increase of five to ten missionaries "in the near future." Yet the death of John J. Coles since the last state session undoubtedly proved a tremendous blow to the mission cause.[22]

The 1895 report of the corresponding secretary of the state convention reveals that the Foreign Mission Convention as a whole still faced a crisis

---

[20]Ibid., 1893, 34-35.

[21]Ibid., 1894, 24.

[22]Ibid.

situation. It was clear to the secretary after his attendance at the 1894 session of the regional convention that it required an organizational restructuring. He pleaded with his fellow Baptists not to abandon African missions. According to the secretary, interest in missions among Baptists was in continual decline.[23] Although it is not absolutely clear from the context whether he referred to state Baptists or Baptists throughout the nation, it can be said with certainty that Virginians now realized that once again some major innovative step had to be taken to advance their mission program for Africa.

## NORTH CAROLINA

The Baptists of North Carolina were not as prominent nor as pioneering with regard to regional and national support of the mission enterprise as their neighbors to the north. But evidence does indicate a very early, enthusiastic, and sustained interest in the evangelization of Africa, although their support of the regional BFMC would best be described in less-glowing terms. As early as October 1880 (one month prior to the organization of the BFMC), J. O. Crosby, corresponding secretary of the Baptist State Convention of North Carolina, reported that the interest in African missions in North Carolina was great. Like his Virginia counterparts, he designated the clergy in the state as one great, obvious hindrance to more effective organization and fund raising.

Many of these individuals indeed did serve as a hindrance, since the local congregation in the Baptist polity had ultimate authority concerning the involvement of the people. A local pastor's opposition because of his commitment to other noble goals (such as domestic mission work or construction of churches) or for more self-centered reasons could spell doom for any foreign mission enterprise others would seek to organize in his community. But the North Carolinians, also like the Virginians, discovered that their state leaders could often circumvent the opposition of the local pastor and appeal directly to the laypeople, who would cooperate much more readily. Realizing this, leaders of the mission movement reasoned

---

[23]Ibid., 1895, 17.

that means could be found to sponsor one missionary on the continent. To do so required proper organization, however.[24]

At their 1881 session the North Carolinians made note of the recently organized Foreign Mission Convention and spoke of cooperating with it to maintain a missionary in Africa. They requested that the Foreign Mission contribute $300 for the missionary in question, J. O. Hayes, during the year, a request that in principle was compatible with the wishes of the BFMC. In a letter to the state convention dated 20 December 1881 (1880?), Hayes acknowledged that he had received Colley's communication inquiring whether he would take the station of the late Solomon Cosby, who had been sent out by the Virginia Baptists years earlier. Hayes was making plans to comply with that request, believing that through black Baptist unity much would be accomplished in the field.[25] It seems that in the midst of financial difficulties and conflicts with Hayes (as described in chapter 2), the Foreign Mission Convention Executive Board dropped support of the North Carolina missionary. Unlike South Carolina's H. N. Bouey, James O. Hayes did not withdraw from the field in Africa, but continued with the financial support of his state convention. His continued presence there helped maintain active interest and support for African missions on the part of North Carolina Baptists comparable to the missionary enthusiasm among their fellow Baptists in Virginia.

The 1882 minutes of the state convention indicate the persistent strength of African mission sentiment in this state. Organizationally, the number of Foreign Mission Board members of the state convention doubled that of any of the other three important boards of the convention. The Foreign Mission Board had twenty-seven members; the Home Mission Board, thirteen; and the Executive Board, eleven. These minutes also show that the North Carolina black Baptists, while pursuing an independent line in state and national movements for African missions, nonetheless maintained connections with the white Baptists of the state. M. C. Ransom, N. F. Roberts, J. Perry, and President Caesar Johnson—all prominent leaders in the state convention—served as corresponding delegates to the white state

[24]Annual Minutes, Baptist State Convention of North Carolina (BSC-NC), 1880, pp. 13-14.

[25]Ibid., 1881, 27.

convention.[26] As a later chapter will reveal, this close relationship between white and black Baptists in North Carolina would be a major factor in the division of black Baptists of the state in subsequent years.

But the decline in missionary support affected North Carolinians as it did Baptists in other states. At the 1889 meeting of the Hayes-Fleming Foreign Mission Society, the treasurer, N. F. Roberts of Raleigh, announced that the organization had raised only $55.21 of the $75 for Hayes's quarterly salary.[27] At the 1890 session of the society, Roberts reported that Hayes had received no salary during the former fiscal year.[28] Only a partial amount of the salary was reported as paid when the 1891 session of the society met. Because of the lack of missionary support, the state Executive Board, subsequent to the 1891 meeting of the convention, ordered Hayes's return to the U.S. so that he might encourage more support for his Liberian mission work. The missionary's visit to the country would be brief, just taking sufficient time for him to visit various churches to appeal for support.[29]

The lack of financial support among members of the Hayes-Fleming Society mirrored the situation of the larger body of North Carolina Baptists. A. W. Pegues, the corresponding secretary of the state convention, reported in 1892 that contributions came from a very small number of churches. In his opinion, the problem was the manner in which the cause of foreign missions was presented to Baptists in the state. If only each church would contribute one dollar annually, that state convention would be much closer to fulfilling its financial obligations. A goal of $1,000 for the work of foreign missions in the ensuing year was set before the convention.[30]

But the minutes of the state convention a year later reveal that, contrary to high expectations, the great upsurge in financial contributions had not materialized. Earnestly, mission leaders appealed to the African missionary tradition in the hopes of igniting a renewed, vigorous commitment that would result in greater outlay of financial resources. The convention mem-

---

[26]Ibid., 1882, 2, 19.

[27]Annual Minutes, Hayes-Fleming Foreign Missionary Society, 1889, p. 29.

[28]Annual Minutes, Baptist Educational and Missionary Convention of North Carolina (BEMC-NC), 1890, p. 28.

[29]Ibid., 1891, 33, 35.

[30]Ibid., 11-12.

bers were urged to remember their responsibility to this "forgotten field," "our mission field by natural right of heredity."[31] Millions of Africans were perishing for want of the gospel. "Shall we not fly to the rescue of our fatherland? Shall we not assist in redeeming that glorious land of antiquity from wretchedness and idolatry? Can we be true to God and at the same time repudiate our obligation to Bro. Hayes and the African work?"[32]

In 1894 there were further references to the field having been "neglected" and "forgotten." Also, the foreign mission enterprise had met resistance from anti-mission elements in the state as it had in Virginia. Apparently these anti-mission advocates were more theological in their opposition than their counterparts in Virginia. Foreign mission opponents in Virginia appear to have advanced the more practical argument that foreign mission efforts hampered the vital work needed within the U.S., especially among blacks in the Southern states. According to the minutes, the North Carolina opponents had attempted to convey to the black Baptists of the state the idea that the foreign mission movement was an alien enterprise that should be shunned. They seem to be spiritual ancestors of Baptist landmarkism, which asserted that organized mission programs contradicted the will of God by introducing and building structures among Christians that they believed had no direct, explicit scriptural basis.

This sentiment never dominated either the white or the black Baptist conventions. But two points should be made. First, if employed selectively, this sentiment could have buttressed the position of those who opposed African missions out of fear that it would deprive the home mission program or the local church of necessary funds. Second, the logic of this anti-mission argument calls into question a very vital portion of black Baptists' self-understanding and the mission they believed they had. For this second reason, the anti-mission argument could never capture a substantial segment of black Christians and thus cannot be counted as a major factor in the decline of missions in the 1880s and 1890s.

Whether the convention leaders saw anti-missionism as a real threat or as a convenient straw man, they attributed to its advocates some of the

[31]Ibid., 1892, 14.
[32]Ibid.

basest motives. Pro-mission Baptists stated that anti-missionism was "high treason" to the work of the denomination and should not be condoned. "Ignorance on the part of leaders is inexcusable, and downright meanness must not be mistaken for ignorance."[33] Despite such fervent defenses, foreign missions continued to decline as in other states.

## SOUTH CAROLINA

South Carolina was the only Southern state to reject cooperation with the black BFMC because of cooperative commitments with a white body, the American Baptist Missionary Union. That story and the reasons for that decision on the part of black South Carolina Baptists were treated in chapter 2. Suffice it to note here that the union welcomed this desire for cooperation on the part of the Baptist Educational, Missionary, and Sunday-School Convention of South Carolina.[34]

The fact that as early as 1880 the American Baptist Missionary Union and the black state convention were seriously discussing cooperation points to the obvious. South Carolina black Baptists, like their counterparts in North Carolina and Virginia, had determined to embark upon mission work in Africa before the formation of the Foreign Mission Convention. In 1880 Edward M. Brawley, eminent black Baptist divine of that state, described interest in African mission work among black Baptists of South Carolina as "wide and deep." Looking over financial contributions to the cause reveals that South Carolina compared favorably with the record of the Virginians, the foremost leaders in the movement. Brawley reported to the Missionary Union:

> The year that closed April 1—the Convention's year—gave us $1,000.52 for African missions; and we raised, in addition to this, funds for State missions and education, besides a collection for the [American Baptist] Publication Society. I am confident that South Carolina will raise not less than fifteen [hundred?] dollars this year for this work, and it is but two years since we concluded to engage in it.[35]

---

[33]Ibid., 1894, 29.

[34]Annual Minutes, ABMU, 1881, in *American Baptist Missionary Magazine* 61 (July 1881): 176-77.

[35]Annual Minutes, ABMU, 1880, xv.

In the early 1880s, the South Carolina missionary, H. N. Bouey, re-signed from the field and returned to the U.S. At this point, the financial contributions of the state convention began to decline, demonstrating the BFMC leaders' suspicion that the absence of a missionary in the field clearly hampered support for the cause. Also, the Foreign Mission Convention at this point was a relative success in terms of placing a number of mission-aries in Africa. With no missionary of their own to support, the black Baptists of South Carolina, understandably, turned to a black convention in order to maintain what they believed to be their God-commanded duty to spread the gospel in Africa, a conviction that had already succeeded in uniting many black Baptists across state lines.

Thus, in 1886 the Foreign Mission Board of the state convention rec-ommended the continued support of African mission work and directed that financial support be channeled through the Foreign Mission Convention by way of Joseph E. Jones, the corresponding secretary of the national convention. In noting that the black Baptists of the state "for some time" had neglected African missions, the board apparently hoped and expected that this shift might increase financial giving.[36]

Yet, as with the Foreign Mission Convention, Virginia, and North Carolina, the attempt to revive support for foreign missions met obstacles, including apathy, in the late 1880s and in the 1890s. In 1887 the Foreign Mission Committee of the state convention noted that the Foreign Mission Convention had placed the state in the Third Missionary District along with Alabama and Georgia, and that H. N. Bouey, the former South Carolina missionary, had been placed in charge of this segment of the larger con-vention's work as general agent for the district. The committee again rec-ommended that the state convention support the Foreign Mission Convention. The Board of Managers also took note of the decline in sup-port for foreign missions and recalled that such had been the case since Bouey returned from Africa. The board challenged convention members to honor their earlier slogan, "South Carolina and Africa for Jesus," and to raise the sum of $500. This amount, the board claimed, would maintain one missionary in the African mission field.[37]

---

[36]Annual Minutes, Baptist Educational, Missionary, and Sunday-School Convention of South Carolina (BCSC), 1886, pp. 17-18.

[37]Ibid., 1887, 23.

In 1888 the Committee on Foreign Fields observed that South Carolinians in earlier years ventured upon the African continent without the cooperative support of any other state, only trusting in God. Surely, now they
must be even more zealous for the cause given the existence of a *national*
foreign mission convention. Reciting a refrain that was being echoed in the
BFMC and the state conventions of North Carolina and Virginia, the committee said that South Carolina had to remember that they were ''a denomination of African descent'' and thus owed a special debt to the African
continent.[38] Yet the decline of support for African missions did not abate.
In 1893 the Board of Managers of the state convention reported feeling
embarrassed because of the small amount of money that South Carolina
had turned over to the treasury of the Foreign Mission Convention. Though
some states in the past year reported from $600 to $900, the African mission-minded state of South Carolina had fallen below the small sum of
$100.[39]

## GEORGIA

Earlier in the book it was shown that Georgia Baptists during the years
1880 and 1881 took a cautious, wait-and-see attitude toward affiliating with
the newly organized BFMC. By the time of their May 1882 meeting, they
had shifted to glowing approval of the work of the new convention. W. J.
White, the corresponding secretary, reported that he had attended the 1881
meeting of the BFMC in Knoxville, Tennessee. Though he was unavoid-
ably late for the meeting, he was warmly received. ''We are all in hearty
accord with the movement put on foot by that body to send the gospel to
Africa; . . . I recommend that our Convention put itself in such relations
with that body, by sending delegates, as will assure them of our deep interest in the evangelization of Africa.''[40] Though White gave his hearty
endorsement, he still felt that there was a need for ''some changes in the
machinery, essentially necessary.''[41] Perhaps White was referring to the

[38]Ibid., 1888, 12-13.

[39]Ibid., 1893, 27-28.

[40]Annual Minutes, Missionary Baptist Convention of Georgia (MBCG), 1881, p. 31.

[41]Ibid.

preponderance of Virginians on the Executive Board. This seems quite possible, since White had gone on record questioning whether the concerns of other states besides Virginia would be equally addressed.

White was joined in this endorsement by the Committee on African Missions. In urging support for the Foreign Mission Convention, the committee members said that the new organization was the only mission group whose "sole object" was the redemption of Africa, "Our Father Land." They called upon Georgia Baptists not to trail other states in support for African missions. The group recommended that the convention president, the corresponding secretary, and others attend the next meeting of the Foreign Mission Convention. They asked that churches and missionary societies contribute to the movement.[42]

In the 1884 session of the state convention, the Reverend Gad S. Johnson in his missionary sermon urged increased support for African missions on the part of black Baptists in Georgia. "How can we, who have plenty to spare, suffer our brothers in Africa to live upon such as the swine become fat [?]."[43] The Foreign Mission Committee of 1887 promised to do more after their 1888 Centennial Celebration.[44] There is no record, however, that the state ever commissioned a missionary for Africa. With no missionary as an inducement for fund raising and the declining support for the cause throughout the Southern states, Georgia appears never to have participated as actively as the states of Virginia, North Carolina, and South Carolina.

## MISSISSIPPI

Black Baptists of Mississippi manifested a strong sense of support for African missions during this period. Unlike Georgia and South Carolina, Mississippi participated in the work of the Foreign Mission Convention from its inception in 1880. T. L. Jordan, the corresponding secretary of the General Baptist Missionary Association of Mississippi, attended this founding session of the organization and noted the movement in his 1881

[42]Ibid., 45-46.
[43]Ibid., 1884, 35.
[44]Ibid., 1887, 29.

report to his fellow Mississippians. "I attended with others the Foreign
Mission Convention held last November in Montgomery, Ala., whose
motto is that 'the field is the world, but Africa is our special field—the land
of our fathers' pride.' Now that such a Convention is organized, they look
for Mississippi Baptists to be among those that do. 'Blessed are those that
do his commandments.' "[45]

As early as 1883, this Mississippi Convention had an active foreign
missions committee made up of notable state leaders such as Henderson
McKinney, H. Woodsmall, and T. L. Jordan.[46] The convention had appointed a Foreign Mission Board with headquarters in Meridian, the same
city in which the Foreign Mission Convention held its fifth meeting in September 1884. Considering the work of African missions a top priority, the
members of the convention approved the call for liberal contributions and
the organization of appropriate societies to advance the cause.[47]

Certainly the knowledge that Henderson McKinney, a fellow Mississippian, had received appointment as a missionary and had been scheduled
to sail in December 1883 added to the fervor for African missions among
the Baptists of the state. Indeed, Jordan mentioned in his 1884 report that
the knowledge that McKinney was educated and churched in the state of
Mississippi should make the zeal of Mississippi Baptists for this work
"unequalled by any."[48] Jordan observed that Mississippi had a goal of $700
to meet and stated, "I intend to lead off with thirty of this amount."[49] In
an eloquent appeal for support of African missions, Jordan demonstrated
his belief in the sad state of religion among African peoples and the responsibility of Afro-Americans to aid in the uplift of their kinspeople.

> There is no such thing as ease to the conscience, or resting at ease in Zion
> while, from across the dark blue waters we hear a voice, in accents such
> as human tongues only utter; looking over into this land that has the bread
> of life, enough and to spare, and with outstretched hands and uplifted, and

---

[45]Annual Minutes, General Baptist Missionary Association of Mississippi (GBMAM),
1881, p. 10.

[46]Ibid., 1883, 3.

[47]Ibid., 1884, 23.

[48]Ibid., 16-17.

[49]Ibid., 17.

mournful tongue, calls to us, ''come over and help us;'' it is the cry of your
brother, it is a native cry from a land prized for everything but religion.[50]

Though economic and other problems began to set in during the mid-
1880s, the General Missionary Baptist Association of the State of Mississippi received a report from its corresponding secretary that African missions was ''in a prosperous condition.'' The secretary noted with pride that
the Foreign Mission Convention had selected the husband-and-wife teams
of E. B. and Mattie Topp and Mr. and Mrs. J. J. Diggs to replace Joseph
H. Presley of Virginia, who had returned because of illness. Colley and
his wife had returned due to illness and a summons by the Foreign Mission
Board of the Foreign Mission Convention. Since Mississippians now held
all but one of the missionary appointments in Africa (the other belonged
to the then-unmarried J. J. Coles), that state had an even greater responsibility to support the work. The state Foreign Mission Board observed with
joy that Mississippi held such a prominent place in mission work.[51]

By the late 1880s, however, mission support began to take a down-
ward turn. The Executive Board's report of 1888 noted that progress in
missions had moved only ''moderately'' because of a lack of workers and
financial resources. The board also disapproved of Topp's method of using African children for fund-raising purposes in the U.S., believing that
the technique might backfire: many Baptists might feel compelled to give
only if they saw an African child. In subsequent years the momentum for
missions in Mississippi appears to have declined as elsewhere, especially
after the return of all missionaries to America in 1888.[52]

## FLORIDA

The first major movement for foreign missions on the state level among
black Baptists of Florida appears to have begun in 1888. By that time, the
regional mission movement of the Foreign Mission Convention was on the
decline and all its missionaries to Africa had returned to the U.S. One of
those missionaries, E. B. Topp of Mississippi, attended the Baptist Gen-

---

[50]Ibid.
[51]Ibid., 1886, 20-21, 24.
[52]Ibid., 1888, 13.

eral Convention of Florida that year. His presentation seems to have been a vital catalyst in soliciting support for African missions. The convention was very impressed and convicted by his sermon entitled "Should the Christians in America Be Interested in Sending the Gospel to the Heathen in Africa?" In it, he asked: "Did not our hearts melt within us, as he depicted the horrors of darkness that hang over our brethren in our Fatherland, and set forth the many reasons why we who have the light should send it to those who have it not?"[53]

Like other mission advocates before him, Topp appealed in the clearest terms to the tradition of African missions among black American Christians. He conveyed to those assembled that Afro-Americans had obligations to uplift Africa, obligations both religious and racial in nature. This point was given added force by the presence of a young African boy. He had brought Jah from Africa at the request of his late fellow missionary, Henderson McKinney, so that the boy might be "educated and christianized to bear the Bread of Life to our perishing kindred." The missionary's presentation of "wooden idols to which they [Africans] are said to bend the knee in adoration" moved the convention most of all.[54] Though his methods of raising funds and his knowledge of African religions were questionable, Topp undoubtedly was successful in lifting Florida from what appears to have been an indifferent attitude toward the mission program. After this presentation J. H. Ballou offered a resolution that, when later reported from the Committee on Resolutions, pledged the state convention to cooperate with the Foreign Mission Convention to the fullest extent in spreading the gospel in Africa. The convention also agreed to the district plan of the Foreign Mission Convention, which placed Florida in the Fourth Missionary District with Topp as general agent.[55]

In 1889 Topp wrote a letter to the annual session of Florida Baptists expressing his regrets concerning his inability to attend the meeting and wishing them God's blessings. The Floridians maintained a concern for African missions by collecting $40 for foreign missions and authorizing

---

[53]Annual Minutes, Baptist General Convention and Baptist Sabbath School Convention of Florida (BGCF), 1888, p. 9.

[54]Ibid.

[55]Ibid., 22-23.

four delegates to attend the annual meeting of the Foreign Mission Convention.[56] But, ironically, the Floridians had begun their short-lived effort at the precise time that mission support was dramatically decreasing in the other states of the region. For the next several years, financial contributions to the cause by Floridians were not very substantial.

Clearly, then, the early 1880s were the years of most active and promising support for African missions on both the regional and the state levels. By the mid-1890s the effort existed mainly in name only. The time was ripe for a bolder, fresher attempt to redeem Afro-Americans' racial home.

## THE PRESENCE OF WOMEN
## IN THE AFRICAN MISSION MOVEMENT, 1880–1894

The story of the African mission movement would not be complete without a consideration of the role of women Baptists. Male ministers dominated and controlled the Baptist Foreign Mission Convention and the state conventions. Still, the presence and influence of women were felt from the very beginning of the Foreign Mission Convention. Of the 151 delegates to the 1880 founding session in Montgomery, Alabama, only two were women. But both E. F. Cassidy and J. P. Moore, a white missionary highly regarded by black Baptists, served on the Committee on the Selection of Officers. Neither was selected as an officer nor as a member of the Executive Board. Nor in subsequent sessions of the Foreign Mission Convention do the minutes list women as officers of the convention or as members of the significant Executive and Foreign Mission Boards.[57] Furthermore, BFMC minutes indicate that the attendance of women at these sessions was always quite minimal. For example, at the 1889 meeting only nine of the 149 delegates were women. Of that nine, six came from the Southern states of Alabama (1), Georgia (3), Tennessee (1), and Louisiana (1). The others hailed from Kentucky (3).

But the same minutes also indicate that these few women played active, public roles in the business of the convention by serving on various committees and, more important, delivering public addresses on the work

---

[56]Ibid., 1889, 15, 17-18.

[57]Lewis G. Jordan, *Negro Baptist History, U.S.A., 1750-1930* (Nashville: Sunday School Publishing Board, National Baptist Convention, U.S.A., 1936) 159.

of African missions. Many of the addresses that women delivered at the
sessions dealt specifically with the role of women in African mission work:
for example, "What Should Baptist Women Do to Redeem Africa?" by
Mrs. Victoria B. Huff (visitor). But they often centered on African missionary concerns in general: for example, "The Duty of the Sunday School
to Aid in Africa's Redemption," by Mrs. J. Garnette of Georgia; "The
Gospel the Only Means of True Civilization," Mrs. M. M. Monroe, Georgia. The minutes also record that women contributed substantial sums to
the mission enterprise by means of personal pledges, annual and life memberships, and by means of women's foreign mission societies at the state,
local, and congregational levels.[58]

Finally, women were given full credit by supporters of the Foreign
Mission Convention as missionaries along with their husbands in Africa.
Yet the convention minutes are androcentric in this regard, viewing wom-
en's participation in missionary work from the perspective of their husbands, which was indicative of the general customs of the time. Whereas
in one context the Foreign Mission Convention would refer to both husband and wife as missionaries, salaries for the two were paid to the husband. The minutes would speak of the male member of the team returning
home, though the female missionary might be the one who was ill. Also,
it is often difficult or impossible to locate the first name of the wife, since
the two are almost invariably listed, for example, as "J. J. Coles and wife,"
not "J. J. and Lucy A. Coles."

For the most part, male ministers of the Foreign Mission Convention
encouraged the active participation of women in areas such as organizing
women's foreign mission societies. At the founding convention, the Executive Board recommended that women be encouraged to organize societies in the local churches.[59] In the 1881 session the Committee on Ways
and Means of Publication urged the delegates to work toward the organization of executive committees in the state conventions. The committee
asked that the state committees include women.[60] "Our sisters are hereby

---

[58]Annual Minutes, BFMC, 1889, 10-14, 16, 19.

[59]Jordan, *Negro Baptist History,* 162.

[60]Annual Minutes, BFMC, 1881, 26-27.

especially called upon in all the states to help us in this great work.''[61] At
the 1885 session of the convention, President W. A. Brinkley of Memphis
praised women for their support of African missions. Brinkley, following
the tradition and policy of the convention, recommended that women's
missionary societies be established throughout the states. Furthermore, he
called for the recognition of women messengers from various women's societies and church groups, and encouraged women to continue their financial support of the foreign mission cause.[62]

   In 1891 Dr. A. R. Griggs of Dallas sought to act on a decision made
by the convention in 1890 and introduced a resolution that would establish
a nine-member committee to draft plans for the formation of a National
Woman's Foreign Mission Organization. This committee was composed
of four women and notable men involved in the African mission movement such as J. E. Jones and E. B. Topp. Probably the economic difficulties of the convention during this period precluded the execution of these
plans.[63]

   The call for women's involvement in the mission program at the state
level was as strong as it was on the regional level. In religious, educational, and missionary quarters, these Baptists knew the intimate relationship that women had in the life of the church. They knew that the support
of women was crucial to the success of any program of the denomination,
whether local, regional, or national in scope. It is not surprising, therefore,
that T. L. Jordan, the corresponding secretary of the General Baptist Missionary Association of Mississippi, drew up a constitution in 1883 with organizational outlines for women's missionary societies in that state. At the
1884 session of this convention, Jordan emphasized the necessity of securing women's support. In his opinion, which mirrored the thinking of
that time, women felt in ways that men would ''never know.'' In all aspects of religious life, he stated, women's wishes found easy listening from
the larger church.[64]

---

[61]Ibid., 27.

[62]Ibid., 1885, 16.

[63]Ibid., 1891, 10.

[64]Annual Minutes, GBMAM, 1884, 17-18.

That these societies are much needed none will deny. It is said that none can feel, as a women feels, or love as she loves, or is more successful than she in great undertakings, going where man dare not venture bearing what men shrink from and feeling what men never know. They are the controlling power in our Sunday-schools, and their pious wishes are always regarded. In our churches, cannot we combine our strength, and elicit their consecrated souls in this mission work?[65]

In 1886 the Women's General Baptist Missionary Society of Mississippi was organized. In seeking to involve other women in the mission enterprise, these women called for support by saying that the Great Commission to spread the gospel was as applicable and binding upon women as men, though the duty could not always be carried out in the same fashion. R. B. Valentine of Batesville, Mississippi—in a talk entitled "The Duty of Sisters to Engage in Mission Work"—stated the case in the following manner: "In the first place, our Saviour has commanded us to go forth and preach the gospel. I take this commission as directly to the sisters, as the brethren. I do not mean that we should occupy the pulpit, but to do good in all proper ways, in spreading the knowledge of the Redeemer's kingdom."[66] Valentine's call probably arose more in the context of securing women's support for *domestic* missions than foreign missions. Yet the same type of sentiments were applied by black Baptists throughout the South in encouraging women's involvement in the foreign mission movement. Such sentiments, for example, can be found in the 1888 annual address of G. W. Gayles, president of the Baptist Missionary Convention of Mississippi. Gayles called for women's involvement in both domestic *and* foreign mission programs. In proposing that women's home and foreign mission societies be formed, he saw women as making significant contributions to the education of black people and the spread of the gospel to Africa. Furthermore, he advocated that his convention receive "female messengers from churches, Sunday-schools and societies."[67]

In North Carolina and Virginia, women were intricately involved in the mission movement in its early stages. The 1880 minutes of the Baptist State

[65]Ibid.

[66]Annual Minutes, Women's General Baptist Missionary Society of Mississippi (WGBMSM), 1888, p. 15.

[67]Annual Minutes, GBMAM, 1888, 23.

Convention of North Carolina list two women, Miss J. M. Hardy and Mrs. Sallie Mial, as members of the Foreign Mission Board. Indeed, during this period Miss Lula C. Fleming of North Carolina served as a missionary to the Congo under the appointment of the American Baptist Missionary Union. The 1890 minutes of the Hayes-Fleming Foreign Mission Society reveal that both Mrs. Giles Neely of Salisbury and Phoebe Bowden of Wilmington, members of the Women's Home and Foreign Mission Society of North Carolina, addressed the convention.[68]

The 1881 minutes of the Virginia Baptist State Convention show that both the Committee on Fields and the Committee on Missionaries included women (Mrs. M. M. Garrett, Harriet R. Taylor, and Malinda Walker) who served alongside renowned African mission supporters such as W. W. Colley, J. M. Armistead, J. Herndon, and William Troy.[69] The official position of Virginians regarding women's support for the cause was expressed in John W. Kirby's Report of the Corresponding Secretary (1891): "All along the line we are impressed with the efforts put forth to enlist our *women* more in the work of building up *societies* to further the cause of Lord Jesus. Shall not the noble-hearted daughters of Virginia join hands with the Baptist daughters of other states in this grand and glorious work?"[70]

Some observations, however, must be made concerning the above comments. First, the appeal for women's participation was not a universal one among black Baptist males. Though predominant opinion favored their participation, in some instances the observations of H. E. Moody of Mississippi obtained in both domestic and foreign missionary movements. "The right to do mission work is denied women by some of the stronger sex."[71] Second, the invitations to women by men or women were not on terms of equal authority and power in the work of state conventions of the Foreign Mission Convention. Women ministers, for the most part, were not recognized by Baptists of either sex. Women, though participating on various important committees, seldom if ever served on major boards.

---

[68]Annual Minutes, BSC-NC, 1880, 2; Hayes-Fleming Foreign Mission Society (bound with the minutes of the BEMC-NC), 1890, 28.

[69]Annual Minutes, VBSC, 1880, 18-19.

[70]Ibid., 1891, 17.

[71]Annual Minutes, WGBMSM, 1888, 13.

Third, the attitudes and positions of these Southern black Baptists also characterized those of most Baptists, white and black, and indeed most Protestants during this time period.

Even though women—for theological and cultural reasons—were barred from participation in the overt leadership of the Foreign Mission and the state Baptist conventions, they nevertheless provided crucial support for the African missionary enterprise. The support of these Baptist women, monetary and otherwise, did not go unnoticed by their contemporary male counterparts and, as we have seen, was actively encouraged by both male and female supporters of the cause. Men clearly recognized the indispensable assistance that a majority of Baptists could lend to the cause. One might interpret the financial demise of the BFMC in part as the failure of the African mission advocate to secure the mass, grassroots support of women.

Women supporters advocated greater participation by women because of their conviction that black American Christians clearly had a providential destiny to uplift their African kin by sharing with them the blessings of Christianity and Western civilization. But I suggest that we also see here the birth of a movement that had significant ramifications for American women in general. Consistent with trends in other denominations and non-religious circles, a women's consciousness was developing with these early calls for more active support of African missions on the part of their sisters. By the turn of the century, Baptist forces would be more firmly united and established, as would the organizational efforts of women at the state levels. By then the fruition of these and other activities would produce women auxiliaries to major black Baptist conventions and associations at both the regional and national levels. Furthermore, an increased emphasis would be placed on the need for women missionaries to identify more closely with the concerns and needs of African women. These developments were a far cry from what we might normally label feminism. But many Baptists, including those who had been associated with the BFMC, heralded these developments as glorious advancements to the recognition that all of God's children, males and females, had the opportunity and the responsibility to share the gospel throughout the world, and especially in Africa.

## CONCLUSION

This chapter concludes the study of the Baptist Foreign Mission Convention in the years 1880-1894. It has shown that the impetus and organization for foreign mission work on the regional-national level partly had their foundation in missionary interest and activities at the state level, especially in the states of Virginia, North Carolina, Mississippi, and for a while, South Carolina. Second, this chapter has pointed out that the story of the African mission movement cannot be fully comprehended without due recognition being given to women Baptists on both the state and regional-national levels.

Part two examines the African mission movement in the National Baptist and Lott Carey Foreign Mission conventions during the years 1895 to 1915. During these years black Baptists in general and African mission supporters in particular finally accomplished their goal of attaining national unity. The work of men and women through the Baptist Foreign Mission Convention and its constituent state conventions contributed to the realization of this unity, particularly as it applied to African missions.

**PART 2**

# THE AFRICAN MISSION MOVEMENT IN CONFLICT AND GROWTH, 1895–1915

With the establishment of the National Baptist Convention (NBC) in 1895, black Baptists had finally achieved organizational unity on a nationwide basis. This unity has endured and even grown to the present time. This triumph was especially significant, since it occurred during a decade of deteriorating political and economic conditions for blacks, most of whom still resided in the South. During this era, the constitutions of many Southern states were revised, effectively disenfranchising black and poor white voters. At this time there were also the Supreme Court's endorsement of racial segregation, and Tuskegee president and educator Booker T. Washington's acceptance of the principle that blacks should forgo agitating for political rights and liberal arts education and focus instead upon economic development and industrial training.

Perhaps because of the restrictions on the freedoms of blacks in the larger society, they moved more aggressively toward the achievement of unity within ecclesiastical circles. At any rate, it is within the context of increased black disenfranchisement and mounting white supremacy that the National Baptist Convention arose. With the NBC's debut, black African mission advocates also succeeded in their effort to effect a truly national movement. Despite the financial woes of the Baptist Foreign Mission Convention, which was actually a regional body, its very existence and efforts qualified it to be a major forerunner of the NBC in general and the Foreign Mission Board of the NBC in particular. During a period when white American Christians devoted little time and attention to mission work in Africa compared with their activities in other parts of the largely non-Christian world, the involvement of united black Baptists in this enterprise became increasingly significant.

Part two focuses on the national phase of African missions that evolved from local and regional phases. More specifically, chapter 4 examines the organization of the National Baptist Convention in 1895 and the Lott Carey Baptist (Home and) Foreign Mission Convention of the United States (LCC) in 1897 as well as analyzing conflicts and points of cooperation between the two groups. This chapter clearly demonstrates that the transition from the regional to the national phase was not without its difficulties and was even resisted in certain quarters. Chapter 5 portrays the continued active manifestation of concern for the cause among supporters of both the NBC and the LCC. Despite personal and philosophical conflicts within and between these groups, both organizations managed to work independently and in cooperation with each other because of goals they envisioned as mutually related to the material and spiritual advancement of the race throughout the world: racial unity and the evangelization of Africa. The firmly entrenched belief that African missions was a divine mandate given most specifically to Afro-American Christians still motivated the actions of black Baptists during these years.

# CHAPTER 4

# THE MISSION MOVEMENT AMID CONFLICT, 1895–1907

By the mid-1890s, the Foreign Mission Convention represented the most successful attempt by black Baptists to forge themselves into a national organization for conducting foreign mission work. Despite its high standing as a self-supporting, independent black denomination, the convention did have three major limitations. (1) It still remained for the most part a regional organization controlled in policy matters by Southern Baptists, most notably the Virginians. (2) It focused its energies entirely upon the area of foreign missions at a time when many black Baptists yearned for an effective national organization that would deal with the spiritual and material conditions of black Americans. (3) The convention was greatly limited in financial resources.

In short, the combined cry from most black Baptist quarters in the mid-1880s was for the formation of a truly national black Baptist denomination. It needed to be economically sufficient to permit extensive efforts, material and spiritual, on behalf of blacks in both the United States and abroad, and to advance the entire African race toward the ideal of Christian civilization. This union was finally realized with the establishment of the National Baptist Convention in 1895. A significant structural component of this new organization was the Foreign Mission Board, which assumed the responsibility for African missions that had formerly been the province of the (now-defunct) BFMC. African missions had finally moved beyond the local and regional states and had become truly a national, unified enterprise.

But the African mission cause did not merely benefit in a passive manner from the plans and activities of Baptists who had primary loyalties elsewhere. Indeed, some of the impetus for the formation of the NBC actually came from people heavily involved in the mission work of the BFMC.

This was a period when black Christians in general sought greater racial unity and cooperation among themselves. Unsurprisingly, then, we note that African mission advocates often made gestures toward cooperation and unity with other black Baptist bodies, whether local or regional-national. Reading the minutes of the Baptist General Association of Western States and Territories, the Foreign Mission Convention, and the Virginia Baptist State Convention, among others, would reveal that they often shared memberships and sent fraternal delegates to each other's annual sessions.[1]

Furthermore, we must beware of drawing sharp lines of separation between African mission supporters and other Baptists. Though for the purpose of this study we have identified various individuals primarily as mission supporters, many of these individuals and conventions played crucial roles in promoting various religious activities. For example, the Virginia Baptist State Convention led the way in the formation of the BFMC. Yet it also devoted even more time to domestic concerns such as evangelism and supporting black education in the state. In addition, many supporters of the Foreign Mission Convention saw the need to conduct domestic and foreign mission work through one major national organization. In 1893 a group of black Baptists set forth a plan known as the Tripartite Union, which would incorporate the conventions of the New England Convention, the African Foreign Mission Convention (General Association?), and the Foreign Mission Convention. The minutes of the 1894 session of the Foreign Mission Convention reveal that the plan had met with rejection from these members.[2]

By 1894 black Baptists, including those in the BFMC, saw the urgent need for a successful union of black Baptist forces. By this time, not only had financial matters worsened, but the conflict between the Foreign Mission Board of the Foreign Mission Convention and its critics had finally come to a crest. Baptists of other states, as they became more interested in the work of the Virginia-dominated BFMC, seemed to grow bolder in their local opposition

---

[1]The exchange of fraternal visitors and the call for cooperation with other Baptists are common features of the minutes of the various Baptist conventions. See the lists of state and regional minutes in the bibliography.

[2]Lewis G. Jordan, *Negro Baptist History U.S.A., 1750–1930* (Nashville TN: Sunday School Publishing Board, National Baptist Convention, n.d.) 117.

to the manner in which the organization was being run. Dr. L. M. Luke of Kentucky led the attack by accusing the board of "inattention and waste," which had resulted in hardships for missionary personnel and a lack of sustained contributions from black Baptists in the U.S. Sutton E. Griggs—pastor and student at Richmond Theological Seminary, and a Virginian—was employed to defend the board. Griggs did his job aptly, "greatly softening the blows of public criticism thereby." Yet the fact that the board had elected to absent itself from the convention illustrated that tension within the organization had mounted to dangerous heights.[3] This tension could only be resolved by a radical reworking of the BFMC.

Out of this stormy session came the resolution of Albert W. Pegues of North Carolina that contributed to the formation of the National Baptist Convention in 1895. Pegues introduced an idea that had been advanced earlier by the great black Baptist divine, William J. Simmons of Kentucky. He recommended that a nine-member committee be appointed to consult with the executive boards of the American National Baptist Convention (founded in 1886) and the Baptist National Educational Convention (founded in 1893) in a search for unity. According to Pegues, the objectives of all three organizations could be realized through one organization with an economy of "both time and money": the goals of the BFMC, through the Foreign Mission Board; the interests of the Educational Convention, through a Board of Education; and the domestic concerns of the American National Baptist Convention, by way of a Board of Missions.[4]

Pegues advanced this proposal in the Southern city Montgomery, Alabama, where only fourteen years previously black Baptists—in response to a call from black Virginia Baptists—had congregated to form the Foreign Mission Convention. The committee appointed to carry out his plan, however, included a wide geographical spectrum of Southern and border state Baptists: William H. McAlpine and Andrew J. Stokes of Alabama, Joseph E. Jones of Virginia, Wesley G. Parks of Tennessee, and Albert W. Pegues of North Carolina represented the South. J. H. Frank, future

---

[3]Ibid., 18.
[4]Ibid., 19.

chairperson of the NBC Foreign Mission Board, hailed from the South-western state of Texas. Other committee members included: A. Hubbs, also of Texas, A. S. Jackson of Louisiana, and Jacob R. Bennett of Arkansas.[5]

## INFLUENCE OF SOUTHERN BAPTISTS
## IN THE NBC, 1895–1915

The founding of the NBC in Atlanta in 1895 was truly a major advance toward a more national convention of black Baptists that would embrace domestic as well as foreign mission religious concerns. But this statement should be tempered with the following points. First, throughout the period under study, Southern black Baptists as a group continued to play the major roles in conducting the business of the organization. However, the overall influence of these Baptists, unlike in the former Foreign Mission Convention, was diluted somewhat by that of stalwart Baptists from Kentucky and Pennsylvania. Second, black Baptists, notwithstanding an expanding and explicitly stated interest in worldwide foreign missions, still focused their overseas activities and interests primarily upon the African continent. Thus, this early national period of African missions can be characterized as one in which power and influence were gradually dispersed to include non-Southern areas.

This lingering influence of Southern black Baptists manifested itself in a number of ways. First, they had a disproportionate share of seats on the Foreign Mission Board of the NBC, the body charged with establishing procedure and selecting personnel for African evangelization. The makeup of the board in 1897 had shifted radically from that of the Executive Board of the Foreign Mission Convention in previous years. John H. Frank, a Kentuckian rather than a Virginian, held the chair of the board; seven other Kentuckians served as board members. Other non-Southern states represented on the board were: Pennsylvania, Indiana, Kansas, West Virginia, Missouri, Illinois, and Louisiana. But the Southern Baptists could still claim a significant impact on the board. Nearly one-third (seven) of the twenty-five members were from the Southern states already discussed. Two came from Tennessee, and one each from Florida, Alabama, North Carolina, Mississippi, and Georgia. With three members, Texas demonstrated that

[5]Ibid.

it now occupied a prominent place in the execution of foreign mission work. The single representative from Virginia in the previous year had been withdrawn or had resigned.[6]

As shall become clear in the following pages, this dilution of Virginian power revealed two significant things. On one hand, the Baptists of other states, including those outside the South, had become much more openly committed to the task of spreading the gospel in Africa. On the other hand, this abrupt removal of the pioneering Virginians from the board would help to create a permanent rift in the movement.

Second, the places selected by the NBC to host the annual conventions provide illustrations of the influence of the South upon the NBC as well as the geographical diversity of the new convention. Between 1880 and 1894 only three of the Foreign Mission Convention annual sessions took place outside the South. But from 1895–1915, a decided shift occurred. Of the twenty-one annual sessions of the NBC, eight were held in the North, four in the border states, and nine in the South.[7] This shift in the locale of meeting places reflected the migration of Afro-Americans from the increasingly harsh political and economic conditions in the South to the West and North during the 1895–1915 period. But the shift perhaps also indicated that the tradition of American mission support among Southern Baptists was gaining significant strongholds and uniting forces with similar movements in other regions of the country.

Third, the influence of Southern black Baptists upon the work of the NBC reveals itself by the number of Southerners engaging in African mission work during this period. James O. Hayes of North Carolina continued his missionary work in Liberia through most of this period in connection with both the NBC and the Lott Carey Baptist Foreign Mission Convention. L. N. Cheek of Mississippi applied for African mission work in 1899 and journeyed to Central Africa in 1900 under the auspices of the NBC. Miss Emma DeLaney of Florida, with the endorsement and support of her fellow Floridians, applied to the NBC for mission work and arrived in Southern Africa in January 1902. In the same month Harrison N. Bouey,

---

[6]Annual Minutes, NBC, 1897, 2.

[7]Ibid., 1915, 8.

former missionary of the Foreign Mission Convention from South Carolina, returned to Liberia with his three sons. In 1912 Miss DeLaney, after spending a few years in the U.S., departed from Liberia. She was accompanied by Susie M. Taylor of Camden, South Carolina. Southerners did not constitute the exclusive black Baptist presence in Africa. But on a mission field that became overwhelmingly dominated by indigenous missionaries, these American Baptists continued the tradition of a Southern black Baptist presence in Africa.[8]

Finally, and most significantly, Southern black Baptists contributed generously to NBC foreign missions during this period, 1895–1915. In 1906, one year after the return of the Lott Carey Baptists to the NBC, four of these states led in financial contributions: Florida ($1,488.08), Alabama ($1,346.34), Virginia ($1,299.94), and Mississippi ($967.65), along with Texas ($1,438.13), which ranked second. Four Southern states led in mission support in 1909: South Carolina ($1,650.44), Florida ($1,284.78), Alabama ($1,283.50), and Mississippi ($1,281.37). In 1911 the amounts of Texas ($2,292.32) and Pennsylvania ($2,017.05) exceeded those of any other states, and the Southern state of Mississippi ($2,003.15) very closely rivaled these states. The other two major contributors were Alabama ($1,557.15) and South Carolina ($1,225.96).[9] The above is not meant to imply that Southern Baptists dominated the fund-raising campaigns for foreign missions within the NBC. It is clear, however, that years after the African mission movement had become truly national, these largely poor, rural states still played a major part in financially supporting the movement.

## DIVISION IN BAPTIST RANKS

The formation of the NBC and consequently the systematic, national organization of the African missions enterprise constituted quite an accomplishment for black Baptists. Undoubtedly, most of them felt a deep sense of pride knowing that, even as the federal government neglected Afro-Americans and white reactionaries in Southern governments limited blacks' freedom, black people had made a statement about the need and possibility

---

[8]Ibid., 1902, 34.
[9]Ibid., 1911, 233.

for racial unity. But within a few years, the leaders of the NBC made two significant decisions that shattered the unity which had been so long in the making. More specifically, two actions drove many Baptists—particularly those on the eastern seaboard—to form the Lott Carey Baptist Foreign Mission Convention in 1897. (1) The NBC eliminated all Virginians from the Foreign Mission Board except one and transferred the headquarters from Richmond to Louisville, Kentucky. (2) The NBC decided that it would write and publish its own religious literature rather than subscribe to materials produced by white Baptists.

The first set of actions certainly paved the way for the exodus of most of the Virginians. It is unclear why the NBC elected such a course, but several reasons suggest themselves. The Virginia-dominated board encountered criticisms in the late 1880s and the early 1890s about its efficiency in the conduct of foreign missions. Quite possibly, the leaders of the new organization blamed the Virginians for the demise and ineffectiveness of the BFMC and hoped to improve matters by placing a new team in charge. Second, the NBC was a product of years of black Baptists' hopes to organize an independent, united black denomination. In that light, the new organization of the board certainly contributed to such a goal by guaranteeing greater representation by all states involved and making the board more geographically accessible to black Baptists nationwide. Finally, it seems that the issue of denominational cooperation with white Baptists had never disappeared. It is possible that the NBC viewed the Virginia Baptist board members as too closely aligned to the idea of cooperation with whites.

Whatever the reason or combination of reasons, this set of actions effectively eliminated Virginia Baptists from significant influence in the formulation and execution of foreign mission policies. It is not difficult to comprehend why this came as a heavy blow to Virginians. Virginia led all states in the number of black Baptists. Since the days of slavery, the Virginians had been the pioneers in black Baptist mission work in Africa. Finally, Virginia was the chief state in the organization and support of the Foreign Mission Convention in the amount of financial contributions, human hours expended in policy making, and lives given and lost in active mission service in Africa.

At their 1896 session the Virginia Baptists responded to their treatment in Atlanta nearly a year earlier: "Our representative men were treated discourteously and ejected from their positions unceremoniously. The brethren further south wanted all, they took all, now Virginia is willing for the same set of brethren to *run all*—Virginia excepted.''[10] The state convention moved to the verge of breaking all connections with the NBC. The Committee on the President's Address advised that the convention should seriously consider returning to the work of conducting foreign missions through the state board. A resolution proposed by Anthony Binga, Jr.— one of the most avid supporters of foreign missions in the state and former chairperson of the Executive Board of the Foreign Mission Convention— offered to do just that. Binga termed the NBC's foreign mission program a waste of money and a discouragement to the Baptist people. He resolved that the Virginia Convention could best perform African mission work through its own board.[11] One wonders whether Binga acted from a mere concern for the better execution of foreign mission work or whether he might also have been reacting with hurt Virginian pride.

Binga's resolution was tabled and a more conciliatory motion was adopted in its place. Joseph E. Jones, another veteran supporter of African missions, moved that a committee be organized to meet with the Foreign Mission Board of the NBC and to gather facts concerning the execution of foreign missions by that body. Joseph E. Jones, W. F. Graham, Anthony Binga, Jr., and J. M. Armistead constituted the committee that was charged with delivering their findings to the state convention.[12] This move was apparently attempted as a final effort to secure modifications or compromises from the NBC and so end the rift between the state convention and that body.

The minutes of the 1897 session of the state group make clear the depth of support within that convention for cooperation with the NBC. True, Joseph E. Jones did not attend, as planned, the 1896 meeting of the NBC to present the VBSC's concerns because of ''a failure to receive the wherewithal to go.''[13] But there were positive signs for cooperation between the

---

[10]Annual Minutes, VBSC, 1896, 15.

[11]Ibid., 29-30.

[12]Ibid., 30.

[13]Ibid., 1897, 21.

two bodies. The Committee on the President's Address reversed its 1896 position and appeared to take a broader perspective on the whole issue. The committee seemed to indicate the value of mutual support when it stated that the withdrawal of Virginia's aid from the NBC was a "hasty" action that sadly portrayed an "inability to adjust difficulties among ourselves." Furthermore, the committee asserted that "many of these objections raised by this convention have been removed."[14] The committee did not go into great detail on this last point. Perhaps it meant that although the NBC's mission program had once been conducted in a wasteful and inefficient manner, things had improved under the direction of the new corresponding secretary, Lewis G. Jordan.

Finally, the committee, composed of notable African mission supporters such as Richard Spiller and E. Watts, recommended that the state convention send a group of delegates to the next NBC annual session with complete authority to settle the difficulties between the two conventions and to report the results to the 1898 meeting of the Virginia Convention.[15] Anthony Binga, Jr. moved that the delegates selected to attend the NBC meeting not be permitted to "commit this body." The motion carried. On the other hand, the Virginians approved a motion by Sutton E. Griggs that the state Foreign Mission Board be empowered to pay money to the NBC Foreign Mission Board "if the delegates to the National Convention so recommend."[16]

It appears that the rift between the Virginia Baptists and the NBC came close to a successful resolution. But the NBC decided on another plan of action that drove both the Virginians and the North Carolinians from its ranks and thus paved the way for the formation of the LCC and divisions among Baptists in Virginia and North Carolina.

## THE "COOPERATION" ISSUE

The conflicting opinions among black Baptists as to the advisability of publishing their own religious literature or of relying upon the Northern, white

---

[14]Ibid., 52.

[15]Ibid.

[16]Ibid., 53.

American Baptist Publication Society (ABPS) reflected the broader question of cooperation in religious work, and most particularly for this study, cooperation in foreign missions. For some time the "independents" had pointed out the discriminatory treatment that black Baptists had received at the hands of many Northern white Baptists and the need for blacks to minister to their own needs rather than rely upon others. Black Baptists, they insisted, should publish their own literature and avoid any cooperative arrangements whereby they were relegated to subordinate positions.

The cooperationists, on the other hand, had called attention to the great amount of humanitarian and religious work that Northern white Baptists had performed on behalf of Southern blacks in the post–Civil War South. These Baptists understandably felt a deep sense of gratitude to Northern white Baptists for the latter's sacrifices and sharing of resources. It would be an act of hostility, they argued, for black Baptists to pursue their own course in religious publications. Furthermore, the cooperationists agreed with many white Northern Baptists that black Baptists were not fully capable at that point of pursuing an independent course in certain religious activities.[17]

The cooperation-independent argument among black Baptists found its way into the new organization. As early as 1895 the independents made an effort to include a provision within the NBC constitution that would explicitly mandate that the convention publish its own literature. This attempt by the independents failed and many black Baptists, according to Jordan, dearly hoped that the matter would rest at that point.[18] In the following year, however, the independents prevailed. The NBC delegates approved a resolution establishing a Publishing Committee under the auspices of the Home Mission Board headquartered in Little Rock, Arkansas. This committee had full authority to begin immediate steps to provide Sunday school literature for black Baptist churches as soon as January 1897.[19]

---

[17]For an account of the cooperationist-independent controversy, see Carter G. Woodson, *The History of the Negro Church*, 3d ed. (Washington: Associated Publishers, 1921; rpt., 1972) 235-37.

[18]Jordan, *Negro Baptist History*, 119.

[19]Ibid.

Among the Southern states, Virginia and North Carolina contained the greatest number of cooperationists. Thus, the black Baptists of these two states quickly responded to the action of the NBC. Virginia responded rather mildly by simply reaffirming its gratefulness, appreciation, and confidence in the religious work and contributions of the American Baptist Home Mission Society and the American Baptist Publication Society.[20] Thus, the NBC decision to publish separate religious literature appears to have had the most devastating impact upon the cooperationists in the Tarheel state. A year prior to the action of the NBC, in 1895, the Board of Managers of the Baptist Educational and Missionary Convention of North Carolina had reported a plan of cooperation adopted at the Oxford (North Carolina) Convention that would involve the support of both Northern and Southern white Baptists with the black Baptists of the state. North Carolinians believed that this plan would be a vital stimulant to local and state work that had been hampered too long by "poor organization, poor management, and poor opportunities."[21]

To be sure, the dissatisfaction among black Baptists of North Carolina with the mission work of the NBC Foreign Mission Board played a role in the controversy between the state and the national body. According to the 1897 proceedings of the state convention, the Committee on Dividing the United States into Missionary Districts pointed out the need to minimize or eradicate the waste of foreign mission monies and to dispatch the greatest amount of funds to the mission field as directly and quickly as possible. The most appropriate means for achieving this goal, the committee members reasoned, was the districting of the country into foreign mission districts as under the old Foreign Mission Convention plan,[22] a proposal the NBC-at-large rejected.[23]

But the cooperation issue played an equal, if not a more important, role in the decision of the North Carolina Baptists to separate from the NBC.

[20]Annual Minutes, VBSC, 1897, 22-23, 53.

[21]Annual Minutes, Baptist Educational and Missionary Convention of North Carolina (BEMC-NC), 1897, pp. 19-20.

[22]Annual Minutes, LCC, 1899, 5.

[23]Perhaps this plan met with rejection by the NBC because a similar earlier proposal had failed to alter appreciably the fortunes of the financially troubled Foreign Mission Convention.

The above-named committee noted that Baptists in Virginia, District of Columbia, and certain New England and Middle Atlantic states wanted to cooperate with white Baptists. Thus, the Board of Managers of the state Baptist group was directed to extend an invitation to these Baptists to assemble in Washington, D.C. on 15 December 1897 to consider the wisdom of organizing a regional convention devoted to the work of foreign missions.[24]

This invitation proved to be the clarion call for the formation of the LCC. Note, then, that the call for a separate convention did not originate among the Virginia Baptists, as Jordan's statements imply.[25] The minutes of the North Carolina and Virginia conventions of 1897 reveal a vast difference in response to the actions of the NBC. Despite its firm support for cooperation with Northern white Baptists, Virginia had not decisively ruled out the possibility of continued (or renewed) alignment with the NBC, as we have seen. Virginia Baptists apparently left the NBC as a direct response to the call of North Carolina rather than because of a determined intention on their part to separate from the national Baptists. Evidently, Baptist contemporaries credited Virginia with spearheading the formation because of the large Baptist population in and great influence of that state.

## NORTH CAROLINA AND VIRGINIA IN THE LCC

On 16 and 17 December 1897 delegates gathered in the Shiloh Baptist Church of Washington, D.C. to organize the LCC. Responding to the call from black Baptists of North Carolina, representatives came from black Baptists of North Carolina, the District of Columbia, "Virginia, . . . Maryland, Delaware, Pennsylvania, New Jersey, New York, and the New England States."[26] Some of the most prominent black Baptists in the foreign mission movement transferred their allegiance from the NBC to this organization. Among the ranks of notables at this founding session were: J. Anderson Taylor, P. F. Morris, H. H. Mitchell, Richard Spiller, Wil-

---

[24]Annual Minutes, BEMC-NC, 1897, 19-20.

[25]See Lewis G. Jordan, *On Two Hemispheres: Bits from the Life Story of Lewis G. Jordan as Told by Himself* (N.p., n.d.) 26.

[26]Minutes, Organizational Meeting of the LCC, 1897, 19; bound with the Annual Minutes, LCC, 1898.

liam Richard Wells, and Joseph E. Jones of Virginia; Albert W. Pegues, S. N. Vass, C. S. Brown, J. A. Whitted of North Carolina; A. Truett of the District of Columbia; W. M. Alexander of Maryland; and W. T. Dixon of New York.[27]

Baptists from the states of Virginia and North Carolina heavily influenced this session. Of the sixty-three registered delegates attending this meeting, twenty-nine, or nearly half, were from the states of Virginia and North Carolina. Virginia demonstrated that foreign missions still held high priority among its Baptists by sending twenty-three delegates, the largest of any other single delegation. North Carolinians and Virginians filled most of the nonceremonial posts created at this convention: P. F. Morris of Virginia was selected as president; A. W. Pegues of North Carolina, recording secretary; C. S. Brown of North Carolina, treasurer; and Sutton E. Griggs of Virginia, statistical secretary. Later P. F. Morris abdicated the office of president. C. S. Brown then assumed the position, which he maintained for the remainder of the period under study.[28]

The proceedings of the 1899 session of the LCC reveal that the formulation and execution of policies still was to a great extent in the hands of the North Carolinians and the Virginians. Of the six nonceremonial offices, two were held by North Carolinians and two by Virginians. In addition, the Virginians controlled the Executive Board of the new organization. In 1899, for example, more than half of the Executive Board positions (thirteen) were held by Virginians, three by North Carolinians, and three by Pennsylvanians.[29]

Though North Carolina had provided the call and would, through C. S. Brown, furnish most of the theological rationale for the LCC, the state of Virginia supplied the chief means (funds) for the execution of the convention's work. The 1910 proceedings of the black Lott Carey-affiliated General (Baptist) Association of Virginia (GAV) reveal that Virginians were still aware of their crucial role in the support of African missions. ''We hope the day will come when Virginia will receive due recognition for the

---

[27]Ibid., 19-23.

[28]Ibid.

[29]Annual Minutes, LCC, 1899, 1.

work which she is doing for Africa. The Lott Carey Foreign Missionary
Convention owes its financial standing largely to Virginia.''[30] These proceedings cited the Virginians as having contributed $698.23 of the
$1,137.46 reported at the 1910 annual session of the LCC held in Durham,
North Carolina. The women of Virginia collected $446.71 of the $676.66
reported by the Women's Auxiliary to the Lott Carey Convention. Thus,
Baptists from Virginia had contributed in excess of sixty percent of the total monies raised, or $1,144.94 from a sum total of $1,813.13.[31]

The minutes of this session also demonstrate that Virginians—with or
without the assistance of other states—always stood ready to conduct foreign mission work. ''We believe . . . Virginia would support two or three
more missionaries on the foreign field. . . . We therefore recommend that
our Board be authorized to devise plans whereby our General Association
will be able to support a missionary or missionaries upon the foreign
field.''[32]

The minutes of the 1911 session of the GAV show that Virginians were
still providing crucial support for the LCC. Virginia Baptists contributed
$1,429.04 to an LCC total of $2,386.52. Also, the Foreign Mission Board of
the GAV noted efforts by its members to conduct a greater investigative study
of the mission situation in Africa in order to improve upon the amount of financial support for the cause. True to the history of foreign mission interest
in Virginia, the board urged that foreign missions continue to play a vital role
in the intents, thoughts, and activities of the people of Virginia.[33]

## THE LCC AND THE COOPERATION ISSUE, 1897–1907

Disenchanted black Baptists of the Southeast had several reasons to
withdraw from the NBC, as I have pointed out. Among them were the
NBC's treatment of the Virginians and a belief that the NBC was ineffec-
tively carrying out the foreign mission program. The LCC, supported by
the Virginians, was organized to collect and to distribute funds specifically
for foreign missions and to do so more efficiently.

---

[30]Annual Minutes, GAV (black), 1910, p. 54.

[31]Ibid., 55.

[32]Ibid.

[33]Annual Minutes, GAV, 1911, 34-35.

But it was the issue of cooperation with white Baptists in denominational activities that captured the most attention in the 1897–1907 debate between the LCC and the NBC. Perhaps no Baptist better expounded the LCC's position than its president, Calvin S. Brown of North Carolina.[34] Born in Salisbury, North Carolina, the very able Brown served as president of the LCC practically from its inception in 1897 throughout the period under study. Brown also served as the president of the Baptist Educational and Missionary Convention of North Carolina and the Waters Normal Institute. A valedictorian graduate of Shaw University in the Tarheel state, Brown also served as pastor for some of the largest and most prosperous churches in North Carolina; editor of the newspaper *The Good Samaritan;* and editor and founder of the *Baptist Pilot.* The LCC constantly commended his annual addresses before the convention and authorized their publication in the local media. In sum, Brown was a well-versed, articulate, and highly respected clergyman whose ideas could not pass unnoticed by even his fiercest opponents.

The question of cooperation went beyond the mere issue of publishing Sunday school literature. It concerned how black Baptists should relate to their white counterparts in all areas of religious work, including foreign missions. Brown and other members of the LCC strongly favored cooperation for moral, theological, and practical reasons.[35] Morally speaking, to abrogate cooperative ventures made some LCC Baptists feel that they were behaving ungratefully toward white Baptists. After all, white Baptists had done a great amount of humanitarian, educational, and religious work for them in the post–Civil War South. Practically speaking, Brown believed that black Baptists had not reached the point in their development at which they could adequately execute major religious operations without the active, sustained guidance of white Baptists. Addressing the LCC convention in 1900, Brown stated: "We are weak, they are strong. We are poor, they are rich. We are ignorant, they are educated. We have no where to lay our heads; they own cattle on a thousand hills. We are a nonentity

[34]For a biography of Calvin S. Brown, see Albert W. Pegues, *Our Baptist Ministers and Schools* (Springfield MA: Wiley & Company, 1892) 95-98.

[35]For a good exposition of Brown's and the LCC's stance on cooperation, see Brown's annual presidential address in the Annual Minutes, LCC, 1900, 8-14.

in politics, but they rule with iron. Destiny has shaped the situation, and I must accept it.''[36] In Brown's mind, another practical consideration was that only in the arena of religious affairs could blacks and whites meet on common ground. Cooperation in religious matters could be used to override human pettiness and to allow human beings to aim for the most noble ideals and practices.[37]

Theologically speaking, Brown argued that black Baptists' refusal to cooperate with white Baptists was contradictory to the expressed will of God. Brown and the LCC laid heavy emphasis upon the universal focus of Christianity. For Brown, race should not count as a valid factor in the life of the church.[38] The duty to evangelize the world was incumbent upon all Christians. Christians had to avoid hampering their mission by realizing that the whole family of Christians was one—regardless of their race or geographical location. Scriptures taught no doctrines of racial differences in the pursuit of the church's work; such things were mere human inventions and accretions to the gospel message.[39]

Brown condemned calls for independence and noncooperation with whites as symptoms of racial prejudice on the part of NBC Baptists. In his opinion, many independent preachers were men of ''narrow'' attitudes who acted contrary to biblical principles.[40] What was quite upsetting to many independent-minded Baptists in the NBC was the downplaying of racism by some Lott Carey Baptists. Brown advocated a course of action that would only be defensible if the church were devoid of racism. He saw no need, in other words, for a particular application of the gospel to the needs of the race. ''It is not a question of race, it is a question of grace. I am not responsible for my race. . . . This race and color business as preached in many of our churches was 'born in sin and conceived in iniquity.' ''[41]

Like the Tuskegee educator Booker T. Washington, Brown tended to minimize the significance of political activity by blacks. He adopted the

---

[36]Ibid., 12.

[37]Ibid.

[38]Ibid.

[39]Ibid.

[40]Ibid,, 1902, 26-27.

[41]Annual Minutes, BEMC-NC, 1903, 11.

idea that the proper way to deal with racial oppression was to spread true Christian principles. Men and women would know the duty of loving all people regardless of race, and thus oppression would come to an end. Similarly, although Brown expressed delight in black business development for the material enrichment and general progress of black people, he did not believe—as did the NBC Baptists—that the black church should act as a means to promote businesses. The first and most important duty of the church was the preaching of the gospel. Preaching the gospel and sacrificing for the cause of Christ did not entail ecclesiastical support for black secular enterprises.[42]

For many Baptists in the NBC, Brown and the cooperationists often separated too sharply the secular struggle of blacks and the cause of Christianity. Less diplomatically, NBC members often pictured the LCC Baptists as willing to lower themselves to the level of subserviency and as sacrificing their racial integrity and pride for the monetary support of white Baptists. Comments from Brown like the following served as powerful reinforcements for such a negative viewpoint. "I have made up my mind to help the man who undertakes the job to improve my condition, and I am not going to waste time quarreling over the plan and especially if he proposes to furnish the instrument and the means and requires me to furnish simply the subject. He may turn the mill to suit himself if he allows me to hold the sack and catch the meal."[43]

Brown's description requires some comment. It appears that Brown and many leaders of the LCC adopted an attitude of superiority toward the masses of black Baptists. In part this attitude was based upon color: Brown and most LCC leaders were mulattoes. In other instances, some LCC Baptists took pride in the sense that they were "pure" Africans. Also, many of these Baptists were products of schools founded and supported in the South by the white Home Mission Society. This fact accounts not only for the sense on their part that they were academically better trained than the "uneducated" black leaders in the independent movement, but it explains their tendency to favor close cooperative arrangements with white Bap-

---

[42]Ibid.

[43]Annual Minutes, LCC, 1900, 12-13.

tists. In short, much of the theological verbiage concerning the Christian virtues of cooperation camouflages a deeper belief on the part of many LCC Baptists that they were superior to their black Baptist counterparts, who still required the guiding hands of whites to lift them from their lowly stations.[44]

Circumstances in time, however, caused LCC Baptists to modify their position on cooperation. Political events such as Jim Crow laws pointed to the need for greater unity among blacks. The tendency of Northern white Baptists to prefer ties with Southern *white* Baptists convinced many black Baptists, cooperationists and independents, that the attitudes of Northern white Baptists were hardening toward them.[45] Many LCC Baptists eventually realized that cooperation with whites was not an easy attainment, no matter how much it had been discussed in theory.

For example, in 1900 the LCC and the American Baptist Missionary Union made plans for their first joint missionary appointments in Africa. Despite the enthusiastic remarks that LCC spokespersons had made in favor of cooperation, correspondence between Henry C. Mabie, the corresponding secretary of the union, and Brown[46] indicates that cooperation between the two bodies materialized with less alacrity and smoothness than one would imagine. It seems that Brown had agreed to a plan of cooperation that granted the union a decided advantage on the managerial level. When he presented the plan to the Executive Board of the LCC, however, the members registered their strong disapproval. In a letter to Mabie, Brown commented upon their response.

The brethren understand from the terms sent us that your board is willing to co-operate with us as a subordinate body instead of a coordinate body.

[44]For an account of the role that the independent-cooperationist debate played in the unification of black Baptist forces in the late nineteenth century, see James Melvin Washington, ''The Origins and Emergence of Black Baptist Separatism, 1863–1897'' (Ph.D. diss., Yale University, 1979) ch. 5. See especially 228-29, 239-43.

[45]See ibid., 226-29 for a discussion of the Fortress Monroe Agreement between the representatives of the Home Mission Society and the SBC.

[46]See Brown's letters to Henry C. Mabie, dated 13 October and 10 November 1900 in the correspondence of the Lott Carey Baptist Foreign Mission Convention, which is part of the papers of the American Baptist Foreign Mission Society, microfilm no. 197 in the American Baptist Historical Society in Rochester, New York. The American Baptist Missionary Union officially took the name American Baptist Foreign Mission Society in 1910.

This feature does not meet the approval of our board. From the terms sent us, the brethren seem to get the impression that all of our efforts and doings must be submitted for your approval, and at the same time, we shall be expected to assume all responsibility so far as expenses go.[47]

It was only after the union had approved a more equitable arrangement that cooperation between the groups became a reality. This critical stance of the LCC board toward cooperation is not surprising given that many of its members—for example, Anthony Binga, Jr., Joseph Endom Jones, Richard Spiller, James Holmes, J. W. Kirby, and J. A. Whitted—were among the members of the board of the Baptist Foreign Mission Convention in the 1880s when that body rejected what it considered to be an unequal cooperative plan with the union. Despite their energetic endorsement of a colorless Christianity, LCC Baptists were graphically reminded of the color consciousness of their white counterparts. Now they not only were voicing many of the same things as their rivals in the NBC, but they also were advocating arguments they had put forth a decade earlier as members of the BFMC—arguments that had led to the formation of the NBC in the first place.

## NBC AND THE COOPERATION ISSUE, 1897–1907

Emmanuel K. Love of Georgia was among those black Baptists who defended the independent principles of the NBC. Born in the vicinity of Marion, Alabama, in 1850, Love attended Lincoln University in that city and graduated in 1877 from Augusta Institute in Georgia. During his ministerial career he served as a missionary of the Home Mission Society for the entire state of Georgia; pastor of the historic First African Baptist Church in Savannah, Georgia; associate editor of the *Georgia Sentinel;* and president of the Foreign Mission Convention.[48]

Love, an active proponent of African missions, rose to defend the NBC's decision to print its own Sunday school literature. Although the comments of Love referred to below were specifically addressed to the issue of religious publication, his rationales for independency reflect the NBC

---

[47]Brown's letter to Mabie, 13 October 1900, p. 1.

[48]For a biography of Love, see Pegues, *Baptist Ministers,* 319-21.

Baptists' views toward cooperation with white Baptists in all areas, including African missions. In an address delivered in St. Louis, Missouri, in September 1896, Love asserted that he held firm affections for the American Baptist Publication Society. Yet since the majority of the NBC delegates had voted to issue separate literature, he would support both the NBC and the black race. But it was more than simply a sense of denominational and racial loyalty that motivated this Georgia Baptist. He could think of no compelling reason why black Baptists should forgo producing their own religious literature. It was natural and "fair," he maintained, that a people would desire to control certain institutions for themselves.[49]

NBC spokespersons could not allow their belief in the universal demands of the Christian faith (in terms of evangelization and religious practice) to obscure the concrete reality of racism on the part of many whites. Blacks might be ever ready to associate and work with whites on an equal footing, disregarding color and race. But in whatever walks of life the races met, NBC leaders contended, black people encountered discrimination and second-class treatment.[50] Furthermore, Love claimed, independent black institutions allowed his people to reach certain potentials that would elude them in a white-controlled institution. Echoing arguments advanced by the Foreign Mission Convention when it rejected cooperation with the union in the mid-1880s, NBC leaders asserted that there were certain necessary qualities that black people had to develop for themselves. According to Love, the willingness of any people to do for themselves gained the attention and admiration of others.[51]

But the National Baptists did not adhere to a policy of racial prejudice, as some LCC Baptists claimed. During these years of NBC-LCC separation, NBC Baptists remained open to cooperative overtures from white Baptists when those proposals were established on bases of equality. Additionally, they took concrete steps to manifest their belief in the universalism of the Christian faith. For example, the NBC Foreign Mission Board as early as 1899 noted that black missionaries had never been sent

---

[49]Jordan, *Negro Baptist History,* 124.

[50]Ibid.

[51]Ibid.

by white denominations to any foreign lands but Africa. Also, the board stated that whites taught immigrants to regard black people as inferior beings. Consequently, these people were rendered inaccessible to the NBC's evangelical activities. Nevertheless, the board stated that the Christian teaching of love for all human beings compelled all Christians to do some service for the salvation of all people. Thus, the board urged the convention to contribute on a yearly basis to the white Baptist denominations, the Baptist Missionary Union and SBC, for foreign mission work in countries where the NBC did not operate mission stations.[52] Perhaps this latter action could be interpreted as merely a token one. It nonetheless carried symbolic significance in that it concretely manifested the NBC convictions about the universality of the gospel and the need for all Christians to support its extension everywhere in the world.

## CONFLICTS AT THE STATE LEVEL, 1897–1907

The separation of the NBC and the LCC over the issue of cooperation had a profound effect upon the movement for missions. This division among supporters of African missions occurred not only between the LCC and the NBC, but among Baptists on the state level and between individuals. Therefore, it is important for us to investigate these rifts if we are to gather a fuller understanding of the impact of the broader division of Baptists, particularly as it related to African missions. In the Southeast the conflict was most severe in the states of North Carolina and Virginia where rival forces contended for the support of the NBC and the LCC as the most viable instrument to carry out African missions.

Perhaps the more dramatic split happened among the black Baptists of the Old Dominion. The conflicts that set the stage for the final division of the Virginia Baptist State Convention (VBSC) in 1899 involved some of the most prominent African mission supporters in Virginia. The bitter debate between Lucy Coles and Z. D. Lewis reflected the acrimony that surfaced between the two camps.

NBC supporter Coles had served along with her husband (J. J. Coles) as a missionary to Liberia in the late 1880s and early 1890s under the aus-

---

[52]Annual Minutes, NBC, 1899, 27-28.

pices of the Foreign Mission Convention. The 22 October 1898 issue of
the *Richmond Planet*[53] carried a letter to the editor written by Mrs. Coles.
The letter described a conflict between her and the prominent African mission supporter and Richmond pastor Z. D. Lewis, who favored the LCC.
Lewis, moderator of the Richmond Ministers' Conference, had recently
opposed an effort by Mrs. Coles to enlist conference support in collecting
funds for the erection of a mission building in Liberia in honor of her late
husband. According to Coles, Lewis delivered a "fiery speech" in which
he claimed that the enterprise fostered by her was an attempt by the NBC
to gain the support of the conference by clandestine methods. Most of the
ministers were absent from the conference.

Coles noted that other prominent Baptist leaders as well as laypersons
in the state had promised their cooperation in the project. She accused Lewis
of being unable to cope with the fact that the NBC had moved the foreign
mission headquarters from Richmond to Louisville and had also displaced
his membership on the board before he could make any contributions to
the evangelization of Africa. Other former members of the Executive Board
of the Foreign Mission Convention had accepted this turn of events with
"dignity," but the same could not be said of Lewis.

Coles defended the fiscal record of the NBC. The former missionary
asserted that Lewis lacked an adequate grasp of the foreign mission business affairs of the NBC, the Foreign Mission Convention, or the LCC. True,
as Lewis had claimed, the NBC owed a debt of $600 to the missionaries
presently stationed in the field in Africa. But Mrs. Coles noted that her recollection of African mission work of the late 1880s and early 1890s (when
"Mr. Lewis was then only a school-boy") was very vivid. During this time
the Foreign Mission Convention had only two missionaries in the field, Mr.
and Mrs. Coles, but owed them a debt of $1,000. In comparison, the vet-
eran missionary wrote, the NBC indebtedness of $600 in support of four-
teen missionaries represented a very paltry sum.[54]

If such debates had centered solely on the points at issue, perhaps the
breach between independents and cooperationists would not have widened so

---

[53]For Lucy A. Coles's account of her conflict with Z. D. Lewis, see *The Richmond
Planet*, 22 October 1893, p. 1.

[54]Ibid.

greatly. Such was not the case, however. Coles, justified or not, continued with attacks upon Lewis's character. She described Lewis as possessing a "continual fault finding, distasteful and meddlesome disposition." In Coles's reckoning, Lewis was "by nature one-sided and not responsible for much he does." She further asserted that he had been hypocritical in his dealings with the NBC African missionary stationed in South Africa, R. L. Stewart.[55] Although I have been unable to locate Lewis's account of this debate, the information presented serves to illustrate the depth of personal conflict and bitterness that surfaced because of the cooperationist issue.

The battle—personality- and issue-wise—involved other prominent black Virginia Baptists, and it finally rent the Virginia Convention in 1899. The cooperationists (and supporters of the LCC) found themselves outnumbered at the 1899 session held at Lexington, Virginia.[56] The independents took advantage of their numerical majority and dissolved all cooperative arrangements with the white Baptists of the North and South as well as with the white General Association of Virginia. The dissidents refused to surrender to this new situation. Five months after the Lexington Convention, in October 1899, these cooperationists gathered and formed a separate black Baptist state organization, the General Association of Virginia (GAV). The arguments between the two groups practically mirrored those of the LCC Baptists and the NBC Baptists. But the charges of personal misconduct were much more pointed. For one thing, the GAV accused the members of the regular state convention of dominating the session and employing "trickery and political methods of bygone days." Furthermore, the Virginia Baptist State Convention, the GAV Baptists claimed, had not been representative of its former constituency.[57]

North Carolina, another member state of the LCC, was able to avoid outright schism until 1903. The state minutes of this year show C. S. Brown (also president of this convention) to be surprised and distressed over actions taken by Baptists in the eastern portion of the state to form their own convention. He recalled that through many years and struggles the North

---

[55]Ibid.

[56]Minutes, Founding Session, GAV, 1899, esp. 5-7.

[57]Ibid.

Carolina Baptists' "fears, hopes and aims have been one." He wished to avoid a disruption of this Baptist unity over "imaginary differences," for any division "would be a calamity of disastrous consequences." So concerned was Brown with the new movement that he had personally gone to the supporters of the new organization in an effort to halt the division.[58]

## REUNION, 1905

Despite the sharp division, neither the NBC nor the LCC ever ruled out some form of reunion for a number of reasons. First, there was a general feeling in both groups that unity should exist among blacks. In an obvious reference to the deteriorating political situation of blacks in the South, Brown, for example, in 1903 spoke in broad terms about certain secular events that had increased blacks' need to achieve as much unity among themselves as possible.[59] There was undoubtedly a powerful interest in attaining some form of denominational unity among Baptists in both groups, since some Baptists in each organization, as former members of the Foreign Mission Convention, had advocated and worked for such a goal. Furthermore, the commitment to redeem the African continent was so powerful that it transcended geographical and ideological boundaries and was thus a strong inducement for cooperation between the two groups. Finally, the financial problems of both groups served to heighten interest in reconciliation. The NBC found that it suffered from the lack of generous contributions by the Baptists in the LCC, especially those of Virginia. Similarly, the LCC probably realized that it had unintentionally exaggerated monetary and other perceived benefits that were to flow from cooperation with white Baptists.

Once rhetoric was decreased and an increased understanding of (if not approval of) the viewpoints of the other's position surfaced, progress toward reconciliation moved with greater alacrity. The Lott Carey Baptists refused to dissolve their organization and to allow themselves to be completely absorbed within the NBC. Instead the two groups agreed that the LCC would maintain a coordinate existence as a district foreign mission

---

[58]Annual Minutes, BEMC-NC, 1903, 11-12.

[59]*National Baptist Union-Review* 5 (7 October 1903): 11.

group within the NBC. In that regard, the LCC retained the right to enter a cooperative arrangement with any other Baptist group. The LCC secured the pledge of the NBC that the convention-at-large would be open to cooperative possibilities with other Baptists, white and black,[60] and that local congregations would retain the right to select their own Sunday school literature.[61] Of course, such an arrangement assured the leaders of the LCC that they would continue exercising a significant degree of leadership and power instead of being totally subsumed under the authority of the NBC. Also, fervent and conscientious African mission supporters in the LCC could maintain efforts to operate what they conceived as a more efficient handling of mission revenues.

For its own part, the NBC, while granting a degree of organizational jurisdiction to the work of the LCC, exerted overall authority over the Foreign Mission Board and the work of foreign missions. The National Baptists perhaps also delighted, if only secretly, in the observation of LCC Baptists that the benefits of cooperation with white Baptists did not preclude the necessity of racial unity and solidarity.

Yet this new relationship effected in 1905 was short-lived. In 1916 a controversy over the ownership of the denominational publishing house split the NBC into two rival conventions: the National Baptist Convention, U.S.A., Incorporated and the new and smaller group, the National Baptist Convention of America. After years of negotiation, the NBC-Unincorporated and the LCC settled on an agreement whereby the latter group would conduct foreign missions for the Unincorporated Baptists. Notwithstanding the LCC's legal prerogative under the LCC-NBC accord to establish such links with other Baptist organizations, this alliance with the rival Unincorporated group spelled doom for the LCC's continued relationship with the Incorporated Baptists. Since 1924 the NBC-Incorporated and the LCC have followed separate paths.[62]

---

[60]Annual Minutes, LCC, 1903, 30.

[61]*National Baptist Union-Review* 5 (7 October 1903): 11.

[62]Leroy Fitts, *Lott Carey: First Black Missionary to Africa* (Valley Forge PA: Judson Press, 1978) 97-98.

## CONCLUSION

The unity of black Baptist forces that Afro-American Baptists within and without the Foreign Mission Convention had sought for years finally materialized in 1895 with the establishment of the NBC. But the decisions of the NBC to reorganize and to transfer the Foreign Mission Board and to cease subscription of Sunday school literature from the white American Baptist Publication Society caused many Baptists of the Southeast to desert the organization. Concern for racial and denominational unity, however, brought Baptists of North Carolina, Virginia, and other members of the LCC into a short-lived coordinate relationship (not a merger) with the NBC in 1905.

For black Baptists, a unity of efforts had its disadvantages as well as its advantages. To a great extent, one could argue rather persuasively that the advent of the LCC represented the need for many Baptists, especially those in Virginia and North Carolina, to maintain an organizational apparatus more accessible to and influenced by them. In other words, though racial and denominational unity was quite palatable as a goal, its attainment pointed out a great need of many Baptists—to have a religious organization geographically close to them. The formation of the LCC, among other things, revealed that some Baptists were simply not totally prepared for the transition of the African mission movement from the regional to the national stage.

But the events as described in this chapter also indicate another vital truth. The desire to labor for the redemption of Africa because of the conviction that God was working through this missionary movement to accomplish a great end for all African peoples was maintained by both the NBC and the LCC. It is noteworthy that the LCC was founded originally for the explicitly designated task of conducting foreign, especially African, missions. The NBC, though it obviously suffered a loss in revenue because of the secession of a great number of Baptists in some of the eastern seaboard states, aggressively continued its efforts to conduct foreign missions. It was supported by many former members of the BFMC, including persons and conventions in states where the LCC was strong, such as Mrs. Lucy Coles and the original Virginia Convention. Chapter 6 focuses upon this continuing African missionary tradition among Baptists in both the LCC and the NBC between 1895 and 1915.

# CHAPTER 5

# THE NBC, THE LCC,
# AND THE AFRICAN MISSION MOVEMENT,
# 1895–1915

The previous chapter highlighted the conflicts and dissension between the two major black Baptist groups, the LCC and the NBC—actions that had serious ramifications for black Baptist unity on the domestic and the African fields of operation. Nevertheless, the commitment of black Christians to evangelize the continent for both spiritual and material reasons prevented such troubles from halting their mission endeavors in Africa. The present chapter focuses on both the NBC's and the LCC's efforts to keep this missionary tradition alive throughout the period under study. As we approach the closing years of our study, we see black Baptists still united in principle, if not organizationally, in the pursuit of bringing the gospel to their African kin.

Granted, there were significant differences between the two groups. In terms of its membership, the NBC was naturally more national in scope than the regional LCC. The NBC conducted most of its foreign mission work in the South African field; the LCC, on the other hand, continued the Foreign Mission Convention's and Southern black Baptist traditions since the 1820s of concentrating mission stations in West Africa, particularly Liberia. It is within the LCC, therefore, that we find the greatest impact of *Southern* Baptist mission concern for West Africa, a commitment dating to antebellum times. Consistent with previous emphasis upon the Southern region as the cradle of the African mission program of black Baptists, this chapter shall follow the LCC with greater detail.

## NBC ORGANIZATIONAL GROWTH
## AND THE AFRICAN MISSION PROGRAM

Considering the low economic status of black Americans in the years 1895–1915, the NBC made commendable progress in organizational growth and foreign mission work. Organizationally, the newly formed NBC quickly expanded its basic structure and policy concerns. Lewis G. Jordan has provided a concise history of these early years of the NBC.[1] In 1895 the NBC had only three major boards: Education, Foreign Missions, and Home Missions. In 1899 the Baptist Young People's Union (BYPU) was formed. In 1900 the Women's Auxiliary to the convention was organized, an event that demonstrated the increasing role of women.

This study has emphasized the sense of racial consciousness of black Christians during this period. They viewed the African mission movement as an obligation placed upon them by God to secure the spiritual and material uplift of people of African descent throughout the world. But in forming separate, independent organizations, black Christians in neither the NBC nor the LCC intended to sever religious ties of cooperation with other Christian groups. Though the NBC had been characterized as advocating a racially exclusive gospel by its rival, the LCC, note that the former organization participated in a number of historically significant, worldwide ecumenical ventures during this period. In 1905 the NBC sent forty delegates to the first meeting of the Baptist World Alliance in London. The NBC also demonstrated their ecumenical propensities by commissioning twenty-five delegates to the Ecumenical Missionary Conference held in Edinburgh, Scotland, in 1910.

Like one of its major forerunners, the American National Baptist Convention, the NBC in these years indicated that its interests involved the political as well as the ecclesiastical concerns of the black Baptist community. These black Baptists protested the deteriorating political fortunes of blacks in the early years of the twentieth century. In 1907, for example, the NBC voiced its opposition to Jim Crow laws being enacted across the South. In 1911 the NBC founded the Committee on the State of the Country, a return to a tradition among black Baptists. The committee's primary task was to investigate and to assess the conditions of black people throughout the nation and to prepare annual reports of its findings to the larger convention. In 1913 the NBC commissioned a history of black Americans and black

---

[1]For a concise account of the early history of the NBC, consult Lewis G. Jordan, *Negro Baptist History, U.S.A., 1750–1940* (Nashville TN: The Sunday School Publishing Board, National Baptist Convention, n.d.) 261-62.

Baptists. Funds collected from the sale of this book were to be used to advance African missions.

Though the NBC had troubling conflicts with the Lott Carey Baptists, its foreign mission program in other ways began on positive and encouraging notes. In 1896 the Baptist General Association of Western States and Territories united with the NBC, bringing the support of many black Baptists of the West and Midwest to the foreign and domestic programs of the NBC. In the same year the NBC founded the *Afro-American Mission Herald* (subsequently known as *The Mission Herald*) to facilitate the development of foreign mission interest and financial support among black Baptists.[2]

The appointment of the very able Lewis Garnett Jordan in 1896 as the corresponding secretary of the Foreign Mission Board ranks as one of the major and best decisions of the new organization. This giant in the history of Baptists in the U.S. succeeded Dr. Lucius M. Luke of Kentucky, who was one of the major critics of the former Foreign Mission Convention Executive Board's conduct of African missions. Luke was chosen as the first corresponding secretary in 1895, but died in December, three months after assuming his new post. On 13 February 1896 the board elected Jordan, who at the time was pastoring Union Baptist Church in Philadelphia. He had exhibited great interest in African missions and had journeyed to West Africa in the 1880s, meeting personally with many of the Foreign Mission Convention missionaries in the field at that time. A Mississippian by birth and a prolific writer, he very ably served the NBC foreign mission cause as corresponding secretary for the board for twenty-five years.[3]

At the beginning of Jordan's tenure, the Foreign Mission Board faced a number of problems that had plagued its predecessor, the BFMC: heavy financial difficulties, missionaries in Africa inadequately supported, and a lagging interest in foreign missions among Afro-American Baptists. The corresponding secretary perhaps did not exaggerate the situation very

---

[2]See William H. Moses, *The Colored Baptists' Family Tree: A Compendium of Organized Negro Baptist Church History* (Nashville TN: The Sunday School Publishing Board, National Baptist Convention, n.d.) 16; and Lewis G. Jordan, *On Two Hemispheres: Bits from the Life Story of Lewis G. Jordan as Told by Himself* (N.p., n.d.) 43.

[3]For an autobiography of Jordan, consult Jordan, *On Two Hemispheres.* For other publications by Jordan, see the bibliography.

greatly, if any, when he described the state of the African mission program: "The whole enterprise was at the vanishing point."[4] He recalled his personal sacrifice in leaving a salaried pastoral position to assume duties "for a work without a dime in the treasury and not even a lead pencil to work with," and he recalled his hurt occasioned by the withdrawal of Virginia Baptists from the convention.[5]

As with the BFMC, the NBC directed its predominant interest in foreign mission matters to Africa. Although the period 1895–1915 saw the placement of NBC missionaries (and/or persons supported by the organization) in Cuba, the West Indies, South America, and even Russia, the economic resources invested and the number of missionary personnel stationed on the mother continent clearly excelled those in all other areas of the world. But two points should be borne in mind. One, during much of this period most missionary personnel were indigenous rather than American-born missionaries. Two, the NBC effected a notable shift in the focus of mission operations from West Africa to southern Africa. The NBC's emphasis upon southern Africa manifested itself in a number of ways: (1) the amount of property and assets owned by the convention in southern Africa as compared to other missionary areas in the world; (2) the number of southern African as opposed to West African students matriculated in black American, Baptist-supported colleges; and (3) the number of NBC missionaries in the southern African field.

Concerning financial holdings, the NBC Foreign Mission Board in 1910, for example, reported its total assets from foreign fields as follows: west coast of Africa, $1,575; Central Africa, $4,400; South America, $5,450; West Indies, $1,500; and South Africa, $14,615. The latter amount represents more than half of the total assets ($27,540). As for expenditures, the board for the fiscal year September–August 1911 allotted more monies for buildings, salaries, and debts to southern Africa than to West Africa. Indeed, the sum of $6,002 for southern Africa nearly doubled the sum of $3,400 for West Africa.[6]

---

[4]Ibid., 73.

[5]Ibid., 26.

[6]Annual Minutes, NBC, 1910, 90-92.

During the 1895–1915 period a significant tradition emerged whereby African students financially supported by the respective denominations ventured to the U.S. for study in black American colleges. In 1899 the NBC in particular established a fund to provide for the education of African students in the United States with the understanding that these students would return as missionaries to the African continent. By 1910 it was abundantly clear that southern African students outnumbered all other African scholars. Of the nineteen NBC-supported foreign students listed at U.S. colleges, twelve came from southern Africa.[7] These statistics are another indication that the NBC focused attention on this region of Africa.

Finally, the south African field proved a better attraction to individual NBC missionaries, as illustrated by the 1905 report of the Foreign Mission Board. In West Africa the NBC supported only six persons: H. N. Bouey in Cape Mound, Dr. N. C. and Georgia Faulkner of Monrovia, and James O. Hayes and wife in Brewerville—all in Liberia. The NBC also gave at least partial support to Majola Agbebi of Nigeria, a leader in the indigenous Baptist church movement in the 1880s and 1890s in that country. On the other hand, the NBC maintained twenty-one missionaries in southern Africa. If the Chiradzulu region of British Central Africa is included, the figure climbs to twenty-four. While at least four of these missionaries were Afro-American, the overwhelming majority were indigenous.[8] Increasingly during this period, both black and white mission supporters accepted as a maxim that overseas missionary societies must train and depend upon indigenous Africans to evangelize the continent, as exemplified in their sponsoring African students for study in American institutions.

Several significant factors contributed to the appeal of southern Africa as a region for mission work by black American Baptists. One, as in Liberia, many inhabitants were members of the Christian church, which provided a moral if not always financial context of support. This factor played some role in persuading black Baptists to come to this section of Africa despite the fact that many white missionaries discriminated against black American missionaries and the white supremacist government placed them

---

[7]Ibid., 81.

[8]Annual Minutes, NBC, 1905, 38-39.

under heavy suspicion. Two, the climate was more temperate than in West Africa. Three, on the whole, transportational facilities were better than in West Africa.[9] In a word, these missionaries considered this region a more comfortable field in which to operate.

## THE APPEAL OF LIBERIA

Some NBC Baptists still contended for their first love, Liberia in West Africa. The call for missionary support for Liberia came most strongly from Southern Baptists. These Baptists—particularly those from the Carolinas and Virginia—were nurtured in environments that had had the strongest connections with West Africa (i.e., Liberia), politically and religiously, because of the nineteenth-century legacies of colonization and missionary activities. One of these Southern Baptists who not only journeyed to Liberia but appealed vigorously for more support from the NBC for the field was Harrison N. Bouey of South Carolina, who went to Liberia as a missionary in 1879. In 1882 he returned to the U.S. and served as a missionary of the American Baptist Publication Society, an associate editor of the *Baptist Pioneer* in Alabama, and worked actively on behalf of the Foreign Mission Convention to engender missionary interest in Africa.[10]

In 1902 Bouey returned to Liberia after a twenty-year absence from the field. The missionary expressed disappointment with the role of the NBC in Liberian mission work. In a letter dated 21 June 1902, he stated that the NBC should place twenty missionaries in the black republic. In comparison to other Christian denominations active in Liberia, he claimed, American black Baptists were doing little. In an attempt to persuade the NBC to adopt a more active role, Bouey spoke of the "reflex influence" deriving from foreign mission work. If the NBC Baptists would devote more attention to the welfare of the non-Christian Liberians, he argued, the black American Baptists would see that their local, state, and "national work would all prosper."[11]

---

[9]In other words, South Africa, like Liberia, in addition to its indigenous population, was occupied by Western Christians.

[10]For a biography of Harrison N. Bouey, see William J. Simmons, *Men of Mark, Eminent, Progressive, and Rising* (New York: George M. Revell & Co., 1887; rpt., Chicago: Johnson Publishing Company, 1970) 675-76.

[11]*The Mission Herald* 8 (July 1902): 2.

A letter the NBC received on 3 December 1902 illustrates Bouey's concern that the NBC had neglected Liberia in favor of other missionary fields. He wrote: "I wish to make no charge against my brethren in America; but, it does seem, that mission work in Liberia, has no such attraction as elsewhere."[12] While other American denominations contributed substantially to their mission work in Liberia, American Baptists had failed to maintain the splendid tradition begun by Lott Carey in the early 1820s. "When I was here twenty years ago, the Baptists were ahead in every respect; but the strong and progressive work of the American Christian denominations has put us in the shade badly. This ought not to be so. We need not less than four good strong spirited men here at present."[13]

During his previous missionary tenure in Liberia, Bouey had heavily involved himself in the activities of the Baptist churches in that country. This missionary had departed Liberia with the promise that he would work to increase the support of Afro-American Baptists for the mission cause there. Upon his return in 1902, he had to give an account for the failure of black American Baptists and himself. As he recalled in a letter to Jordan in 1904, W. F. Gibson, former pastor in Marshall, Liberia, and a close friend of Bouey in the 1870s and 1880s, questioned Bouey as to why he had not fulfilled an earlier pledge to return sooner to Africa. Furthermore, Gibson, still desiring a plan for closer cooperation between American black Baptists and Liberian Baptists, wished to know why the former Baptist had allowed other groups to better them in Liberian mission work. All of the American Baptists had seemingly deserted the field. Neither the American Baptist Missionary Union nor the SBC maintained active missions in the field. As a result, Liberian Baptist students, faced with a lack of Baptist-supported schools, were often lost to the denomination because they had to attend schools operated by other denominations in order to continue their formal education.[14]

Bouey expressed repentance for his personal inaction and called upon the NBC to take a greater interest in Liberian work. The veteran mission-

---

[12]Ibid. (March 1903): 6.

[13]*National Baptist Union-Review* 18 (June 1904): 4.

[14]*The Mission Herald* 9 (January 1905): 1.

ary promised his lifelong, unflinching service to the cause of Christianity in general and to the promotion of closer bonds of cooperation between American Baptists and Liberian Baptists in particular.[15] Whether the above is a precise recollection of an authentic conversation or a literary device, it does demonstrate Bouey's deep sense of commitment to the Liberian mission field.

Other Southern Baptists followed Bouey to the Liberian field. On 8 June 1912 Emma B. DeLaney of Fernandina, Florida, and Susie M. Taylor of Camden, South Carolina, journeyed to the continent to replace the recently deceased Bouey. DeLaney, a graduate of Spelman College in Atlanta, Georgia, first ventured to Africa in 1902 when she journeyed as an NBC missionary to southern Africa. They were followed in December 1912 by a southwesterner, Miss Eliza L. Davis of Texas. In July 1914 Davis and Taylor were planning, with the support of the NBC, to construct an industrial school in the African nation. Also, the NBC Foreign Mission Board reported in the same month that under the ministries of Taylor and Davis, 300 persons had been converted to Christianity.[16] A Baptist leader in Liberia, A. C. Reeves, described the religious revival that was taking place in a letter to the board: "The awakening in Liberia is regarded as more widespread than any spiritual awakening ever known in the history of this part of Africa."[17] But the mission was still taking its toll upon the health of missionaries. In March 1915 the board reported that Taylor had been ordered home because of poor health.[18]

Southerners in the 1895–1915 period continued to draw attention to West Africa, but the NBC as a whole had shifted foreign mission sentiment and activity to southern Africa. It was mainly within the LCC that the Southern Baptists most persistently expressed missionary interest in West Africa.

**THE LCC—EARLY GROWTH AND AFRICAN MISSIONS**

It was noted in a previous chapter that the LCC was formed as a regional organization with the specific task of promoting foreign missions,

---

[15]Ibid.

[16]Ibid., 18 (July 1914): 3.

[17]Ibid.

[18]Ibid., 19 (March 1915): 1.

especially African missions, among its constituents on the eastern seaboard. In the early years the LCC made substantial progress in the following areas: (1) the establishment of cooperative ties with the American
Baptist Missionary Union in 1900 and with the NBC in 1905; and (2) the
addition of a women's auxiliary in 1902. The LCC added a Home Mission
Department in 1903. This act, however, did not deflect the organization
from its support of African missions.

True to its basic policy of cooperation, the LCC, like the NBC, estab-
lished significant connections for the furtherance of missionary work in
Africa. In 1900 the LCC effected an agreement with the American Baptist
Missionary Union to support mutually the Reverend Clinton C. Boone and
his wife, Eva Coles Boone (daughter of Lucy and the late John Coles), in
Central Africa. The LCC and the NBC three years after their reconciliation
(1908) arranged terms to cosponsor E. D. Murff. Murff was an indigenous
African returning to southern Africa after a period of study in the U.S. The
LCC Baptists believed that they had a commission—as all Christians did—
to spread Christianity to all parts of the non-Christian world. Because
"conditions prevented" them from actively engaging in mission work in
other foreign fields, they would lend financial support to the cause by supporting those Baptist organizations that were involved in those lands. Consequently, the LCC in 1908 agreed to contribute to the mission of the NBC
in South America.[19] Consistent with ecumenical trends among Christians
at the time and because of their own understanding of the faith, these black
Baptists, both in the LCC and the NBC, refused to allow their deeply held
commitment to uplift Africa to separate them from a sense of the universal
message of the gospel. Indeed, black Baptists during this period constantly
managed to contribute at least a small portion from their meager resources
for mission work in non-African fields.

As with the NBC, women individually and collectively played a major
role in fostering foreign missions during this period. As early as 1899, only
two years after the founding of the LCC, a movement was undertaken to
promote a women's auxiliary to the Lott Carey Convention (LCC-W). On
21 August women attending the LCC annual session met in a "Woman's

---

[19]Annual Minutes, LCC, 1908, 31-33.

Meeting'' and discussed the necessity of women having specific responsibility for some phase of foreign mission work. Miss C. B. Person of North
Carolina cited the significant financial contributions of women in black
Baptist congregations and asserted that women could be of valuable assistance to the foreign mission cause. Person encouraged women to form organizations for foreign missions in each of their churches.[20]

Mrs. C. S. Brown, wife of the president of the LCC and also a North
Carolinian, called attention to the number of people in foreign places who
had ''no churches or preachers or missionaries such as we have to dispel
darkness and ignorance.'' Though every Baptist could not become a missionary, he or she could offer financial assistance for the cause. At this
meeting a sum of $20 was collected for the assistance of Mrs. Mamie
Branton Tule, a missionary to South Africa.[21] Perhaps the most significant
event of the meeting was the decision to form a committee that would consider the merit of organizing a women's auxiliary group. The committee
included four men and three women, among them Mrs. P. G. Shepard and
Mrs. C. S. Brown of North Carolina.[22]

The LCC-W basically reflected the heavy Southern, and particularly
Southeastern, influence characteristic of the LCC as a whole. For example, of the twenty delegates to the 1903 session of the LCC-W, fifteen were
from Virginia and North Carolina.[23] Though non-Southeasterners often held
the presidency during this period, the 1913 minutes demonstrate that
Southeasterners often predominated in the LCC-W as well as the LCC
general organization. In that year three of the five officers were citizens of
North Carolina and Virginia.[24]

The Women's Auxiliary formed at the 1900 session of the LCC in Al-
exandria, Virginia, proved to be a vital participant in the execution of African missions. For example, the 1909 minutes of the LCC credit the LCC-W
for contributing substantially toward the travel expenses incurred by the

[20]Ibid., 1899, 16.

[21]Ibid., 17-18.

[22]Ibid., 17.

[23]Ibid., 1903, 44.

[24]Ibid., 1913, 47.

Reverend W. H. and Mrs. Cora P. Thomas's departure to Liberia. Women were also active in African mission movements on the state level. For example, the Women's Auxiliary of the Baptist Educational and Missionary Convention of North Carolina pledged to provide the full salary of Mrs. Thomas during her stay in Africa. In short, the minutes of the LCC (as well as the NBC) are replete with praise for the Baptist women's support of African missions.[25]

## HOME MISSION DEPARTMENT

From the very beginning of the LCC, there were those who sought to make the LCC both a home- and foreign-mission society. For example, distinguished North Carolinian clergyman J. A. Whitted, acting as temporary moderator at the inaugural session of the LCC in 1897, stated that North Carolina Baptists had extended invitations to the Baptists assembled for the express purpose of forming a convention embracing both realms of religious concerns. But minutes of the assembly indicate that it focused exclusively on the aspects of foreign mission work.[26]

In 1902 the convention officially became the Lott Carey Baptist Home and Foreign Mission Convention of the United States. This change emerged as a result of persistent pleadings from a number "of the wisest and most loyal brethren of our Convention." Advocates for a home mission department believed that the establishment of such a branch would increase the LCC membership. Many clergymen and churches, though in full sympathy with the principles of the LCC, withheld their support from the organization because they considered the convention "incomplete without a Home Mission Department." Also, many Baptists felt that Baptist-supported schools that shared in the cooperation theology of the LCC would have a closer association with the convention by means of a home missions department.[27]

This development in an organization founded with the primary, explicit purpose of conducting a foreign mission program represents a fas-

[25]Ibid., 1909, 28.
[26]Ibid., Organizational Meeting, 1897, 19-20; bound with Annual Minutes, LCC, 1898.
[27]Ibid., 1902, 21.

cinating turn of events in the history of black Baptists. In the past African mission supporters had urged their fellow Baptists to understand the intimate connection between domestic mission and foreign mission work. They had insisted on the "reflex influence" that African evangelization would have on the vitality and growth of churches in the U.S. Now domestic mission advocates were posing similar arguments relative to that work. Both of these historical circumstances demonstrate the powerful tradition in black Christian history that refused to allow a too-sharp dichotomy between domestic missions on the one hand and African missions on the other.

## FOCUS ON WEST AFRICA

Notwithstanding this change, the major focus of the convention remained on the cause of foreign missions, particularly African missions. As C. S. Brown stated in his annual address in September 1908: "Our chief desire is to see the great Negro people thoroughly united in their efforts to save Africa. And, while we favor other organized adventures for denominational good, yet the sole and dominant purpose of this organization is the spread of the gospel in heathen lands."[28]

Despite the strong emphasis that LCC Baptists placed upon the universality of the gospel message and the divine commission to spread the gospel to all non-Christian peoples, the attention of black LCC Baptists remained on Africa for a number of reasons. According to the LCC corresponding secretary, William M. Alexander of Maryland, there were five reasons why black Baptists had "special obligations" to Africa: (1) its huge size, (2) a great neglect of Africa by Christian missionary societies, (3) the legacy of Lott Carey and other black American Baptists who gave their lives for the redemption of the mother continent, (4) the appeals of many converted Africans for help from their African kin in the U.S., (5) and the common destiny of Africans and Afro-Americans[29] (a point discussed in greater detail in part three). In addition, the paucity of financial resources for both the LCC and the NBC served to limit their missionary activities to Africa. Also, there was a tendency among white missionary organiza-

---

[28]Ibid., 1908, 38.
[29]Ibid., 1899, 36-37.

tions to support black missionaries only when they served at mission stations in Africa.

By 1903, six years after the organization of the LCC, all four of its missionaries were stationed in Africa: one in Liberia, two in the Congo, and one in southern Africa.[30] Yet unlike the NBC, the LCC by 1915 had placed most of its missionary personnel in West Africa, primarily in Liberia. Liberia especially held major sway in the minds of many LCC Baptists—again including, most notably, C. S. Brown. In 1907 Brown described the African republic as "the most inviting field" because of the political influence of Baptists in that country. The Liberian Baptist Association included "old established and well organized churches" within its ranks. He stated that the LCC could establish cooperative agreements with these bodies and pursue more aggressive mission work among interior, non-Christian ethnic groups. Also, the LCC had the advantage in Liberia of building upon the foundation laid by James O. Hayes, a North Carolina missionary stationed in Africa for twenty years and who at that time was connected with the LCC.[31]

Brown's heavy and practical emphasis upon the Liberian field for missionary endeavors appears to have caused concern on the part of other members of the convention who were still dedicated to the theological, racial, and perhaps overly ambitious aim of spreading the Christian message throughout the entire continent. In 1908 the LCC president made a number of suggestions for improving mission work. Among those was the recommendation: "Strengthen our work in Liberia and concentrate our efforts mainly there." The Committee on the President's Report gave Brown high praise. But in responding to the president's suggestion relative to Liberia, the committee stated that, when feasible, the work "should be increased, but not to the exclusion of other portions of Africa." The committee agreed with Brown on filling the vacancy in Central Africa caused by the death of Mrs. Boone in 1902 and Mr. Boone's return to the U.S. in 1906 by sending the LCC's newest missionaries, the Reverend W. H. Thomas and Miss Cora Pair, to that field.[32]

---

[30]Ibid., 1903, 27.

[31]Ibid., 1907, 30.

[32]Ibid., 1908, 42-44.

In 1913 Brown again called upon the convention to give special consideration to Liberia. The committee agreed with most of his recommendations, including the suggestions to enlarge and to make permanent Liberian mission work and to establish a mission station in the black nation of Haiti. Brown's suggestion to send a foreign mission commissioner to Liberia or elect "a foreign secretary for the supervision of the field work of the missionaries" was rejected by the committee. According to the committee, limited financial resources precluded such a venture. The committee, therefore, deferred the matter until the following session of the LCC.[33]

## LCC MISSIONARIES IN WEST AFRICA

Brown and the committee appear to have been contending merely over a matter of principle. In practical terms, most of the American-born LCC foreign missionaries were stationed in Liberia by the end of 1915. The missionaries who served in the Liberian field were: James O. and Mrs. Hayes, W. H. and Cora A. (Pair) Thomas, G. D. Gayles, and C. C. Boone. All of these missionaries hailed from the South (and North Carolina!) except G. D. Gayles of Baltimore, Maryland.

After spending two years laying the groundwork for its missionary labors in West Africa, the LCC in 1899 arranged to support James O. Hayes. Hayes (mentioned previously) had been commissioned by the black Baptists of North Carolina about twenty years earlier. In 1899 the North Carolina Baptists agreed to support their missionary through the Executive Board of the LCC.[34] Although Hayes at this time was also under appointment of the NBC, this group had no quarrel with the LCC's support of him. Jordan, the corresponding secretary for the NBC Foreign Mission Board, assured him by letter that the NBC would not object to this collateral appointment by the LCC. Hayes, for his part, gladly accepted the LCC appointment while making clear that he did so from a simple desire to obtain additional financial assistance for his missionary endeavors. He did not wish to sow seeds of conflict between the LCC and the NBC.[35] Available evi-

---

[33]Ibid., 1913, 44-45.

[34]Ibid., 1899, 34.

[35]Ibid.

dence suggests that this arrangement caused no strife between the two conventions. It is an indication of nobility on the part of black Baptists that during the height of the controversy between the LCC and the NBC, they placed the financial needs of a missionary in the field above their theological and organizational disputes.

The LCC appointed a missionary who after a twenty-year service in Liberia had acquired a position of honor and prominence among Americo-Liberians. Hayes in the early 1900s pastored a church in Brewerville to which an industrial school was attached for the training of Liberian young people. The LCC minutes made note that Mrs. Hayes assisted her husband in the execution of mission work.[36] But Hayes was also active outside his local congregation. He served as a member of the Liberia Baptist Association and, according to the 1909 proceedings of the LCC, repeatedly served as moderator (an elective office) of this group.[37] By 1914 Hayes, respected in both the religious and political circles of Liberia, had to restrict his work because of old age.[38]

In 1908 the LCC appointed three new missionaries for service in Africa. The Reverend G. D. Gayles of Baltimore was to be transported to his station in Liberia at the expense of the Baptists of his home city. Both Cora A. Pair and the Reverend W. H. Thomas (the future Mr. and Mrs. Thomas) hailed from North Carolina. The Woman's Baptist Missionary Convention in that state pledged to pay both the salary and the transportation expenses of Miss Pair,[39] an indication of the increased assertiveness of women as a group in many Christian denominations during this period. W. H. and Cora Thomas originally sailed to Liberia with the understanding that they would be reassigned to the Congo when expedient. Yet once in Liberia, the Thomases decided to remain, believing that duty demanded their staying in the field that had so long been overlooked in American Baptist missionary circles. The Reverend Thomas took the position of preacher to the in-

---

[36]Ibid., 1902, 24; 1909, 25.

[37]Ibid., 1909, 25.

[38]Report of the Corresponding Secretary of the LCC, 1914, 7-8; printed separately from the Annual Minutes.

[39]Annual Minutes, LCC, 1908, 36.

digenous peoples while Mrs. Thomas taught in the industrial school.[40] This
was an arrangement that often obtained with married couples, black and
white, in the mission field.

In the mission field missionaries served as a vital support group for each
other. For example, when the Thomases arrived in Liberia, they had the
pleasure of being received by Hayes and Dr. Ernest Lyons, a native-born
West Indian and the United States minister to Liberia. When G. D. Gayles
sailed six months later (7 May 1909), he found the Hayes and Thomases
waiting to receive him in Brewerville.[41] All four of these missionaries by
1914 were stationed in Brewerville. Such interaction serves as one explanation for the attractiveness of Liberia as a mission field.

But all LCC missionaries did not venture to Liberia or other parts of
West Africa. C. C. and Eva Boone first went to Central Africa rather than
West Africa under the cooperative agreement between the LCC and the
predominantly white American Baptist Missionary Union in 1900. Boone
graduated from Virginia Union University in 1900 and was highly es-
teemed by his pastor, the renowned C. S. Brown. Eva Boone graduated
from Hartshorn Memorial College and also was highly praised among
Baptist church people.[42] Three of the most prominent Southern black clergymen active in the foreign mission movement—Anthony Binga, Jr., J. A.
Whitted, and C. S. Brown—assisted the corresponding secretary of the
LCC, William Alexander, in arranging terms of cooperation between the
Baptist Missionary Union and the LCC for the Boones's departure to Africa. These men also joined the couple in canvassing the South for funds.
Brown and Whitted aided them in North Carolina and Virginia, while Binga
assisted the two missionary designees in the historically significant city of
Richmond.[43] But the LCC also sought funds outside the South. For example, in New York City Baptists gathered in the historic Abyssinian Baptist Church, collected $53.72, and pledged their continued assistance in the
evangelization of Africa.[44]

---

[40]Ibid., 1909, 25-26.

[41]Ibid.

[42]Ibid., 1900, 35.

[43]Ibid., 1901, 37-38.

[44]Ibid., 38.

In 1906 C. C. Boone, now a widower, returned to the U.S. after five years of service in Africa. Impressed with the medical needs of the peoples on the continent, he took a course in medicine at the Baptist-supported Shaw University in Raleigh, North Carolina. According to the 1908 LCC proceedings, the missionary wished "to be able to minister to the bodies as well as the souls of the people" and planned to return to Africa. During his stay in the U.S., Boone completed *The Congo as I Saw It,* in which the missionary set forth his impressions on the spiritual state, customs, and needs of peoples in the Congo. The LCC hoped that a huge circulation of the book would aid financially in the quest to promote African missions.[45]

When Boone returned to Africa in 1913, however, he went to Liberia rather than the Congo. Whether this change of mission stations was because of cooperation problems with the white American Baptist Missionary Union, the belief that he was needed more in Liberia than the Congo, or some other reason (possibly it was a combination of the above) is not clear. But rather than remain in Brewerville where the other Afro-American Baptist missionaries were, he sought permission to concentrate his efforts among the Americo-Liberians instead of the indigenous peoples. According to Boone, the Americo-Liberians had warmly welcomed him. He had had occasion to visit the Providence Baptist Association, the Sunday school convention, and the "Union Meeting." In his opinion, these peoples wished to do good, but were hampered by circumstances.[46] His decision was not motivated by unconcern for the indigenous peoples. Boone wanted to direct his energies toward Americo-Liberians because he believed that such efforts would have a concomitant benefit for the indigenous peoples. According to him, Americo-Liberians, if converted and sufficiently nourished in the Christian faith, would provide examples and so win the indigenous peoples to the faith.[47]

## SOUTHERN AFRICA

Besides Liberia and Central Africa, the other major geographical area of missionary concern for the LCC during the period 1900–1915 was

---

[45]Ibid., 1908, 34-35.

[46]Report of the Corresponding Secretary of the LCC, 1914, 12-13.

[47]Ibid.

southern Africa. In 1899 the LCC reported that it supported the former NBC missionary R. A. Jackson at Cape Town. But the following year the convention announced that it had dropped the assistance for the missionary at his request. No reason was given for Jackson's action.[48]

A convert of Jackson, John Tule, an indigenous South African, and his wife, Mrs. Mamie Branton Tule, accepted appointment by the LCC Executive Board on 30 March 1900. It appears that the conflict between the NBC and the LCC had grown to the extent that, unlike one year earlier, the two conventions were unwilling to support the same missionary. On the other hand, perhaps the LCC's hesitancy to support the Tules derived from a concern about duplicating financial outlays to missionaries. At any rate, Mrs. Tule, a graduate of Shaw University, was instrumental in securing their appointments only after she convinced the LCC that they had resigned from the employment of the NBC Foreign Mission Board.[49] In 1905 the LCC commissioned another South African, F. B. Mdodona, for service in that part of Africa.[50] As mentioned earlier, the LCC agreed to cooperate with the NBC in 1908 to support E. D. Murff.[51] Predominant LCC foreign mission interest, notwithstanding my comments about southern Africa, remained focused on West Africa.

## FINANCIAL DIFFICULTIES

For all of the successes and sincere efforts, both the NBC and LCC faced financial difficulties during this era. True, financial support for missions never plummeted to a low level comparable to that of the Foreign Mission Convention in the early 1880s. Nevertheless, the black Baptist church people generally had severely limited monetary means, and this financial status was reflected in their contributions to foreign missions. Consequently, the activities of African missionaries had to be drastically circumscribed.

---

[48]Ibid., 1900, 33.

[49]Ibid., 34-35.

[50]*A History of the Lott Carey District Baptist Foreign Mission Convention, 1897–1907,* p. 8. Supplement to the collection of Annual Minutes of the LCC, located in the papers of the American Baptist Historical Society, Rochester, New York.

[51]Annual Minutes, LCC, 1908, 31.

In 1909 Brown called attention to the low amount of financial support for African missions. Whether the limited financial support for missions was because of ignorance or the indebtedness occasioned by a desire for expensive and unnecessary construction work on the local churches, the black American minister, he claimed, had to take complete responsibility as the leader of his people. According to Brown's analysis, three major hindrances prevented greater effectiveness in foreign mission work: (1) ignorance and lack of real concern for the spiritual state of non-Christians, (2) a failure to realize that African missionaries carried responsibility equal to that of local ministers, (3) and dissension within local churches and other Baptist bodies that robbed the mission movement of much of its support.[52]

Of course, there were accomplishments for which the organization could be proud. The LCC corresponding secretary in his 1914 report extolled the work of the convention. In its seventeen-year history, the convention collected $40,000 for purposes of foreign missions. True to the inaugural goals of the LCC, the convention sought to be efficient in its work by making certain that seventy-five percent of all those funds collected went directly to missionaries for transportation, salaries, and expenses. The secretary noted that ten missionaries had been commissioned for African work and that they had baptized 3,500 converts.[53]

Yet C. S. Brown, a year earlier in his annual address, had provided a very thorough if rather harsh critique of the African mission enterprise. The LCC leader appears to have directed his attention to all black Baptists, not only those of the LCC, when he expressed "shame" at the failures of black American Baptists. Though black Baptists had been involved in the mission enterprise for forty years "of service and experience," the wonderful intellectual and financial advancements of the Baptists could not conceal that the African mission program was also "vague and indefinite—little more than a comity on missions."[54] He continued to point out the faults of the enterprise and to urge a new, improved systematic approach to the endeavor.[55]

---

[52]Ibid., 1909, 31-32.

[53]Report of the Corresponding Secretary of the LCC, 1914, 15.

[54]Annual Minutes, LCC, 1913, 40.

[55]Ibid.

## CONCLUSION

This chapter completes my description of the origins of the black Baptists' organization of African mission work. It is noteworthy that both the LCC and the NBC, the two major black Baptist bodies dedicated to the evangelization of the mother continent, continued to pursue their goal in an aggressive manner during the 1895–1915 period. Despite their inability to maintain or effect organic union between them, their commitment to carry the gospel to Africa as a means of achieving spiritual and material uplift of their African kin united them, at least in spirit. The dedication to African evangelization survived the tensions, the acrimony, and the divisions and played a significant role in the organizations of black American Baptists for decades beyond the period outlined in this study.

Actually, the separation of the LCC and the NBC Baptists may have contributed to broadening Afro-American Baptists' contact with African peoples. Prior to the split, the overwhelming mission activities of these Baptists had been in West Africa, notably Liberia and to a significantly lesser degree, Nigeria. There had, of course, been missionaries assigned to Central Africa, especially by the Baptist General Association of Western States and Territories. But during the late 1890s and the early 1900s Afro-American Baptists began to focus their attention on southern Africa. This new trend in Baptist circles on one hand represented a move by Afro-American Christians in general to become more active in this area. It is still interesting to note, however, that the LCC concentrated its efforts in West Africa, especially Liberia, while the NBC operated mainly in southern Africa. The effect was to solidify black Baptist mission stations in both areas. During the 1880–1915 period Afro-American Baptists organized their mission movement to such an extent that they progressed beyond Liberia to other portions of "black" Africa—that is, Central and southern Africa.

But the value of this study lies not only in commenting upon the number of African converts, churches built, or missionaries commissioned. This work has focused upon the *American* dimension of this movement, observing it as a phenomenon in black religious history rather than a strict accounting of missionary successes and failures in the field. C. S. Brown, the LCC president, was correct to chastise black Baptists for not maximizing their potentials. But given the factors of economics, the political climate of the times, the concentration on problems relating to organization and development of black denominations, and the demands that the domestic scene placed upon the energies and resources of black church people, the African missionary movement may be judged a reasonable success.

Besides, an even more significant consideration for this study—and for many of us interested in American and Afro-American general and religious history—is the idea permeating this movement: that African missionary work was divinely ordained for black Christians to uplift their African kin spiritually and materially. This motivation indicates a lot about the images that Afro-Americans had of themselves and African peoples.

**PART 3**

# MISSION IDEOLOGY, 1880–1915

# CHAPTER 6

# MISSION IDEOLOGY, 1880–1915

In previous chapters I have outlined the origins and development of the African mission program among Afro-American Baptists, concentrating upon black Baptists in the South during this period. Those chapters revealed how the African mission sentiment, which originated during the years of enslavement, crystallized into independent state conventions, the Baptist Foreign Mission Convention, the National Baptist Convention, and the Lott Carey Baptist Convention. Primarily focusing upon organizational development, I have demonstrated continually the underlying basic motive of these African mission supporters: their endeavor to spread the Christian gospel to their African kin in the belief that it would serve to enlighten the indigenous peoples and thus advance them spiritually and materially.

The purpose of this chapter is to examine in greater detail the religious thinking and ideas of black Baptists relative to four crucial areas of concern: (1) African religions, cultures, and customs; (2) the presence of European colonialism and the response of black Baptist mission supporters; (3) "practical Christianity" and its relationship to the effort to promote Westernized education in the mission fields; and (4) the continuing significance of Liberia as an outpost of "Christian civilization" for many mission supporters.

The reader will observe several overall conclusions with reference to these broad areas of concern. First, black Baptists agreed with most American Christians of that period that African societies and religions were decidedly inferior to Christianity and Western culture and had very few, if any, meaningful contributions to make to understanding, applying, or critiquing the latter two. Though an ardent sympathizer of overseas missions, I wonder if these mission supporters could have demonstrated greater sympathy with and understanding of positive features of African religions and cultures.

Second, there was a curious silence in the missionary letters, minutes, and reports of black Baptists concerning the ethics of the system of colonialism in Africa during most of this period. Since Afro-American Baptists were ex-slaves or descendants of former slaves and were themselves the victims of increasingly reactionary political pressure in the South, such a silence appears strange. Third, despite the above observations, these mission supporters demonstrated a sense of racial identification with the conditions and destiny of indigenous Africans that their white counterparts could not, for obvious reasons, match. Fourth, and related to the third point, in expounding their theology of "practical Christianity" and their philosophy of the nature and role of education relative to African missions, black Baptists demonstrated that they pursued the evangelization of Africa as a means to improve the material conditions of Africans in a more vigorous manner than their white counterparts.

## AFRICAN RELIGIONS

In line with the general missionary attitudes of the time, black Baptists approached the mission enterprise with an overall negative appraisal of the African traditional religions and Islam. Of course, persons who seek to convert persons from one religion to another usually operate from one of the following bases. (1) The religion to be introduced is the one and only means to salvation or pleasing God. All other religions are idolatrous, heathenistic, and superstitious at worst and lacking certain crucial elements at best. (2) The religion to be introduced is superior to all other religions or at least the ones available to the target group of people. According to this line of reasoning, other religions might have many good and noble elements and even be means to gain salvation if pursued with sincerity and conviction. The appeal of the religion being introduced is its superior values. During the long history of Christianity, the first line of theological thought has been clearly preeminent.

Understandably, most black and white Baptists and other Christians viewed the traditional religions of Africa in the first manner. Actually, African religions were considered in the most negative light. Baptists found little of redeemable value in them. Islam, also encountered by many missionaries in Africa, has many common religious ideas with Christianity,

such as a strong emphasis upon monotheism and a recognition of many of
the central ideas and personalities of the Judeo-Christian tradition. But it
too was rejected as a false religion, a position perfectly consistent with
mainstream Christian traditions and history. In addition, Baptists, black
and white, during this period made little, if any, distinction among the various religions they encountered. On one hand, this position may illustrate
the commonalities among the indigenous religions. On the other hand, this
tendency to lump all religions into one category bespeaks unconcern for
the value of the traditional religions.

John J. Coles, one of the first missionaries commissioned by the Baptist Foreign Mission Convention in the 1880s, exemplifies the negative
image that both African traditional religion and Islam held in the minds of
black Baptists. Coles's farewell address, scheduled for the day of his departure for Liberia, outlined his mission as one to free the continent "from
ignorance, superstition, nakedness, domestic slavery, human sacrifices,
idols, cannibalism, and a million other vices which now prey upon our
heathen brothers."[1] He did note that all African peoples whom he had encountered believed in one Supreme Being. But other than viewing this idea
as an effective avenue to introduce Africans to the monotheism of Christianity, the missionary seemingly found little of substantial worth in this
theological tenet of African religion. Indeed, the missionary maintained
that the adherents of the traditional religions as well as the devotees of Islam practiced false worship.[2]

Some missionaries delighted at the presence of Islam in Africa because
they considered it a religion that would pave the way for the acceptance of
Christianity, given its greater affinity with the ideas and traditions of
Christianity than with African religions. Coles's analysis of the value of
Islam, however, appears to be more negative. He wrote that Islamic missionaries were persuading the people to follow "the religion of the False
Prophet." Most Christians—black and white, Baptists and non-Baptists—
would have agreed with this characterization of Islam. But Coles went fur-
ther and rejected the notion that the presence of Islam prepared the people

---

[1]John J. Coles, *Africa in Brief* (New York: Freeman Steam Printing Establishment, 1886)
xii.

[2]Ibid., 11.

to accept Christianity. Instead, he asserted, this religion had the detrimental effect of actually leading the people farther from the redemption of Jesus "than heathenism" or indigenous African religions.[3] Perhaps he took this position because he thought the similarities between Islam and Christianity made it much more difficult for the missionaries to draw a sharp distinction between the two. Indeed, Coles at one point wrote that he battled daily with Islamic followers, who he described as "the opposers of Christianity."[4]

Finally, Coles believed, Christian missionaries faced a clear-cut struggle between good and evil in their efforts to advance the Christian religion. He believed that his racial family in Africa were "as servants and soldiers for hell." The battle lines between Christianity and traditional African religion were quite clearly defined; he permitted no points of compromise, conciliation, or mutual sharing and borrowing between the two groups.[5] In brief, he saw little that Christians could learn about God and religion from African peoples.

Nearly twenty years later, black Baptists continued to embrace similar ideas about African religions. Some missionaries basically shared Coles's analysis of Islam, but evidenced a significantly higher measure of respect and appreciation for the sincerity and devotion of Moslems in African societies. Harrison N. Bouey, an NBC missionary, demonstrated such in a letter from Cape Mount, Liberia, dated 29 June 1902. According to Bouey, a group of influential Moslem leaders held a ceremony blessing him for his preaching against the importation of alcoholic beverages into the territory. He felt awkward at the service because he did not subscribe to the tenets of Islam and, as a consequence, did not feel comfortable with their commending him to Allah. Notwithstanding, he sensed an obligation to honor "their reverence."[6]

Nevertheless, Bouey agreed with his fellow Baptists and the predominant opinion among European and American mission-minded people that devotees of either Islam or traditional African faiths were people to be pitied because they did not claim the centrality of Jesus Christ for their reli-

---

[3]Ibid., 38.
[4]Ibid., 47.
[5]Ibid., 58.
[6]*The Mission Herald* 8 (July 1902): 2.

gious life: "But, brethren these poor, blind people are led into a Christless devotion. If you could only see Mohammedanism [Islam] on the one side and that miserable alligatorism on the other, you would thank God for what you have done, and ask him to do more for Foreign Missions."[7]

It is true that missionaries often exaggerated situations in order to draw greater support for the mission cause. Thus, we are safe in assuming that they tended to point out only what they and most Christians considered to be negative aspects. We simply do not know whether missionaries held a more balanced attitude toward African religious systems than they manifested in writings and speeches. It should be reiterated, however, that the idea that Christians should conduct dialogue with adherents of other religions rather than convert them is a fairly recent one. Basic Christian traditions in the time period under study called for the conversion of all non-Christian peoples to the faith. Missionaries, before leaving for their field of operation, had been so conditioned. Black Baptist missionaries, like other Christian missionaries, shared this theology and outlook. All non-Christians were lost and in need of Christianity; and Africans, they generally thought, were among the most "lost" people in the world. As C. S. Brown, president of the LCC, said concerning Africa in 1909: "Here heathenism finds its rankest growth; here superstition finds its most devout followers; here Mohammedanism has riveted its strongest bonds."[8]

## CULTURES AND CUSTOMS

Black Baptists, like most Christians, also expressed disdain for African cultures and customs. Afro-American Baptists, like most European and American missionaries, very seldom noted any crucial differentiation among the cultures or religions of African peoples during this period. To the extent that they perceived differences among the various sections and ethnic groups in Africa, they considered those variations to be of minor relevance. In the minutes and reports of black Baptist groups—at national, regional, or state levels—the *whole* of Africa was seen as void of adequate and commendable civilization and religion. The emphasis seldom, if ever,

---

[7]Ibid.

[8]Annual Minutes, LCC, 1909, 30.

fell upon a certain section of Africa as requiring cultural or religious redemption to the exclusion of other sections.

Black Baptists occasionally pointed to certain aspects of African societies that commanded their admiration: for example, the physical beauty
of the inhabitants, the hospitality of the local people,[9] or the firmness of
the indigenous legal systems.[10] Yet, the overall evaluation was a negative
one. Coles applied the terms *heathen* and *savage* to the cultural as well as
the religious sphere of African societies. One of the most immediate and
distressing things that greeted Coles upon his arrival in Liberia was the
practical nakedness of the people. He viewed traditional family life in Africa with dismay, dissatisfied with the respective roles of African men and
women with whom he lived and worked. Most of the manual work and
actual subsistence for the family were provided by women.[11] Disparag-
ingly, he wrote, "Men are expected to do the mental labor, trade and carry
on wars. They make no provision for the family."[12]

Coles found it impossible to justify the African system of polygamy
that he encountered. Religiously speaking, he accepted the basic Christian
position that God approved only of monogamy. From a practical point of
view, he saw polygamy as one expression of the low regard he believed
African men had for African women. In a polygamous society, Coles wrote,
the number of wives that a man possessed usually indicated the degree of
his wealth.[13] Whereas some modern scholars of African cultures might take
a more sympathetic (though not necessarily approving) position vis-à-vis
the dowry system[14] that was an integral part of African family arrangement, Coles viewed the system much more negatively. He regarded it as
a manifestation of slavery, especially in light of his allegation that women

---

[9] Coles, *Africa,* 67-68, 96, 104.

[10] Ibid., 72; C. C. Boone, *Congo as I Saw It* (New York: J. J. Little and Ives Company,
1927) 31, 33.

[11] Coles, *Africa,* 33, 65.

[12] Ibid., 65.

[13] Ibid., 93.

[14] For a modern, more sympathetic critique of traditional African societies, see E. A.
Ayandele, *The Missionary Impact on Modern Nigeria, 1842-1914: A Political and Social
Analysis* (London: Longmans, Green and Co., 1966) 334-37.

performed the greater bulk of manual labor. He saw little ritual symbolism or worth in the practice and considered it merely the selling of a human being.[15]

Black Baptist missionaries, as members of Western culture, brought from the U.S. an egalitarian perspective on how society should be constructed. As such, they deprecated slavery and monarchy in African cultures. These Baptists were only a matter of decades removed from one of the most cruel and debilitating systems of bondage that any people had experienced. They made no distinctions between the slavery of Europeans and Americans and that of Africans. Whereas some scholars can correctly point out that African slaves were able to maintain their human dignity with little difficulty and had some measure and hope of social mobility, black Baptists paid little attention to these differences. Slavery was slavery; and like many other Christians, they hated it in all its forms and considered the system an evil to be extirpated as soon as possible. Furthermore, these missionaries, theories notwithstanding, had the opportunity to observe the harsher realities of African slavery in actual practice.

These negative portraits of African ways of life were practically universal and constant throughout the period under study. Coles represented the general sentiment of Afro-American Baptists regarding African cultures when he recorded the words of his missionary predecessor, William W. Colley: "Slavery and monarchy are twin babies of hell."[16] Along these lines, one of the strongest accusations W. F. Graham of Virginia launched against many black Baptist pastors was his 1908 declaration that they ruled their "churches like despots ruled their tribes in the jungles of Africa."[17] C. C. Boone, an LCC missionary to the Congo, also rated African cultures in an extremely negative fashion. Boone, like his father-in-law, J. J. Coles, was dismayed with the low status of women in the African household. In his opinion, they were mere "slaves" forced to perform "drudgery work." Society was completely segregated by sex in work, play, and school. From his observations, there appeared to be little real affection existing between

---

[15]Coles, *Africa*, 66.

[16]Ibid., 39.

[17]*National Baptist Union-Review* 9 (28 March 1908): 7.

husband and wife, parents and children, and among the children themselves. Boone characterized Congolese life as dry and routine.[18]

> There is not love existing between man and wife as we realize it in this
> country. Indeed love to them is scarcely known. You never see a man ca-
> ress his wife or the woman her child. They do not even play with their chil-
> dren. And it is seldom that you see the children playing. I mean the little
> children. Life seems to mean but little to them until they get twelve or
> fourteen years old.[19]

## COLONIALISM

These black Baptists' viewpoints toward African cultures and religions
can elicit quite a measure of discomfort in an age more tolerant of cultural
differences. Also, their stance on European colonialism in Africa may raise
puzzling and troubling queries concerning their fidelity to the principle of
material progress for African peoples. To a great extent there is a strange
silence on the part of these Baptists with regard to European ventures in
Africa. For the most part, black Baptists were not constant agitators against
the establishment or for the disestablishment of colonial governments in
Africa. As I already noted, this silence appears odd given the legacy of
brutal American slavery, the triumph of reactionaries in Southern state
governments, and the rising tide of fear and intimidation precipitated by
lynchings and other violent acts by white vigilantes during this period.

Some black Baptists, though, did offer impressive and stinging critiques of the colonial system. In less than a decade after the famous Berlin
Conference of European Powers, President J. J. Worlds of the Baptist Educational and Missionary Convention of North Carolina in 1890 demonstrated that the black Baptists in his state understood the selfish economic
motives of European merchants and entrepreneurs. In Worlds's opinion,
there was little interest on the part of these Europeans to lift Africans from
their "cradle of ignorance and superstitions." Rather, in search of the natural resources of the continent, the Europeans carried "clanking chains of
wretched slavery" to foist upon the indigenous peoples. Without provid-

---

[18]Boone, *Congo,* 36-37.
[19]Ibid., 37.

ing details, Worlds claimed that black Baptists in America, including those of North Carolina, could best prevent this enslavement of Africans and rescue them from their servitude by supporting the foreign mission enterprise[20]: "If we would strike those shackles from their feet, hands and souls, if we would dispel the long and dreary night of darkness, if we would cause her rivers to flow with peace and her lands from vale to mountains [to] rejoice in liberty, then go water the Rose of Sharon, already planted in her great valleys and skirting her mountain summits."[21] Thus, in accordance with classic black Christian thought of that period, the Baptist leader believed that the evangelization of Africa would assure both the political and spiritual redemption of Africa.

In 1907 C. S. Brown, a North Carolinian and president and spokesperson for the LCC, called for European governments to become more benevolent in their rule in Africa. Speaking before the 1907 Foreign Mission Institute meeting in Kentucky, Brown described King Leopold's and the Belgians' ventures in the Congo as greedy and atrocious. Brown did not omit Britain from his attacks. He queried, "And what shall we say of those sections where Anglo-Saxon supremacy has placed its iron [heel] and the natives have been crushed into submission?"[22] Europeans, argued Brown, should promote the material growth and progress of African peoples because whites had extracted riches from the continent in the form of "rubber, ivory, and diamonds" as well as by "blood money" and by means of the "iniquitous slave business." Europeans should offer an "atonement" to Africans and to God by collecting funds to erect schools and churches and by dispatching "teachers and preachers" to work in them.[23]

Brown apparently subscribed in part at least to the concept of "the white man's burden," the duty of white Europeans and Americans to elevate the darker peoples of the world. But whether because of a firm belief in this doctrine or because it was a diplomatic means to secure the support of whites, he claimed that the Europeans' debt to Africa went beyond repay-

---

[20]Annual Minutes, BEMC-NC, 1890, 8-9.

[21]Ibid.

[22]*The Mission Herald* 12 (June 1907): 1.

[23]Ibid.

ment for riches and human beings taken from the continent. He appealed
to a principle of just government, asserting that the aim of any government
should be the uplift of those subject to it, "to promote the material, social,
and moral welfare of the people." According to Brown, none of the European powers had made sufficient efforts to achieve these ends for African peoples.[24] He continued his criticism of colonial powers in 1909.

> And here [in Africa], in the name of christianity and civilization, the great
> governments are inflicting cruelties upon the natives seldom surpassed by
> barbarians in their most savage condition. In some cases the natives are
> brutalized into subjection and deprived by legal enactments to hope for the
> restoration of their manhood rights in the land of their nativity.[25]

Brown offered an interesting contrast between the behavior of the European and American governments in relation to Africa. Whereas European nations had struggled to engulf Liberia, the United States had
intervened to assure Liberia that it would retain at least a sizable amount
of its territorial integrity in the face of European encroachments in West
Africa. The United States, in addition, had taken a greater interest in the
evangelization of Africa.[26]

The Christian world was practically unanimous in its condemnation of the
Belgian atrocities in the Congo. The black Baptists of the LCC shared in the
expression of this outrage, as illustrated by C. S. Brown's statements above.
But in 1909 these Baptists advanced beyond humanitarian and religious de-
nunciation of the affair and expressed a sense of racial kinship and solidarity
with the peoples of the Congo. C. C. Boone of North Carolina, a former missionary to the Congo, sounded these themes in a resolution subsequently
adopted by the general convention. Boone's preamble and resolutions decried
the "indescribable cruelties" and "oppression" of the indigenous peoples by
the Belgian government. In asserting his concern for the political status of the
peoples, he stated: "We believe in freedom and equal rights for all, and . . .
the natives of [the] Congo are being deprived of their homes, their country

---

[24]Ibid.

[25]Annual Minutes, LCC, 1909, 30, 31.

[26]Ibid., 26.

and their lives."[27] He pledged the cooperation of the LCC "with the American and English Congo Reform Association in giving liberty to the Congo people." Finally, the former missionary displayed the strong sense of kinship that many Afro-Americans felt toward Africans when he stated that the LCC deplored "the wanton cruelties that are being committed against *our people.*"[28]

Black Baptists firmly believed in a divine and beneficent Providence who actively intervened in world affairs to rectify wrongs and punish the guilty. Some Afro-American Baptists viewed the outbreak of World War I as a punishment inflicted upon European powers, especially Belgium, for their sins of greed and brutality. For example, in the 14 November 1914 issue of *National Baptist Union-Review,* a writer interpreted the Germans' devastation of Belgium as just retribution for King Leopold's brutal reign in the Congo. The government, having reaped rewards through the sufferings of others, had to pay for its callousness and oppression.[29]

## THE SILENCE

As I have demonstrated, some black Baptists expressed clear and strong displeasure about European colonial rule in Africa, especially its harsher aspects. There is, nevertheless, an interesting silence in much of their organizational minutes with regard to the Europeans' activities on the continent and to the very principle of colonialism and its usurpation of African political and economic rights. There are a number of interpretations for this silence. First, some black Baptists might have condoned the establishment and maintenance of the colonial regime. This position would stand at apparent odds with American black Baptists' insistence on their own political and economic rights in the United States, especially given their powerful declarations of racial kinship with Africans. Yet Afro-American Baptists could have found means to circumvent this seeming contradiction in political ideology.

Lewis G. Jordan, the corresponding secretary to the Foreign Mission Board of the NBC throughout this period, was a prime example of an Afro-

[27]Ibid., 16.

[28]Ibid.

[29]*National Baptist Union-Review* 16 (14 November 1914).

American Baptist who on the one hand criticized the European colonial policies but concomitantly appeared to endorse the principle of the system. He sounded a rather surprising theme. He did not debate the rightness of the Europeans' course in partitioning Africa. That right was obvious. European rule served to obliterate barbarism, something from which all of humanity would benefit. Since Africans had been "unable to use" their lands to the greater benefit of humankind, Jordan reasoned, they had forfeited their right of possession. He wrote: "There is no question involved as to whether Europe had a right to carve up Africa; . . . it is for the good of the world that large sections of the world should not be left in barbarism; that no race has a right to territory which it is unable to use or which it uses in such a way as to prove detrimental to mankind."[30]

Yet if so-called civilized nations would rule over "barbarians," they must provide benevolent services for the latter group encompassing both the spiritual and physical spheres: just compensation for labor, promotion of material advancement, lifting the indigenous peoples to a higher moral and spiritual plane, and the "preservation of the race."[31] Thus, colonialism should benefit both Europeans and Africans and lead to self-rule for the latter. "In short, Europe has no business in Africa unless it is for the good of the Africans as well as for the good of the Europeans."[32]

Some reservations concerning this procolonial sentiment should be expressed. (1) It does not appear to be a universally held idea among black Baptists. Actually, I have found no evidence that any other black Baptist shared this philosophy. (2) Jordan's book *Pebbles from an African Beach* was published in 1918, three years after the last date of this study. But I have found no evidence to suggest that Jordan's view was a novel one for him. It is interesting that a person as learned about the peoples and lands of Africa and as involved in the work of African missions as Jordan should subscribe so completely to such a version of the white man's burden. It is significant that—notwithstanding his critique of the actual administration

---

[30]Lewis G. Jordan, *Pebbles from an African Beach* (Philadelphia: Lisle-Carey Press, 1918) 43.

[31]Ibid.

[32]Ibid.

of colonial authority for the material, political, and economic progress of Africans—a black American would endorse the principle of colonialism.

There is another category of possible reasons for this silence. It might have arisen out of the belief that European nations, "civilized and Christian," would in the long run serve the interests of African peoples. I have shown that the overwhelming majority of mission-minded black Baptists considered the religions and cultures of Africa markedly inferior to those of Europe and America. Indeed, throughout the period under study the republic of Liberia, founded as a colony to spread Western civilization and Christianity, was still considered one of the few outposts of these principles in Africa by most black Baptists. Logically, black Baptists would view European nations, regardless of the latter's own selfish political and economic motives, as harbingers of progress. Though the colonial experience might be one that few black people unqualifiably endorsed, yet it, like slavery, could work for the ultimate spiritual and material progress of the Africans. This argument carries considerable weight if we recall the basic premise of black and white Christians of the era that true religion (i.e., Christianity) ensured temporal as well as spiritual progress for societies and that, conversely, false religion (e.g., any African religion or Islam) contributed to backwardness.

Third, during the 1880s and 1890s many black Baptists perhaps considered the continent of Africa impenetrable. Since the fifteenth and sixteenth centuries Europeans had been in continuous contact with coastal Africa. But the Sahara desert, fear of the climate, and the active resistance of the indigenous peoples themselves had impeded penetration of the continent. With the discovery of the treatment for malaria and the persistence of the traders, missionaries, and explorers, the walls of resistance were eventually shattered in the latter half of the nineteenth century.

Yet as late as the early 1900s, C. C. Boone, the Lott Carey Convention missionary, voiced what was perhaps the opinion of many American Christians. He believed that foreign armies would never succeed in conquering Africa; only the Bible would. "In almost every case and in every section, the man of God has been the pioneer, enduring the hardships, opening up the country. In so many cases, he alone could do it with the gospel."[33] Thus, during these early years, many black Baptists perhaps remained silent about European intervention because they believed that complete occupation by the colonial powers would never materialize.

A fourth possible reason for the silence of many black Baptists concerning the colonial system could be a fear of theirs that the European governments would exact reprisals against their missionary activities. Black Baptist missionaries often referred to the discriminatory treatment they received from white authorities, particularly in southern Africa. Apparently colonial authorities throughout Africa feared that black missionaries would ignite rebellion among African peoples. C. S. Brown of the LCC, despite his criticisms of Belgian atrocities, reminded his fellow Baptists in 1909 that they had to be sensitive to the political arrangements in Africa: "We seem to forget that Africa has been parceled out among the leading civilized nations, and that they have regulations that must be complied with. . . . We cannot hope to succeed if our loyalty to the existing government is suspected."[34]

With an event in 1915 that involved the NBC, South African officials believed that their fears had been realized. In that year an African, John Chilembwe, led an ill-fated uprising of indigenous Africans in Nyasaland against the South African government. The government crushed the rebellion and confiscated NBC property. Obviously, this uprising had significant ramifications for the National Baptist Convention and black Christians in general relative to their missionary activities in Africa and especially southern Africa.

Besides the fact that Afro-American Baptists had officially commissioned Chilembwe as a missionary, they also had provided for his education at a black Baptist school, Virginia Theological Seminary and College in Lynchburg. Shepperson and Price believe that Chilembwe's political outlook and decision to revolt violently might have been influenced by his experience in Lynchburg. These authors note that he had had first-hand experience of segregation and discrimination in the Southeast and that he was exposed to the problack, "independent" thinking of such prominent black

---

[33]Boone, *Congo*, 89.

[34]Annual Minutes, LCC, 1909, 34.

Baptists as Charles S. Morris of New York and Lewis G. Jordan. Furthermore, Chilembwe had been acquainted with similar racial attitudes in the "independent" Virginia Theological Seminary and College.[35] This series of experiences either fashioned Chilembwe's political outlook or served as a vital reinforcement to a philosophy originating from his experience in southern Africa.

The official response of black American Baptists is instructive. For the most part, black Baptists merely noted the event and lamented Chilembwe's death and the loss of his missionary services. The official 1915 minutes of the NBC are most interesting of all, however. The minutes blamed Joseph Boothe for misleading Chilembwe. Boothe was an English missionary who established the Zambezi Industrial Mission in South Africa and had introduced Chilembwe to Jordan and other black Baptists in the U.S. In their minutes the NBC Baptists stated that Chilembwe had been misled by Boothe to commit "this awful, wicked blunder."[36]

The minutes noted that the missionaries had always been instructed to be loyal to the governments under which they worked, that they should seek the welfare and progress of indigenous peoples by means of the gospel, not by violence.[37] Whether because of a theological abhorrence to violence or because of practical strategy, black Baptists, despite criticizing colonialism, never advocated violence as a means of political change.

Fifth, black Baptists believed firmly in the inevitable progress of the black race. Staunch believers in the literal fulfillment of biblical prophecy, they approached the future with confidence that racism would be overshadowed by the fulfillment of Psalms 68:31, which they interpreted to guarantee the political progress as well as the spiritual redemption of the African race. Having full confidence in the abilities of blacks, these Baptists believed that the black race, like other races, could progress by means

---

[35]See George Shepperson and Thomas Price, *Independent African: John Chilembwe and the Origins, Setting and Significance of the Nyasaland Native Rising of 1915* (Edinburgh, Scotland: Edinburgh University Press, 1958) 93-108, 112-18.

[36]Annual Minutes, NBC, 1915, 112-13.

[37]Ibid., 113.

of education and Christianity.[38] The Emancipation Proclamation and the political privileges of Reconstruction had been concrete manifestations to them of God's active involvement in human history on behalf of the black race. Thus, even amid the setbacks of the post-Reconstruction era, black Christians still retained the belief that by hard work, the acquisition of education, and loyalty to God, the African race would eventually overcome any human obstacles such as colonialism and racism. Indeed, colonialism, as slavery, could under the Providence of God actually serve as a guarantee of the progress of the African race.

Finally, one could argue that colonialism as a system had not reached its organizational apex in Africa during the 1880–1915 period and, consequently, it would be inappropriate to expect Afro-American Baptists or any other group to have developed detailed critiques of the system. Two objections could be attached to this argument: (1) I am not seeking detailed, philosophically symmetrical critiques as such, but rather a greater amount of evidence stating black Baptists' abhorrence of the principle of colonialism. (2) Though colonialism had not reached the height of its power and influence on the Continent, the process of European occupation, partition, and domination had certainly begun by the 1890s. The records of the period do indicate, as demonstrated in this chapter, that black Baptists were informed about these developments. Therefore, this argument hardly suffices as a persuasive rationale for their silence concerning colonialism. Instead, we are on a much more solid foundation in basing the explanation for this silence upon one, several, or all of the previous five points.

## MODERATING INFLUENCES

As discussed above, black Baptists' acceptance, toleration, or silence concerning colonialism was moderated by their insistence that the material and economic well-being of the indigenous peoples should be recognized.

---

[38]For expositions on the relationship between formal education and the inevitable progress of the black race, see E. R. Carter, *Biographical Sketches of Our Pulpit* (1888; rpt., Chicago: Afro-American Press, 1969) 82-83; and W. Bishop Johnson, *The Scourging of a Race and Other Sermons and Addresses* (Washington: Beresford, Printer, 1904). For an example of black Baptists' belief that the destiny of blacks lay in the Providence of God if they would submit to the divine will, see especially Johnson's sermon ''The Scourging of a Race,'' 1-16.

There were also moderating influences to their strongly negative evaluations of traditional African religion and culture. Despite their negative appraisals of Africans, black Baptists felt a special identity with Africans that often eluded their white counterparts, Baptist and non-Baptist. The black Baptists were maintaining a theological tradition that antedated the black missionary Lott Carey.

Perhaps no black Baptist missionary better expressed disdain for the cultures and religions of Africa than John J. Coles. Nonetheless, even Coles exhibited a profound, sentimental attachment to and identification with the land and peoples of Africa. He considered Africa the natural homeland for all persons of African descent. According to Coles, blacks traveling to Asia and Europe sojourned as mere visitors. Even the U.S., which had been a haven for the oppressed Pilgrim fathers, was a country of race problems, with people clamoring for and clashing over a host of "rights." In Africa, the missionary claimed, blacks were not visitors nor did they have to struggle for rights;[39] they could find a refuge in the land of their ancestors.

If Africa was "home," then Coles and other black Baptist missionaries were bearing the gospel to their own racial family. As such, these missionaries exhibited a keen personal and racial attachment to the indigenous peoples that went beyond the aim of simply converting nonbelievers to Christianity. It is at this point that Afro-American and white Baptists differed the most in their appraisal of African peoples. White Baptists and other white Christians generally transferred their already acquired beliefs about the racial inferiority of black peoples to the mission fields. Afro-American Baptists and other black Christians would have difficulty subscribing to any doctrine of African inferiority without implicating themselves. Black Baptists agreed that African culture was "savage" and African religion was "heathen." But these terms were cultural and theological descriptions of the peoples, not biological claims. This "heathenism" and "savagery" did not obtain due to innate black inferiority, but because Africans had not been exposed to the blessings of Christianity and Western civilization. Once these were acquired, Africans would emerge from their "savagery" and develop a respectable civilization.

---

[39]Coles, *Africa,* xii-xiii.

Concomitantly, black Baptists had little difficulty forging an explicit, special identity with Africans that most white missionaries were unable to duplicate. The more these black missionaries encountered what they termed degradation and misery, the more they determined to rescue their peoples from such circumstances. For example, upon witnessing the mistreatment of a slave, Coles lamented, "Being identified with the African race, I thus exclaimed from mingled grief and pity: Oh, my people, my people, for them I can but sit here and weep."[40]

It might be argued that this identification with Africa originated from the simple fact that white American society and ecclesiastical structures had excluded blacks; therefore, they identified with African peoples by default. Yet the available data indicate that the predominant feeling of Afro-American Baptists was of racial solidarity. They also exhibited confidence that God intended to use the entire race for a great and noble purpose. Hence, there was not simply identification by default. In addition, it must be remembered that the African missionary enterprise represented an extension of the evangelistic activities of the black churches. Current critical studies and traditional apologetic literature underscore that the black churches were not merely imitating white churches as they patiently waited to be included within that fellowship. Instead, Afro-American Christians were creating an independent Christianity that, though doctrinally consonant with that of their white counterparts, had its own uniqueness and agenda. The same is true of the African missionary movement in particular.

This sense of racial solidarity and identification with African peoples reflected itself in and is explained by the belief of Afro-American Christians, including black Baptists, that they had a special, divine role to play in the redemption of Africa. These Baptists glorified the God who had rescued black American Christians from the "barbarism," "paganism," "cannibalism," and "savagery" of Africa. Like most black Christians, they insisted that God had disapproved the system of racial slavery that had been practiced in the United States. God had permitted such an atrocity so that blacks could acquire the blessings of Christianity and civilization. Since

---

[40]Ibid., 94-95.

God had emancipated them, black Christians had a special obligation to lift the clouds of heathenism and sin from the land of their fathers and so fulfill the prophecy of Psalms 68:31.

This concept, which began in the early days of slavery and was influenced and reinforced by white proponents of black colonization in Africa and of African missions, was a recurring theme in the missiology of the 1880–1915 period of black Baptist history. In 1889 the president of the Baptist Foreign Mission Convention, Emmanuel K. Love of Georgia, appealed to the Scriptures for a justification of the belief that God often saved or ministered to a given people through representatives of their own race. Love stated that Providence had an overriding purpose in allowing the vicious system of American slavery to provide for the salvation and civilization of the African continent by Afro-American Christians.[41] "There is no doubt in my mind that Africa is our field of operation, and that as Moses was sent to deliver his brethren, as the prophets were members of the race to whom they were sent, so I am convinced that God's purpose is to redeem Africa through us. . . . This work is ours by appointment, by inheritance, and by choice."[42] Similar sentiments were expressed on the state level. The president of the North Carolina Baptists stated in 1893, "Africa is our land, our mission field by the natural right of heredity; . . . shall we not fly to the rescue of our fatherland?"[43]

The leading cooperationist spokespersons of the LCC loudly disclaimed the proclamation of a "racial gospel" and "race religion." One might logically conclude, therefore, that they would be reticent to adopt a strong pro-African foreign mission policy and then to identify it with the racial struggles of Afro-Americans. Yet they, like their pro-independence opponents in the NBC, located most of their foreign mission stations in Africa. During the height of the debate between the cooperationists and the independents in 1899, the LCC Baptists listed several reasons for concentrating their work in Africa. One reason was the conviction that all descendants of Africa shared a common struggle and a common temporal

---

[41]Annual Minutes, BFMC, 1889, 7-8.

[42]Ibid., 7.

[43]Annual Minutes, BEMC-NC, 1893, 14.

destiny. "Africa is the mother country of the [Hamitic] race and her children in other lands will find it more than a struggle to rise to the highest standard of civilization so long as the great body of the race in Africa is wedded to idols."[44] This statement is indicative of a number of things. First, despite a tendency of black Baptists to tread lightly with regard to the issue of colonialism, they nevertheless saw a political connection between themselves and continental Africans. Second, belief in the special calling of black Christians to uplift Africa transcended the idea of "Negro Christianity." (The latter movement's supporters usually came from the ranks of the NBC.)

## PRACTICAL CHRISTIANITY

From the above comments, it could be correctly inferred that black Baptists advocated and attempted to evangelize African peoples on the basis of a "practical Christianity." These Baptists believed that any authentic, wholistic representation of the Christian faith involved an active concern for the physical, intellectual, and spiritual spheres of human life. They promoted the work of foreign missions on the assumption that material as well as spiritual blessings automatically flowed from a life of faith in Jesus. Like most mission-minded Christians, black Baptists believed that false worship and beliefs had both obscured the Africans' view of God and had caused African culture to become degraded. True Christianity would redeem Africans, religiously and culturally.

Dr. Albert W. Pegues during this period served as recording secretary of the LCC and dean of the Theological Department at Baptist-supported Shaw University. In 1915 while serving as the president of the Educational and Missionary Convention of North Carolina, Pegues in his annual address spoke of the significance of developing the intellect. The North Carolina African mission supporter and black Baptist biographer[45] also pointed out the connection many Baptists had observed between Christianity and civilization. "Chris-

---

[44]Annual Minutes, LCC, 1899, 36-37.

[45]For biographical sketches of Albert W. Pegues, consult C. L. Purce's introduction to Pegues's *Our Baptist Ministers and Schools* (Springfield MA: Wiley and Company, 1892) 9-15; and "Lott Carey District Baptist Foreign Mission Convention," a history of the convention and a supplement to the Annual Minutes, LCC, 1907, in the papers of the American Baptist Historical Society, Rochester, New York, p. 5.

tianity includes civilization. The Christian religion touches every phase of human life, every phase of human interest and activity."[46]

Many white Christians during this time period advocated the principle of a practical Christianity. But particularly in reference to the question of the political, economic, and material uplift and progress of the black race, their utterances did not always correspond to those of their black counterparts. Often black Baptists would remind white American Christians that their understanding and practice of Christianity fell far short of what they considered acceptable. C. T. Walker of Augusta, Georgia, spoke for the vast majority of black Baptists when he addressed the NBC in 1914: "The Negro Baptists believe in a practical Christianity; applied Christianity. We believe that America needs a practical Christianity which will settle the trouble that afflicts us if properly supported."[47] Black Baptists believed that black Christians would be major instruments of God to inaugurate a state of affairs in the world where color and race were insignificant in the conduct of human affairs. According to C. T. Walker: "I believe that the Negro will give to the world the highest type of the Christian religion that the world has ever had. . . . we believe that God knows but one race, and that is the human race."[48]

## EDUCATION

This attempt to apply and communicate a practical Christianity manifested itself in the philosophy of education held by African mission supporters. Education played a huge role in their pursuit of African missions not merely because they believed that a proper and continuing appropriation of Christianity required certain elementary academic skills such as reading. They also believed that it was a prerequisite for material progress for any people. During slavery education was denied to people in bondage because it represented a threat to the system. Partly because of this circumstance, black people generally—and black Christians in particular—viewed it then and later as a significant tool for their material advancement. This

[46]*National Baptist Union-Review* 16 (5 December 1914): 2.

[47]Annual Minutes, NBC, 1914, 66.

[48]Ibid.

viewpoint continued into the 1880–1915 period. For the prominent Georgia Baptist and writer E. R. Carter, education was one of those vital factors that guaranteed the progress of any people who possessed it.[49] As early as 1878 the Baptist State Convention of North Carolina described the significance of education in words that remained a credo of black Baptists through the 1880–1915 period: "Education is the only lever by which any race or people can be raised to a high standard of citizenship and civilization."[50] In 1888 the black Baptists of Florida joined in extolling the value of education for the material advancement of the race. "One of the most vital subjects connected with the progress and development of our denomination and race is the subject of education."[51]

When black Baptists referred to education, they meant formal, Western education. But more comprehensively, education included the following features: (1) the intellectual or liberal arts; (2) a moral or spiritual aspect; (3) an emphasis upon benevolent concern, especially as related to the uplift of the black race; (4) and the industrial, or vocational, aspect. The Virginia Baptist State Convention (VBSC) minutes of 1880 illustrate this multifaceted understanding of education. According to the Committee on Education, true education encompassed physical education, which trained the body; intellectual education, which developed the mental faculties; and moral education, which cultivated the proper spiritual sentiments and taught people to live in peace with one another.[52]

Another significant component of education in the minds of black Baptists was the "industrial" segment. Industrial education equipped students with manual skills such as mechanics, bricklaying, cooking, carpentry, and sewing. Booker T. Washington delivered his monumental Atlanta Exposition Address in 1895, counseling blacks to accommodate themselves to the dominance of whites in the political sphere and extolling the value of industrial education for blacks. But even prior to this event, black Baptists referred frequently to a perceived need for industrial education for blacks.

[49]See Carter, *Biographical Sketches,* n. 38.

[50]Annual Minutes, Baptist State Convention of North Carolina (BSC-NC), 1878, 13-14.

[51]Annual Minutes, Baptist General Convention of Florida (BGCF), 1888, 21.

[52]Annual Minutes, VBSC, 1880, 21-22.

For example, the Committee on the President's Address of the VBSC in 1889 suggested that the Virginia Baptist Seminary in Lynchburg add an industrial department. Three of the five committee members were also outstanding advocates of African missions: the chairperson, Richard Wells; Henry Williams, Jr.; and Richard Spiller. All three of these individuals served as members of the Executive Boards of both the VBSC and the BFMC.[53]

Black Baptists would have been very much in line with the general missionary philosophy of education as it was applied to Africans at the time if they had limited their educational goals to the industrial segment. But they recognized the significance of all forms of education and stressed that position as the occasion demanded. For example, the Report of the Corresponding Secretary of the LCC in 1907 lambasted efforts of some states to confine black public schools to primary and industrial education. Blacks, asserted the corresponding secretary, deserved the same access to education as members of any other race; they merited the opportunity to rise to the level most appropriate for their natural abilities. Industrial education was lauded by all blacks, he stated, but not when it was employed by whites to retain educational and economic advantages over blacks.[54] The Committee on the Corresponding Secretary's Report, composed of notable advocates of African missions such as J. A. Whitted and S. N. Vass of North Carolina and W. M. Moss of Virginia, did not dissent from these views.[55]

Black Baptists insisted that benevolence should be a very important ingredient to any educational program and that the emphasis on benevolence should apply particularly to the uplift of the African race. The Educational Board of the VBSC in 1887, for example, reported that true education taught individuals to develop their powers to the fullest capacity and to employ that knowledge to glorify God and to serve the black race. In their quest to uplift the race, blacks had the support of God and their "friends" (sympathetic whites). But trust in neither should eclipse their desire to help themselves. Along those lines, the board recommended that every edu-

[53]Ibid., 1889, 32-33.

[54]Annual Minutes, LCC, 1907, 29.

[55]Ibid., 33.

cational program should include an emphasis upon pride, respect, and confidence in the race and faith that fellow blacks had the requisite abilities and proper judgments to lead the race. "These things are quite essential to our elevation."[56] The Educational Board called for a sustained dedication to the principles of education, racial unity, and cooperation because it would be a most difficult task to erase the imprint of 245 years of slavery.[57]

## EDUCATION AND AFRICAN MISSIONS

Black Baptists attempted to transfer their philosophy of education to the African mission field in concrete ways. There are a number of historical arrangements that explain this transference. First, the same denominational schools, such as Richmond Theological Seminary in Virginia, Shaw University in North Carolina, Benedict College in South Carolina, and Jackson College in Mississippi, that produced prominent educators and church leaders on the domestic front also produced outstanding African mission supporters and trained missionaries—for example, John J. Coles and C. C. Boone.[58] It is not surprising, therefore, that Baptists involved in both domestic and foreign missions would share in the educational ideology that undergirded and was promulgated by these institutions.

Second, prominent African missions advocates such as J. W. Patterson and W. M. Moss of Virginia and J. A. Whitted and C. S. Brown of North Carolina also involved themselves in leadership capacities in other areas of denominational and educational work. Indeed, it would be impossible to refer to these persons solely as African mission supporters. Additionally, such leaders also held key trusteeship and sponsorship positions in the operation of Baptist schools. In short, the persons who spoke most ardently of the need to acquire Western education also were frequently among the most dedicated supporters of African missions. It would be surprising if their view concerning the role of education in the African mission enterprise contradicted the one they had expounded for Afro-Americans.

---

[56]Annual Minutes, VBSC, 1887, 24.

[57]Ibid.

[58]See Pegues, *Baptist Ministers*, for a list of Baptist-supported schools, 27-28. Pegues's work in general will provide specific examples of the interconnections between Baptist leaders, schools, missionaries, and African mission work.

To a greater extent than most white missionaries, black Baptists sought to spread Western education in Africa with the hope of materially uplifting the people, not for the mere purpose of facilitating the acceptance and practice of Christianity. The difference in the philosophy of black Baptists and white Christians is even apparent in the way they approached the issue of religious training for indigenous Africans. For example, whereas the Southern Baptist Convention during these years made little or no effort to encourage and support Africans for study in the U.S., Baptists in both the LCC and the NBC encouraged Africans to attend their schools either on the Continent or in the U.S. so as to equip them better for religious work among their people.[59]

It is therefore in the context of black Baptists' viewpoint on the nature, role, and purpose of Western education that we understand the insistence on the part of African missionaries and mission supporters that African mission stations be constituted with both ecclesiastical and scholastic departments. The Baptist Foreign Mission Convention missionary John J. Coles, during his first missionary sojourn in Africa in the 1880s, sacrificed his own provisions of "proper food and clothes" in order to inaugurate and maintain a school for African boys.[60] Coles commented during his second missionary journey to Africa that proper education must convey both Christianity and Western culture. Coles wrote that mission schools should produce graduates who would exemplify in their life-styles the qualities of good, "civilized," *Western* Christians. These graduates would represent such a marked contrast to the religion and culture of "heathenism" that non-Christian Africans would be converted. Thus, education would introduce a "higher" civilization and improve the material aspects of the peoples' lives.[61]

Finally, the Report of the Corresponding Secretary of the LCC in 1914 is another indication of the crucial place that the school played in the ac-

---

[59] "The Southern American Baptist Mission refused to encourage any of their agents to go to the United States even for advanced courses in theology. The only outstanding Nigerian connected with that mission is Nathaniel David Ayerinde, who, out of his personal savings, made his way to the United States in 1906 and was made to fend for himself until 1916 when he returned to Nigeria" (Ayandele, *Missionary Impact*, 287).

[60] Coles, *Africa*, 49.

[61] Annual Minutes, VBSC, 1890, 29-30.

tivity of African missions. The report, adopted by the general convention, referred to the mission school as "the hope of our work." Liberia was finally making significant progress toward becoming a successful republic. According to the report, common opinion held that "religious training and public education of the children" would serve as appropriate means to ensure material progress in the republic.[62] Furthermore, the report rejoiced in the belief that all five LCC missionaries stationed in Liberia had the qualifications of Christianity, formal education, and American civilization. The report asserted that Liberia had been founded as a colony upon these three principles. The corresponding secretary obviously saw a vital connection between the work of the missionaries and what he saw as a new growth in the "civil progressive life" of the Republic.[63] Thus, even at the conclusion of the 1880–1915 period these Baptists, individually and collectively, regarded Western education as an important means to introduce Africans to both Christianity and Western civilization.

## LIBERIA

Prior to the Civil War, many black Baptists followed the philosophy of the missionary-colonist Lott Carey and proclaimed a strong connection and working relationship between black emigration to and colonization of Liberia on one hand and the evangelization and material uplift of Africans on the other hand. In the period 1880–1915 the concern for the evangelization and material uplift of Africans continued, although the support for emigration to Liberia as a means to accomplish these ends declined perceptibly. The idea of general emigration of blacks, which never acquired overwhelming support from black Baptists, was dealt an even more severe blow with the promulgation of the Emancipation Proclamation and the inauguration of Reconstruction. These events offered Southern blacks—who represented the bulk of Afro-Americans—greater hope for improving their social, economic, and political status in the U.S. Individual missionaries and Baptists might occasionally call for a limited scale of emigration to

---

[62]Annual Minutes, LCC, 1914, 8.

[63]Ibid.

Liberia.[64] But as a whole Liberia lost its appeal as a political haven for oppressed black Americans until the Garvey movement after 1915.

Still, the rejection of any large-scale mass emigration to Africa did not preclude a great number of Baptists from regarding the former American colony of Liberia in West Africa in a special way. Even in the 1880–1915 period a significant number of these Baptists continued to believe that Liberia was the most logical point from which to launch a mission program that would redeem and "civilize" the entire continent of Africa. It was in the state of Virginia and in the Lott Carey Convention that black Baptists voiced the greatest missionary interest and provided the greatest number of missionary personnel for Liberia. As late as 1910 the (black) Baptist General Association of Virginia made the redemption of Africa dependent upon the Republic of Liberia. "We believe that if Africa is to be redeemed; if American Negroes are to play an important part in her redemption[,] the Republic of Liberia must be the strategic point from which American Negro missionaries must operate."[65]

These Virginia Baptists claimed that Liberia offered a splendid blend of Christianity and civilization. This republic would serve as a learning center to which indigenous Africans from across the continent could come and prepare themselves as missionaries to their respective countries. Referring to the cultural and linguistic gap between Afro-American missionaries and Africans, the Virginia Baptists asserted that indigenous Africans could best serve their own people. "They certainly would be better prepared, an equal training given to work among their people than those from our country."[66] As stated previously, this emphasis upon using indigenous Africans to evangelize their peoples is consistent with the general tenor of Christian missions in the U.S., both black and white, during this period.

But for many black Baptists, Liberia still carried hope for the political uplift of Africans and their racial kin throughout the world. In 1913 C. S. Brown of the LCC commented that Liberia represented to the entire world that blacks were capable of self-government. Thus, if this example of black

[64]E.g., see Susie M. Taylor's suggestion in Annual Minutes, NBC, 1912, 147.

[65]Annual Minutes, General Association of Virginia (GAV), 1910, 53.

[66]Ibid., 53-54.

self-rule were to falter, then the entire race would suffer. But, he claimed, the future of Liberia lay in the hands of Afro-American Christians.[67] "If we, the negro Christians of America, would consent to focalize our missionary efforts there and do our duty, the government of Liberia, now the scorn and ridicule of the civilized world, would soon rise in dignity and command universal respect." [68]

Brown, along with other black spokespersons such as W. E. B. DuBois and Edward Wilmot Blyden, spoke of a need for racial distinctiveness. He said that blacks had a special contribution to make to the world. Like the Chinese and Japanese, he argued, the black race must fulfill this racial destiny outside the United States. The Baptist leader appeared almost ready to call for a general exodus of blacks from the country when he claimed that all signs pointed to the black race's accepting Africa as its homeland. According to Brown, the more the ruling whites of the United States heaped insults and humiliation upon blacks, the more those oppressed people would look to a land where they could enjoy full freedom.[69]

Brown undoubtedly made those statements in the context of increasing political repression of blacks in the early twentieth century. Two points should be made concerning his position. One, I have found no evidence to suggest that prior to 1915 Brown ever adopted a pro-emigrationist philosophy. Second, I do not assert that his viewpoints represented the predominant opinion among either black Baptists in general or the LCC in particular, merely that they are representative of a continuing creed among many of these Baptists that Liberia should occupy a special place in any plans to uplift Africans politically, economically, and spiritually.

## CONCLUSION

Whereas previous chapters concentrated upon the organizational aspects of the black Baptists' attempt to evangelize the African continent, this chapter delineated and defined their mission ideology: the religious and philosophical ideas, presuppositions, and objectives that motivated their

---

[67]Annual Minutes, LCC, 1913, 41-42.

[68]Ibid., 42.

[69]Ibid.

active and sustained commitment to this enterprise during the entire 1880–1915 period. Analysis of the data of the period disclosed a number of significant findings. First, black Baptists maintained the missionary tradition that originated during the antebellum years. It was an interpretation of Psalms 68:31 which held that blacks in the U.S., Africa, and throughout the world shared a common temporal (as well as spiritual) struggle and destiny. They explicitly identified with the peoples of Africa and thus transcended their extremely negative impressions, ideas, and feelings about African cultures and religions—all of which were common among most foreign mission-minded American and European Christians during the time. The "heathenism" that black Baptists beheld was not that of an innately inferior, alien race, but the shortcomings of brothers and sisters awaiting freedom from their prisons through the loving ministry of the gospel.

In addition, many black Baptists did not attack the ethics of European colonialism as frequently as one might imagine or expect. But some did advocate more liberal policies regarding the political and economic rights of indigenous Africans under European rule. All appeared to promulgate the idea of a "practical Christianity"—the doctrine that the faith brought this-worldly as well as spiritual benefits to its devotees—and a philosophy of education emphasizing social and benevolent results. Though other areas of Africa began to attract more attention and missionaries during this period, Liberia still occupied major prominence in black Baptists' efforts to evangelize and uplift African peoples and still served as a symbol for the material progress of black peoples. Finally, this chapter has highlighted the mission ideology of black Baptists who, following in the tradition of the black missionary Lott Carey, were motivated to conduct mission work in Africa for both racial and religious, temporal and spiritual reasons.

# CHAPTER 7

# CONCLUSION

One of the most fascinating developments in American religious history was the rise of the African missionary movement among black Christians. This study has provided a case study of that movement by focusing upon black Baptists during the 1880–1915 period with primary emphasis upon the Southern origins of that movement. Efforts were made to evangelize Africa beginning with the west coast of Africa in the regions we know as Liberia and to a secondary degree Nigeria. It is appropriate at this point to review briefly the rise and development of this American movement.

With the founding of the Richmond African Baptist Missionary Society by Lott Carey, Colin Teague, and William Crane in 1815, Baptists—black and white—inaugurated a tradition that for the next 100 years would have profound repercussions for the history of Afro-American Baptists. This missionary tradition was guided by an interpretation of Psalm 68:31 which held that God promised a grand future for peoples of African descent. The purpose of the Richmond Society was to spread Christianity and Western civilization to the continent of Africa. This organization was a missionary society whose ends were both the material and spiritual uplift of the African peoples.

It is not surprising that this new society collaborated with both the General Convention of the Baptist Denomination in the United States for Foreign Missions or the Triennial Convention founded in 1814 and the American Colonization Society (ACS) founded in 1816–1817. Encouraged by white Baptists, the Richmond Society became the core group of support for African missionary work in the Triennial Convention, providing missionaries and funds for the task. Chiefly through the medium of this society, black Baptists and white friends of African missions called attention to the continent of Africa even as Adoniram Judson and Luther Rice were calling attention to Asia. In their cooperation with the ACS, black Baptists sought answers to both the enslavement of Afro-Americans and "redemption" of Africans. Colonization supported the belief current among Christians in that period of history that a "heathen" society must be reconstituted in all of its aspects, culturally as well as spiritually.

Not all black Baptists shared in the belief that blacks should emigrate en masse to the African continent. Most refused to surrender either their identification with, loyalty to, or hope in the land of their birth. But as the early colonizationist-missionary Baptists such as Lott Carey entered and settled western Africa, they developed two somewhat paradoxical notions that influenced black Baptist history and African mission work beyond this period. These convictions were held as strongly by the missionary colonists in the field as by the anticolonizationist mission supporters in the U.S. On the one hand, these Baptists subscribed to the general Western Christian assessment of African religions and cultures as decidedly inferior to Christianity and Western culture. On the other hand, they were sensitively attuned to their rejection by white American society. This fact, combined with their understanding of Psalm 68:31, indissolubly linked black Baptists with the struggle and destiny of the African peoples.

This zeal for African missions work on the part of black Baptists was manifested in and greatly influenced the growth of independent black Baptist ecclesiastical structures after the Civil War. Much of the connection between colonization and African missions had been dissolved by the liberation of blacks from legal slavery and by the ensuing period of political advancement for exslaves and their descendants. But the black Baptists of South Carolina, North Carolina, and Virginia continued to show interest in the material and religious uplift of African peoples by sending missionaries to the west coast of Africa in the years 1875 to 1880. In 1880 this zeal for African redemption reached regional proportions when, under the leadership of the missionary W. W. Colley and his fellow black Virginia Baptists, representatives from eleven states gathered to organize the Baptist Foreign Mission Convention in the United States.

For American religious history, the Foreign Mission Convention was historically significant for a number of reasons. First, this quasi-national organization was founded for the sole purpose of conducting foreign mis-

sions work at a point in history when many black Baptists quite understandably believed that their monies and energies would best be directed
at religious and humanitarian concerns within the U.S. Second, despite the
severe limitation of funds among black Baptists, the missionary organization succeeded in placing several missionaries in Liberia during the years
1883 to 1894. Third, though members of the organization conceived of it
as a national body, its predominant character remained Southern, most
particularly influenced by the Virginians. Indeed, the Baptists of that state
overwhelmingly dominated the policy-making Executive Board headquartered in Richmond.

Fourth, at the height of financial difficulties, the membership of the
Foreign Mission Convention refused repeated offers of cooperation from
the white American Baptist Missionary Union. These black Baptists believed that accepting those offers would compromise their independent
status and deter black Baptists from pursuing essential work that only they,
as black Baptists, could best perform. Fifth, the Foreign Mission Convention in 1895 became one of the major forerunners of the National Baptist
Convention (NBC), founded in 1895, and its major department for the pursuit of foreign missions. This is significant given that the NBC would become the largest and oldest of national black Baptist groups.

Black Baptists from all quarters for years had craved national unity.
This unity materialized in 1895; however, questions concerning the NBC's
willingness to cooperate in religious work with white Baptists, the membership and placement of the Foreign Mission Board, and a general concern with the proper conduct of foreign mission work resulted in North
Carolina's and Virginia's leading other states of the eastern seaboard to
found the Lott Carey Baptist (Home and) Foreign Mission Convention of
the United States (LCC) in 1897. The main issue was cooperation with
white Baptist groups, which also divided black Baptists on the state level
in North Carolina and, most painfully, in Virginia. Yet the same desires
for racial and denominational unity and love for African missions that had
served to unite black Baptists in 1895 were among the factors that reunited
the NBC and the LCC into a coordinate (not merged) relationship in 1907,
a relationship that lasted until the 1920s.

Whether in conflict or cooperation, the LCC and the NBC in the years
1895–1915 continued the precedents of the Foreign Mission Convention

and, before it, the states of North Carolina, South Carolina, and Virginia in focusing their foreign mission attention on the continent of Africa. Furthermore, there remained a great deal of support for West African or Liberian mission work. Thus, the missionary legacy of Lott Carey, linking Southern black Baptists with West Africa, was maintained during these years and became truly a nationally organized movement.

The antebellum theological rationale for mission work in Africa by black Baptists continued in this period. As was the case with most white and black foreign-mission-minded people in the 1880–1915 period, black Baptists considered African cultures inferior to Western culture and African religions inferior to the Christian religion. While white missionaries collaborated with and supported colonialism, these black Baptists for the most part remained silent about the ethics of the system imposed on Africans. Nevertheless, by their criticisms of the system's atrocities, their belief that Christianity and Western education served to uplift people materially, and their strong sense of racial solidarity with the peoples of the continent, black American Baptists demonstrated that they were motivated by a concern to better the lives of Africans in material and religious aspects. With greater intensity than missionary-minded white Christians, these Baptists strove—at least in theory—almost as earnestly for the material benefit of Africans as they did for their Christianization.

In this study, I have been primarily interested in the domestic organization of and motivation for African missions on the part of black Baptists. The academic significance of the mission movement among these Baptists does not depend upon the scope or managerial efficiency of their mission organizations. Their leaders constantly noted that the support for African missions suffered from lack of funds and, as such, fell far short of the member churches' potential. Second, the specific aim of this study has not permitted a systematic and comprehensive assessment of the benefits that accrued to Africans on the basis of black Baptist missionary activities. It is clear, for example, that intimate combination of Western culture with Christianity and religion applied to Afro-American Baptist missionaries and their supporters as it did to other American and European Christians. In other words, black Baptists often saw the necessity to transfer Western cultural norms as well as Christianity to Africans.

Whatever the assessment of the actual influence of the mission program upon African societies, the movement was significant for black Baptist history. The zeal for promoting African missions and the discrimination by white Baptists helped to encourage black Baptists to form independent religious organizations. The state, regional, and national organizations served as refuges from a white world of racial discrimination. Positively, such mission societies gave these Baptists the opportunity to practice their organizational skills, united them, and became instruments of racial pride and proof that blacks could independently practice self-government and management. Finally, the mission program became a vital connection between Afro-Americans and continental Africans. Despite their negative evaluations of African religions and cultures, black Baptist missionaries were able to maintain their identification and association with continental Africans. The significance of that identification and association for Afro-American/African dialogue deserves a separate study.

All of these factors suggest some very positive things about the consciousness of black Baptists in particular and black Christians generally. They had a strong sense of purpose, destiny, and confidence in themselves. It has been demonstrated in the previous pages that black Baptists were not merely imitating white churches. They embraced Christianity and foreign missions, but adjusted or applied them to their own needs and aspirations. One might think that, given the multitude of political and economic woes they faced—particularly during the turbulent 1880–1915 period—black Baptists and other black Christians would have withdrawn completely into the arena of their own domestic concerns.

But these men and women had an understanding of themselves and history, permeated by their strong belief in an all-wise, loving, and beneficent God, that lifted them above such parochialism. These people dared to believe that the God of Abraham and Sarah, Moses and Miriam, and Jesus and Mary was their God. The Lord of history had not overlooked their sufferings, disappointments, and trials. Instead, God was working through these vicissitudes and using these exslaves and their children to usher in an era when such pains would vanish from humankind, and all of Africa's sons and daughters would stand proudly in a new world of freedom, justice, and Christian love. It is this faith in God, themselves, and the African race that remains one of the greatest legacies of the black Baptist missionary movement.

# SELECTED BIBLIOGRAPHY

## I. DENOMINATIONAL MINUTES

### A. Regional and National Minutes

American Baptist Foreign Mission Society (formerly the American Baptist Missionary Union). Annual Minutes. 1910–1916.

American Baptist Missionary Union. Annual Minutes. 1879, 1880, 1881, 1884, 1886–1888, 1892–1901, 1905–1909.

Baptist Foreign Mission Convention of the United States of America. Annual Minutes. 1881–1891.

Baptist General Association of Western States and Territories. Annual Minutes. 1882, 1886–1888, 1890, 1891, 1894.

The Consolidated American Baptist Missionary Convention. Annual Minutes. 1865, 1869, 1872, 1877.

Consolidated American Educational Association. Annual Minutes. 1869.

Lott Carey Baptist (Home and) Foreign Mission Convention. Annual Minutes. 1897–1903, 1907–1913.

_____. The Corresponding Secretary's eighteenth Annual Report. 1914.

National Baptist Convention. Annual Minutes. 1898–1912, 1914, 1915.

The New England Baptist Missionary Convention. Annual Minutes. 1877–1880.

The Southern Baptist Convention. Annual Minutes. 1845, 1846, 1854, 1855, 1860, 1866, 1869, 1872, 1875–1915.

The Founding Assembly of the Liberia Baptist Missionary Convention. Minutes. 1880.

The Triennial Convention or the General Baptist Denomination in the United States for Foreign Missions. Minutes. 1817, 1835, 1842.

### B. State Minutes

Baptist Educational and Missionary Convention of North Carolina. Annual Minutes. 1889–1895, 1897–1899, 1901, 1903, 1904, 1908–1913, 1915.

The Baptist Educational, Missionary, and Sunday School Convention of South Carolina. Annual Minutes. 1878–1881, 1886–1894, 1898.

(Baptist) General Association of Virginia (black). Annual Minutes. 1899, 1900, 1902–1906, 1909–1911.

Baptist General Convention of Florida. Annual Minutes. 1884–1890.

Baptist General State Convention of the State of Florida. Annual Minutes. 1892.

Baptist Missionary State Convention of Mississippi. Annual Minutes. 1888.

Baptist State Convention of North Carolina. Annual Minutes. 1878, 1880–1882, 1884, 1886.

Colored Baptist State Convention of South Carolina. Annual Minutes. 1904–1906, 1908, 1909.

General Baptist Missionary Association of the State of Mississippi. Annual Minutes. 1881, 1883, 1884, 1886, 1888, 1889.

Florida Baptist General State Convention. Annual Minutes. 1891, 1898, 1899, 1901.

Missionary Baptist Convention of Georgia. Annual Minutes. 1880–1897, 1900.

Missionary Baptist Convention of the States of Mississippi, Louisiana, and Arkansas. Annual Minutes. 1888.

The Missionary Baptist State Convention of Tennessee. Annual Minutes. 1895.

Missionary, Educational, and Sunday School Convention of Tennessee. Annual Minutes. 1895, 1897, 1898.

State Convention of the Colored Baptists of South Carolina. Annual Minutes. 1901.

Virginia Baptist State Convention. Annual Minutes. 1878–1897.

Women's Baptist Home and Foreign Mission Convention of North Carolina. Annual Minutes. 1909.

Women's General Baptist Missionary of Mississippi. Annual Minutes. 1887, 1888.

## II. DENOMINATIONAL SOURCES
## ON FOREIGN MISSIONS

Adams, C. C. and A. Marshall Halley. *Negro Baptists and Foreign Missions.* Philadelphia: Foreign Board of the National Baptist Convention, 1944.

Boone, C. C. *The Congo as I Saw It.* New York: J. J. Little and Ives Co., 1927.

Bowen, T. J. *Adventures and Missionary Labours in Several Countries in the Interior of Africa from 1849 to 1856.* Second ed., with a new introduction by E. A. Ayandele. London: Frank Cass & Co., 1968.

Cauthen, Baker J., ed. *Advance: A History of Southern Baptist Foreign Missions.* Nashville: Broadman Press, 1970.

Coles, John J. *Africa in Brief.* New York: New York Freeman Steam Printing Establishment, 1886.

Fisher, Miles Mark. "Lott Carey: The Colonizing Missionary." *Journal of Negro History* 7 (October 1922): 380-418.

Freeman, Edward A. *The Epoch of Negro Baptists and the Foreign Mission Board, National Convention, U.S.A., Inc.* Kansas City KS: Central Seminary Press, 1953.

Green, C. Sylvester. *New Nigeria: Southern Baptists at Work in Africa.* Richmond: Foreign Mission Board, Southern Baptist Convention, 1936.

Harr, Wilbur Christian. "The Negro as an American Protestant Missionary in Africa." (Ph.D. diss., University of Chicago Divinity School, 1946.)

Hervey, G. Winfred. *The Story of Baptist Missions in Foreign Lands, from the Time of Carey to the Present Date.* St. Louis: Chancy R. Barns, 1886.

Jordan, Lewis Garnett. *A Brief Record of Negro Baptist Missionaries Who Heard and Obeyed the Command "Go Ye"; They Went—Preaching the Word.* N.p., n.d.

_____. *Pebbles from an African Beach.* Philadelphia: Lisle-Carey Press, [1918?].

_____. *Up the Ladder in Foreign Missions.* Nashville: National Baptist Publishing Board, 1901.

Maddry, Charles E. *Day Dawn in Yoruba Land.* Nashville: Broadman Press, 1939.

Martin, Sandy Dwayne. "Spelman's Emma B. DeLaney and the African Mission." *Journal of Religious Thought* 41 (Spring-Summer 1984): 22-37.

Poe, William A. "Lott Carey: Man of Purchased Freedom." *Church History* 39 (March 1970): 49-61.

Tupper, H. A. *The Foreign Missions of the Southern Baptist Convention.* Philadelphia: American Baptist Publication Society, 1880.

Weeks, Nan F., comp. *Builders of a New Africa.* Nashville: Broadman Press, 1944.

Wright, Mary Emily. *The Missionary Work of the Southern Baptist Convention.* Philadelphia: American Baptist Publication Society, 1902.

## III. DENOMINATIONAL HISTORY AND BIOGRAPHY

Bacote, Samuel William, ed. *Who's Who among the Colored Baptists of the United States.* Volume 1. Kansas City MO: Franklin Hudson Publishing Company, 1913.

Binga, Anthony, Jr. *Sermons on Several Occasions.* Volume 1. Washington: N.p., 1889.

Boone, Theodore S. *Some Negro Baptist Remarkables of Georgia.* Twenty-Second Annual Report of the Historical and Research Department of the National Baptist Convention, U.S.A., Incorporated, Delivered to the Sixty-Sixth Annual Session of the National Baptist Convention, U.S.A., Inc., Atlanta, Georgia, September 5, 1946.

Boothe, Charles Octavius. *The Cyclopedia of the Colored Baptists of Alabama.* Birmingham: Alabama Publishing Company, 1895.

Brawley, Edward MacKnight, ed. *The Negro Baptist Pulpit.* Philadelphia: American Baptist Publication Society, 1890.

Carter, E. R., writer and collator. *Biographical Sketches of Our Pulpit.* Chicago: Afro-Am Press, 1969. (Reprint of 1888 edition.)

Cook, Richard B. *The Story of the Baptists in All Ages and Countries.* Revised and enlarged by a supplementary chapter on the colored Baptists. Baltimore: H. M. Wharton & Company, 1887.

Correspondence of the Lott Carey Baptist Foreign Mission Convention. American Baptist Foreign Mission Society Papers. Microfilm Number 197. American Baptist Historical Society. Rochester, New York.

Dwelle, J. H. *A Brief History of Black Baptists in North America.* Pittsburgh: Pioneer Printing Company, n.d.

Eighmy, John Lee. *Churches in Cultural Captivity: A History of the Attitudes of Southern Baptists.* Knoxville: University of Tennessee Press, 1972.

Fitts, Leroy. *A History of Black Baptists.* Nashville: Broadman Press, 1985.

_____ . *Lott Carey: First Black Missionary to Africa.* Valley Forge PA: Judson Press, 1978.

Grundman, Adolph H. "Northern Baptists and the Founding of Virginia Union University: The Perils of Paternalism." *Journal of Negro History* 63 (January 1978): 26-41.

Johnson, W. Bishop. *The Scourging of a Race and Other Sermons and Addresses.* Washington: Beresford Printer, 1904.

Jordan, Lewis Garnett. *Negro Baptist History, U.S.A., 1750–1930.* Nashville: Sunday School Publishing Board, National Baptist Convention, U.S.A., [1936?].

_____ . *On Two Hemispheres: Bits from the Life Story of Lewis G. Jordan as Told by Himself.* N.p., n.d.

Moses, William H. *The Colored Baptist Family Tree: A Compendium of Organized Negro Baptist Church History.* Nashville: Sunday School Publishing Board, National Baptist Convention, U.S.A., 1925.

Pegues, Albert W. *Our Baptist Ministers and Schools.* Springfield MA: Wiley and Company, 1892.

Penn, I. Garland and J. W. E. Bowen, eds. *The United Negro: His Problems and His Progress; Containing the Addresses and Proceedings of the Negro Young People's Christian and Educational Congress, Held August 6-11, 1902.* Atlanta: D. E. Luther Publishing Company, 1902.

Pius, N. H. *An Outline of Baptist History.* Nashville: National Baptist Publishing Board, 1911.

Simmons, William J. *Men of Mark: Eminent, Progressive and Rising.* New York: George M. Revell & Co., 1887. Reprint. Chicago: Johnson Publishing Company, 1970.

Sobel, Mechal. *Trabelin' on: The Slave Journey to an Afro-Baptist Faith.* Westport: Greenwood Press, 1979.

Spain, Rufus B. *At Ease in Zion: Social History of Southern Baptists, 1865–1900.* Nashville: Vanderbilt University Press, 1967.

Taylor, James B. *Virginia Baptist Ministers.* Volume 2. Philadelphia: J. B. Lippincott & Co., 1859.

Washington, James Melvin. *Frustrated Fellowship: The Black Baptist Quest for Social Power.* Macon GA: Mercer University Press, 1986.

_____ . "The Origins and Emergence of Black Baptist Separatism, 1863–1897." (Ph.D. diss., Yale University, 1979).

Whitted, J. A. *A History of the Negro Baptists of North Carolina.* Raleigh NC: Edwards & Broughton Printing Company, 1908.

## IV. SOURCES ON AFRICAN MISSIONS AND RELIGIONS

Ajayi, J. F. Ade. *Christian Missions in Nigeria, 1841–1891: The Making of a New Elite.* London: Longmans, Green, and Company, 1965.

Ayandele, E. A. *The Missionary Impact on Modern Nigeria, 1842–1914: A Political and Social Analysis.* London: Longmans, Green and Company, 1966.

Berman, Edward H. *African Reactions to Missionary Education.* New York: Teachers College Press, 1975.

Cason, John Walter. "The Growth of Christianity in the Liberian Environment." (Ph.D. diss., Columbia University and Union Theological Seminary, 1962).

Du Plessis, J. *The Evangelisation of Pagan Africa: A History of Christian Missions to the Pagan Tribes of Central Africa.* Cape Town, South Africa: J. C. Juta & Co., 1929.

Groves, C. P. *The Planting of Christianity in Africa.* Volume 3, 1878–1914. London: Lutterworth Press, 1955.

Harris, Joseph E. *Africans and Their History.* New York: New American Library/ Times Mirror, 1972.

Hastings, Adrian. *Church and Mission in Modern Africa.* Bronx NY: Fordham University Press, 1967.

Idowu, E. Bolaji. *African Traditional Religion: A Definition.* Maryknoll NY: Orbis Books, 1973.

_____ . *Towards an Indigenous Church.* London: Oxford University Press, 1965.

Jacobs, Sylvia M., ed. *Black Americans and the Missionary Movement in Africa.* Westport CT: Greenwood Press, 1982.

July, Robert W. *A History of the African People.* New York: Charles Scribner's Sons, 1970.

King, Noel Q. *Christian and Muslim in Africa.* New York: Harper & Row, 1971.

Lynch, Hollis R. *Edward Wilmot Blyden: Pan-Negro Patriot, 1832–1912.* New York: Oxford University Press, 1970.

Marinelli, Lawrence A. *The New Liberia: A Historical and Political Survey.* London: Pall Mall Press, 1964.

Mbiti, John S. *African Religions and Philosophy.* Garden City NY: Anchor Books, Doubleday & Co., 1970.

_____ . *Introduction to African Religion.* New York: Praeger Publishers, 1975.

Roland, Joan G., ed. *Africa: The Heritage and the Challenge, An Anthology of African History.* Greenwich CT: Fawcett Publications, 1974.

Shepperson, George and Thomas Price. *Independent African: John Chilembwe and the Origins, Setting and Significance of the Nyasaland Native Rising of 1915.* Edinburgh: Edinburgh University Press, 1958.

Spivey, Donald. "The African Crusade for Black Industrial Schooling." *Journal of Negro History* 63 (January 1978): 1-17.

Trimingham, J. Spencer. *The Christian Church and Islam in West Africa.* London: SCM Press, 1955.

Walker, James W. St. G. *The Black Loyalists: The Search for a Promised Land in Nova Scotia and Sierra Leone, 1783–1870.* New York: Africana Publishing Press, 1976.

Webster, James Bertin. *The African Churches among the Yoruba, 1888–1922.* Oxford: Clarendon Press, 1964.

West, Richard. *Back to Africa: A History of Sierra Leone and Liberia.* New York: Holt, Rinehart and Winston, 1970.

Williams, Walter L. *Black Americans and the Evangelization of Africa, 1877–1900.* Madison: University of Wisconsin Press, 1982.

Wilson, Charles Morrow. *Liberia: Black Africa in Microcosm.* New York: Harper & Row, 1971.

## V. GENERAL HISTORICAL AND RELIGIOUS WORKS

Ahlstrom, Sydney E. *A Religious History of the American People.* New Haven: Yale University Press, 1972.

Ajayi, J. F. A. and Michael Crowder, eds. *History of West Africa.* Volume 2. New York: Columbia University Press, 1973.

Bracey, John H., Jr., August Meier, and Elliot Rudwick, eds. *Black Nationalism in America.* New York: Bobbs-Merrill Company, 1970.

Brotz, Howard. *Negro Social and Political Thought, 1850–1920: Representative Texts.* New York: Basic Books, 1966.

Burkett, Randall K. *Black Redemption: Churchmen Speak for the Garvey Movement.* Philadelphia: Temple University Press, 1978.

Chaney, Charles L. *The Birth of Missions in America.* South Pasadena CA: William Carey Library, 1976.

Costas, Orlando E. *The Church and Its Mission: A Shattering Critique from the Third World.* Wheaton IL: Lyndale House Publishers, 1974.

Drake, St. Clair. *The Redemption of Africa and Black Religion.* Chicago: Third World Press, 1977.

Fishel, Leslie H., Jr., and Benjamin Quarles, eds. *The Black American: A Documentary History.* Third ed. Oakland NJ: Scott, Foresman and Company, 1970.

Fordham, Monroe. *Major Themes in Northern Black Religious Thought, 1800–1860.* Hicksville NY: An Exposition-University Book, 1975.

Franklin, John Hope. *From Slavery to Freedom: A History of Negro Americans.* Fourth ed. New York: Alfred A. Knopf, 1974.

Fredrickson, George M. *The Black Image in the White Mind: The Debate on Afro-American Character and Destiny, 1817–1914.* New York: Harper & Row, 1972.

George, Carol V. R. *Segregated Sabbaths: Richard Allen and the Rise of Independent Black Churches, 1760–1840.* New York: Oxford University Press, 1973.

Grant, Joanne, ed. *Black Protest: History, Documents, and Analyses, 1619 to the Present.* Revised ed. Greenwich CT: Fawcett Publications, 1974.

Handy, Robert T. *A Christian America: Protestant Hopes and Historical Realities.* New York: Oxford University Press, 1971.

_____ . *A History of the Churches in the United States and Canada.* New York: Oxford University Press, 1977.

Harris, Shelton H. *Paul Cuffee: Black America and the African Return.* New York: Simon and Schuster, 1972.

Hudson, Winthrop S. *Religion in America: An Historical Account of the Development of American Religious Life.* Second ed. New York: Charles Scribner's Sons, 1973.

Jones, Allen W. "The Role of Tuskegee Institute in the Education of Black Farmers." *Journal of Negro History* 60 (April 1975): 252-67.

Jordan, Winthrop D. *White over Black: American Attitudes toward the Negro, 1550–1812.* Baltimore: Penguin Books, 1971.

*Journal of Daniel Coker.* Baltimore: Edward J. Coale, 1820.

July, Robert W. *The Origins of Modern African Thought: Its Development in West Africa during the Nineteenth and Twentieth Centuries.* New York: Frederick A. Praeger, 1967.

Latourette, Kenneth Scott. *A History of the Expansion of Christianity.* Volume 5: *The Great Century: The Americas, Australasia, and Africa, 1800–1914.* Contemporary Evangelical Perspectives. Grand Rapids: Zondervan, 1970.

Levine, Lawrence W. *Black Culture and Black Consciousness: Afro-American Folk Thought from Slavery to Freedom.* New York: Oxford University Press, 1977.

Lincoln, C. Eric. *The Black Church since Frazier*. New York: Schocken Books, 1974.

_____ , ed. *The Black Experience in Religion*. Garden City NY: Anchor Press/Doubleday, 1974.

Litwack, Leon F. *Been in the Storm so Long: The Aftermath of Slavery*. New York: Vintage Books, 1979.

McBride, Donald. "Africa's Elevation and Changing Racial Thought at Lincoln University, 1854–1888." *Journal of Negro History* 62 (October 1977): 363-77.

Marty, Martin E. *Righteous Empire: The Protestant Experience in America*. New York: Dial Press, 1970.

Mathews, Donald G. *Religion in the Old South*. Chicago: University of Chicago Press, 1977.

Mead, Sidney E. *The Lively Experiment: The Shaping of Christianity in America*. New York: Harper & Row, 1963.

Miller, Floyd J. *The Search for a Black Nationality: Black Emigration and Colonization, 1787–1863*. Urbana IL: University of Illinois Press, 1975.

Noble, Frederic Perry. *The Redemption of Africa*. New York: Young People's Missionary Movement, 1899.

Quarles, Benjamin. *Black Abolitionists*. New York: Oxford University Press, 1975.

Raboteau, Albert J. *Slave Religion: The "Invisible Institution" in the Antebellum South*. New York: Oxford University Press, 1978.

Redkey, Edwin S. *Black Exodus: Black Nationalist and Back-to-Africa Movements, 1890–1910*. New Haven: Yale University Press, 1969.

Scherer, Lester B. *Slavery and the Churches in Early America, 1619–1819*. Grand Rapids: William B. Eerdmans, 1975.

Sernett, Milton C., ed. *Afro-American Religious History: A Documentary Witness*. Durham: Duke University Press, 1985.

_____ . *Black Religion and American Evangelicalism: White Protestants, Plantation Missions, and the Flowering of Negro Christianity, 1787–1865*. Foreword by Martin E. Marty. ATLA Monograph Series, no. 7. Metuchen NJ: Scarecrow Press, and The American Theological Library Association, 1975.

Shick, Tom W. *Behold the Promised Land: A History of Afro-American Settler Society in Nineteenth Century Liberia*. Baltimore: Johns Hopkins University Press, 1977.

Staudenraus, P. J. *The African Colonization Movement, 1816–1865*. New York: Columbia University Press, 1961.

Tuveson, Ernest Lee. *Redeemer Nation: The Idea of America's Millennial Role*. Chicago: University of Chicago Press, 1968.

Tyms, James Daniel. *The Rise of Religious Education among Negro Baptists: A Historical Case Study*. New York: Exposition Press, 1965.

Uya, Okon Edet, ed. *Black Brotherhood: Afro-Americans and Africa*. Lexington MA: D. C. Heath and Company, 1971.

Wilson, Ellen Gibson. *The Loyal Blacks*. New York: Capricorn Books, G. P. Putnam's Sons, 1976.

Woodson, Carter G. *The History of the Negro Church*. Third ed. Washington: Associated Publishers, 1972.

## VI. PERIODICALS

*The African Repository*. Volumes 1-60 (1825–1884).

*The Mission Herald*. 6 (August 1901); 8 (July 1902); supplement. 8 (September 1902); 8 (March 1903); 9 (January 1905); 9 (May–June 1905); 10 (August 1905); 10 (October 1905); 11 (January 1907); 11 (February 1907); 12 (June 1907); supplement. 12 (June 1907); 12 (July 1907); 13 (June 1908); 13 (August 1908); 13 (October 1908); 13 (December 1908); 13 (April 1909); 15 (March 1911); 16 (June 1912); 16 (September 1912); 16 (October 1913); 18 (July 1914); 18 (September 1914); 18 (November 1914); 19 (December 1914); 19 (February 1915); 19 (March 1915); 19 (April 1915); 19 (May 1915); 19 (June 1915); 19 (July 1915); 19 (September 1915).

*The National Baptist*. (Philadelphia). 11 September 1884.

*National Baptist Union Review*. Volumes 3-7 (1901–1907); 9-10 (1908); 16 (1914–1915).

*The Richmond Planet*. 9 June 1897; 19 February; 5 March–9 April; 17 September–31 December 1898; 12 August–9 December 1899; 26 May–9 June; 15 September 1900.

*The Rogerana*. 16 (November 1901); 16 (April 1902); 17 (January 1903); 18 (November 1903).

# AUTHOR INDEX

# SUBJECT INDEX